JUMP Math 8.2

Book 8 Part 2 of 2

Contents

jump math

MULTIPLYING POTENTIAL.

JUMP Math
Toronto, Canada
www.jumpmath.org

Writers: Dr. John Mighton, Dr. Sindi Sabourin, Dr. Anna Klebanov
Contributing Writer: Margaret McClintock
Cover Design: Blakeley Words+Pictures
Text Design: Pam Lostracco
Layout: Laura Brady, Rita Camacho, Nuria Gonzalez, Pam Lostracco, Ilyana Martinez
Cover Photograph: © Gary Blakeley, Blakeley Words+Pictures

ISBN: 978-1-897120-61-3

Second printing May 2010

ANCIENT FOREST™ FRIENDLY

158 trees were saved for our forests

Preserving our environment
JUMP Math chose to print the pages of this book on recycled paper and saved these resources[1]:

energy	water	greenhouse gases	solid waste
83 million BTUs	241,998 L	6,213 kg	2,560 kg

Printed by **Webcom Inc.** on Legacy Book Opaque 100% post-consumer waste.

FSC
Recycled
Supporting responsible use of forest resources

Cert no. SW-COC-002358
www.fsc.org
© 1996 Forest Stewardship Council

[1]Estimates were made using the Environmental Defense Paper Calculator.

Printed and bound in Canada

Welcome to JUMP Math

Entering the world of JUMP Math means believing that every child has the capacity to be fully numerate and to love math. Founder and mathematician John Mighton has used this premise to develop his innovative teaching method. The resulting materials isolate and describe concepts so clearly and incrementally that everyone can understand them.

JUMP Math is comprised of workbooks, teacher's guides, evaluation materials, outreach programs, tutoring support through schools and community organizations, and provincial curriculum correlations. All of this is presented on the JUMP Math website: **www.jumpmath.org**.

Teacher's guides are available on the website for free use. Read the introduction to the teacher's guides before you begin using these materials. This will ensure that you understand both the philosophy and the methodology of JUMP Math. The workbooks are designed for use by students, with adult guidance. Each student will have unique needs and it is important to provide the student with the appropriate support and encouragement as he or she works through the material.

Allow students to discover the concepts on the worksheets by themselves as much as possible. Mathematical discoveries can be made in small, incremental steps. The discovery of a new step is like untangling the parts of a puzzle. It is exciting and rewarding.

Students will need to answer the shaded questions using a notebook. Grid paper and notebooks should always be on hand for answering extra questions or when additional room for calculation is needed. Grid paper is also available in the BLM section of the Teacher's Guide.

Contents

Unit 3: Geometry

Unit 4: Patterns and Algebra

Unit 5: Number Sense

Unit 6: Measurement

Unit 7: Geometry

Unit 8: Probability and Data Management

NS8-75 Relating Fractions and Division

 $\frac{1}{2}$ is one whole divided into 2 parts, so $\frac{1}{2} = 1 \div 2$.

1. a) $\frac{1}{5} = 1 \div$ ____   b) $\frac{1}{4} =$ ____ $\div$ ____   c) $\frac{1}{8} =$ ____ $\div$ ____

2. a) Explain why $24 \div 2$ is three times $8 \div 2$.   b) Explain why $3 \div 8$ is three times $1 \div 8$.

c) Explain why $3 \div 8$ is $3 \times \frac{1}{8}$.   d) Explain why $3 \div 8 = \frac{3}{8}$.

3. Use $\frac{a}{b} = a \div b$ to write the fraction as a decimal. Keep dividing until the remainder is 0.

a) $\frac{1}{5} = 1 \div 5$ b) $\frac{3}{5} =$ ___ $\div$ ___   c) $\frac{4}{10} =$ ___ $\div$ ___   d) $\frac{2}{4} =$ ___ $\div$ ___   e) $\frac{4}{8} =$ ___ $\div$ ___

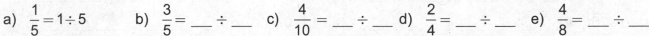

So, $\frac{1}{5} = 0.$___   So, $\frac{3}{5} = 0.$___   So, $\frac{4}{10} = 0.$___   So, $\frac{2}{4} = 0.$___   So, $\frac{4}{8} = 0.$___

f) $\frac{5}{2}$ g) $\frac{7}{4}$ h) $\frac{9}{10}$ i) $\frac{4}{5}$ j) $\frac{24}{40}$

4. a) Change the fraction to a decimal using long division. Keep dividing until the remainder is 0.

$\frac{1}{8} = 8\overline{)1.000} = ?$ $\frac{2}{8} = 8\overline{)2.000} = ?$ $\frac{3}{8} = 8\overline{)3.000} = ?$

b) What is the pattern in the decimal equivalents in part a)?

c) Extend the pattern from part a) to predict the decimals equivalent to $\frac{4}{8}, \frac{5}{8}, \frac{6}{8}, \frac{7}{8}$, and $\frac{8}{8}$.

5. Convert each fraction to a decimal fraction. Then change the fraction to a decimal. Check your answers using a calculator.

a) $\frac{3}{40} = \frac{75}{1000} = 0.075$ b) $\frac{17}{20} = \frac{}{100}$ c) $\frac{19}{125} = \frac{}{1000}$

Check: $3 \div 40 = 0.075$ Check: Check:

d) $\frac{17}{25}$ e) $\frac{7}{20}$ f) $\frac{273}{500}$ g) $\frac{111}{250}$ **BONUS ▶** $\frac{9}{16}$

NS8-76 Repeating Decimals

A **repeating decimal** is a decimal with a digit or group of digits that repeats forever.

The digit or sequence of digits that repeats can be shown by a bar. Example: $4.121212\ldots = 4.\overline{12}$.

A **terminating decimal** is a decimal that does not go on forever. Examples: 5.68, 0.444

Some decimals do not terminate or repeat. Example: $\pi = 3.14159\ldots$

1. Write each decimal to eight decimal places.

   a) $0.\overline{3} \approx 0.\underline{3}$ __ __ __ __ __ __ __

   b) $0.0\overline{3} \approx 0.\underline{0}\ \underline{3}\ \underline{3}\ \underline{3}$ __ __ __ __

   c) $0.00\overline{3} \approx 0.$__ __ __ __ __ __ __ __

   d) $0.\overline{52} \approx 0.$__ __ __ __ __ __ __ __

   e) $0.\overline{817} \approx 0.$__ __ __ __ __ __ __ __

   f) $0.8\overline{17} \approx 0.$__ __ __ __ __ __ __ __

   g) $0.9\overline{26} \approx 0.$__ __ __ __ __ __ __ __

   h) $0.2\overline{537} \approx 0.$__ __ __ __ __ __ __ __

   i) $7.2\overline{3} \approx 7.$__ __ __ __ __ __ __ __

   j) $8.2\overline{539} \approx 8.$__ __ __ __ __ __ __ __

2. Circle the repeating decimals.

   0.123412312   0.77   0.222222222...   0.512512512...   0.123238...

3. Write each repeating decimal using bar notation.

   a) $0.555555\ldots =$ _____

   b) $2.343434\ldots =$ _____

   c) $5.237237\ldots =$ _____

   d) $57.121212\ldots =$ _____

   e) $8.162626\ldots =$ _____

   f) $0.910591059105 =$ _____

4. Find the decimal value of each fraction to 3 decimal places. Then write the fraction as a repeating decimal.

   a) 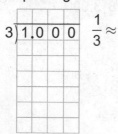 $\dfrac{1}{3} \approx$

   b) 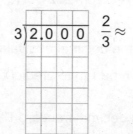 $\dfrac{2}{3} \approx$

5. Use long division to calculate the decimal equivalent of the fraction to 6 decimal places. Then write the decimal using bar notation.

   a) $\dfrac{1}{6}$ b) $\dfrac{4}{9}$ c) $\dfrac{1}{11}$ d) $\dfrac{5}{12}$

6. Match the fractions with their decimal equivalents. Use a calculator.

A $\frac{1}{3}$ B $\frac{55}{99}$ C $\frac{2}{3}$ D $\frac{2}{9}$ ___ $0.\overline{6}$ ___ $0.\overline{2}$ ___ $0.\overline{3}$ ___ $0.\overline{5}$

7. Round the repeating decimals to the nearest tenth, hundredth, and thousandth.

	nearest tenth	nearest hundredth	nearest thousandth
$\frac{2}{7} = 0.285714285714285714285714\ldots$			
$\frac{5}{13} = 0.384615384615384615384615\ldots$			

How to Compare Decimals

Step 1: Write out the first few digits of each decimal.
(Add zeros at the end of terminating decimals.)

Step 2: Circle the first digits where the decimals differ.

Step 3: The decimal with the greater circled digit is greater.

Example:

.678 [?] .67

.6 7 8 0 0 0

.6 7 6 7 6 7

.678 [>] .67

---

8. Compare the decimals.

a) .349 [   ] .3$\overline{49}$

b) .278 [   ] .2$\overline{7}$

c) .$\overline{613}$ [   ] .61$\overline{3}$

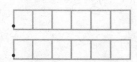

9. Write each group of numbers in order from least to greatest.

a) 0.4   0.4$\overline{2}$ 0.$\overline{42}$ 0.42

b) 0.16   0.1$\overline{6}$ 0.1$\overline{6}$ 0.$\overline{16}$

c) 0.387   0.38$\overline{7}$ 0.3$\overline{87}$ 0.$\overline{387}$

d) 0.546   0.54$\overline{6}$ 0.5$\overline{46}$ 0.$\overline{546}$

e) 0.383   0.38$\overline{3}$ 0.3$\overline{83}$ 0.$\overline{383}$

f) 0.786   0.78$\overline{6}$ 0.7$\overline{86}$ 0.$\overline{786}$

10. a) Use long division to write the fractions as repeating decimals. Copy your answers below.

$\frac{1}{9} =$ $\frac{2}{9} =$ $\frac{3}{9} =$ $\frac{4}{9} =$

b) Use the pattern you found in part a) to find…

$\frac{5}{9} =$ $\frac{6}{9} =$ $\frac{7}{9} =$ $\frac{8}{9} =$ $\frac{9}{9} =$

NS8-77 Using Decimals to Compare Fractions

1. Write each fraction as a decimal. Circle the decimal that is closest to the fraction.

   a) $\frac{1}{4} = \underline{.25}$

   $\frac{1}{4}$ is closest to: 0.2   0.4   0.6

   b) $\frac{3}{4} = \underline{}$

   $\frac{3}{4}$ is closest to: 0.5   0.7   0.9

   c) $\frac{1}{5} = \underline{}$

   $\frac{1}{5}$ is closest to: 0.14   0.25   0.36

   d) $\frac{2}{5} = \underline{}$

   $\frac{2}{5}$ is closest to: 0.25   0.42   0.52

2. Express each fraction as a decimal (round your answer to three decimal places).
   Circle the fraction that is closest to the decimal.

   a) $\frac{4}{5}$ `.800` $\frac{7}{10}$ ☐ $\frac{2}{3}$ ☐   0.65 is closest to: $\frac{4}{5}$ $\frac{7}{10}$ $\frac{2}{3}$

   b) $\frac{1}{7}$ ☐ $\frac{1}{8}$ ☐ $\frac{1}{9}$ ☐   0.125 is closest to: $\frac{1}{7}$ $\frac{1}{8}$ $\frac{1}{9}$

   c) $3\frac{1}{2}$ ☐ $\frac{10}{3}$ ☐ $\frac{8}{3}$ ☐   3.28 is closest to: $3\frac{1}{2}$ $\frac{10}{3}$ $\frac{8}{3}$

3. Use decimal equivalents to order these fractions from greatest to least: $\frac{5}{6}, \frac{13}{17}, \frac{56}{73}, \frac{4}{5}$.

4. a) Compare each fraction and decimal by writing them as fractions with
      a common denominator.

   i) 0.57 and $\frac{3}{5}$ ii) 0.83 and $\frac{4}{5}$ iii) $\frac{2}{3}$ and 0.37

   b) Compare each fraction and decimal from part a) by writing the fraction
      as a decimal.

   c) Do you prefer the method you used in part a) or part b)? Explain.

5. a) Which of $\frac{6}{11}, \frac{23}{45}$, and $\frac{11}{21}$ is closest to $\frac{1}{2}$?   b) Which of 0.285, $0.\overline{286}$, and $0.28\overline{5}$ is closest to $\frac{2}{7}$?

6. 0.24 is close to 0.25, so a fraction close to 0.24 is $\frac{1}{4}$. Write a fraction that is close to...

   a) 0.52   b) 0.32   c) 0.298   d) 0.38   e) 0.59   f) 0.12

7. a) Use a calculator to write each fraction as a decimal: $\frac{8}{13}, \frac{9}{11}, \frac{5}{36}, \frac{3}{17}, \frac{89}{121}$.

   b) Order the fractions in part a) from least to greatest.

NS8-78 Is the Fraction a Terminating or Repeating Decimal?

INVESTIGATION ▶ How can you tell from the fraction whether the equivalent decimal repeats or terminates?

A. Write three different fractions, one with each denominator: 10, 100, and 1 000. Will the decimal representations of these fractions terminate? Explain.

B. Why can a terminating decimal always be written as a decimal fraction?

Examples: $0.3 = \dfrac{3}{10}$, $0.17 = \dfrac{17}{100}$

C. Divide using a calculator. Does the decimal equivalent of the fraction terminate or repeat?

a) $\dfrac{5}{8}$ b) $\dfrac{7}{12}$ c) $\dfrac{6}{13}$ d) $\dfrac{7}{15}$ e) $\dfrac{3}{17}$ f) $\dfrac{13}{2000}$

Write the fractions with equivalent terminating decimals as decimal fractions.

D. $10 = 2 \times 5$. Write 100 and 1 000 as a product of 2s and 5s.

E. Write a fraction with a denominator that is a product of 2s, 5s, or a combination of 2s and 5s. Use a calculator to divide the numerator by the denominator. Does the equivalent decimal terminate?

F. Write $\dfrac{1}{6}, \dfrac{2}{6}, \dfrac{3}{6}, \dfrac{4}{6}$, and $\dfrac{5}{6}$ in simplest form. Why is $\dfrac{3}{6}$ the only one of the sixths that terminates?

How to Decide If a Fraction Is Equivalent to a Terminating Decimal or a Repeating Decimal

Step 1: Write the fraction in **lowest terms**.

Step 2: Look at the **denominator**.
If it can be written as a product of only 2s and/or 5s, the decimal terminates.
If it cannot be written as a product of only 2s and/or 5s, the decimal repeats.

---

1. a) Calculate the first few powers of 3 ($3, 3 \times 3, 3 \times 3 \times 3, \dots$).

b) Are the decimal equivalents for $\dfrac{1}{3}, \dfrac{1}{9}$, and $\dfrac{1}{27}$ repeating decimals? How can you tell without calculating the decimal?

2. a) Write out the twelfths from $\dfrac{1}{12}$ to $\dfrac{11}{12}$. Write them all in lowest terms.

b) Predict which of the twelfths will terminate. Explain.
c) Use a calculator to calculate the decimal equivalents for all the twelfths.
d) Which of the twelfths terminate? Was your prediction in part b) correct?

3. The denominators of $\dfrac{3}{6}, \dfrac{3}{12}, \dfrac{6}{12}, \dfrac{3}{15}, \dfrac{6}{15}, \dfrac{9}{15}$ and $\dfrac{12}{15}$, all have 3 as a factor. But they are all terminating decimals. Why?

NS8-79 Adding and Subtracting Repeating Decimals

1. Add or subtract the decimals by lining up the decimal places.

   a) $.\overline{25} + .\overline{33} = .58\overline{25}$

   b) $.\overline{125} + .\overline{2} =$

   c) $.\overline{34} + .\overline{61} = \underline{\hspace{1cm}}$

   d) $.\overline{342} + .\overline{251} = \underline{\hspace{1cm}}$

   e) $.\overline{52} - .\overline{22} = \underline{\hspace{1cm}}$

   f) $.\overline{345} - .\overline{123} = \underline{\hspace{1cm}}$

2. $\frac{1}{9} = 0.111..., \quad \frac{2}{9} = 0.222..., \quad \frac{3}{9} = 0.333...,$ and so on.

   a) Add the repeating decimals by lining up the decimal places.

   i) $0.\overline{1} + 0.\overline{2} = \underline{\hspace{1cm}}$

   ii) $0.\overline{2} + 0.\overline{5} = \underline{\hspace{1cm}}$

   iii) $0.\overline{4} + 0.\overline{4} = \underline{\hspace{1cm}}$

   b) Add the repeating decimals in part a) by changing them to fractions, adding the fractions, then writing the sum as a decimal.

   c) Do you prefer the method you used in part a) or part b)? Explain.

3. a) Add by lining up the decimal places.

   i) $0.3 + 0.7$ ii) $0.33 + 0.77$ iii) $0.333 + 0.777$ iv) $0.3333 + 0.7777$

   b) Use the pattern in part a) to predict $0.\overline{3} + 0.\overline{7}$.

   c) Why is it not possible to add $0.\overline{3} + 0.\overline{7}$ by lining up the decimal places?

   d) Change the repeating decimals in part b) to fractions. (Hint: Use the pattern in Question 2.)

   Add the fractions. Was your prediction in part b) correct?

4. Add or subtract by...

   a) lining up the decimal places.

   b) changing the decimals to fractions, adding or subtracting the fractions, then changing the fraction to a decimal by dividing.

   i) $0.25 + 0.\overline{3}$ ii) $0.\overline{3} - 0.25$ iii) $0.5 + 0.\overline{4}$ iv) $0.5 - 0.\overline{4}$

NS8-80 Writing Repeating Decimals as Fractions

1. a) Use long division to write $\frac{1}{11}, \frac{2}{11}, \frac{3}{11}$, and $\frac{4}{11}$ as decimals.

   b) Extend the pattern to find $\frac{5}{11}, \frac{6}{11}, \frac{7}{11}, \frac{8}{11}, \frac{9}{11}, \frac{10}{11}$, and $\frac{11}{11}$.

   c) Use $\frac{9}{9} = \frac{11}{11} = 0.\overline{9}$ to show that $0.\overline{9} = 1$.

   d) Calculate the first three products, then predict the fourth.

0.09	0.0909	0.090909	0.$\overline{09}$
×5	×5	×5	×5

   e) Calculate $0.\overline{09} \times 5$ by changing the decimal to a fraction. Then change your answer back to a decimal. Was your prediction correct?

2. a) Use long division to show that $\frac{1}{99} = 0.\overline{01}$.

   b) Calculate the first three products, then predict the fourth.

0.01	0.0101	0.010101	0.$\overline{01}$
×17	×17	×17	×17

   c) Write $\frac{17}{99}$ as a repeating decimal. Explain your answer.

3. Write the fraction as a repeating decimal.

   a) $\frac{25}{99}$ b) $\frac{38}{99}$ c) $\frac{97}{99}$ d) $\frac{86}{99}$ e) $\frac{7}{99}$ f) $\frac{4}{99}$

4. Change the fraction to an equivalent fraction with denominator 9 or 99. Then write the repeating decimal.

   a) $\frac{13}{33}$ b) $\frac{2}{3}$ c) $\frac{4}{11}$ d) $\frac{34}{66}$ e) $\frac{10}{18}$ f) $\frac{30}{55}$

5. Change each repeating decimal to a fraction. Write your answer in lowest terms.

   a) $0.\overline{46}$ b) $0.\overline{07}$ c) $0.\overline{15}$ d) $0.\overline{98}$ e) $0.\overline{6}$ f) $0.\overline{48}$

6. a) We know that $\frac{1}{9} = 0.\overline{1}$ and $\frac{1}{99} = 0.\overline{01}$.   Predict: $\frac{1}{999} = \underline{\hspace{2cm}}$

   Check your answer by long division.

   b) Use your answer in part a) to calculate the equivalent decimal for...

   i) $\frac{34}{999}$ ii) $\frac{8}{999}$ iii) $\frac{734}{999}$ iv) $\frac{46}{999}$ v) $\frac{25}{333}$ vi) $\frac{47}{111}$

1. Write the repeating decimal as a fraction.

a) $0.\overline{7} = \dfrac{}{9}$

b) $0.\overline{23} = \dfrac{}{99}$

c) $0.\overline{05} = \dfrac{}{99}$

d) $0.\overline{441} = \dfrac{}{999}$

e) $0.\overline{652} = \dfrac{}{999}$

f) $0.\overline{98} =$

g) $0.\overline{5} =$

h) $0.\overline{461} =$

i) $0.\overline{38} =$

j) $0.\overline{061} =$

2. Multiply or divide by moving the decimal point the correct number of places, left or right.

a) $25.44444\ldots \times 10$

b) $2.66666\ldots \times 100$

c) $24.919191\ldots \div 10$

d) $0.\overline{32} \times 100$

e) $0.\overline{32} \div 100$

f) $54.\overline{361} \times 100$

g) $0.\overline{341} \div 10$

h) $7.\overline{432} \div 1000$

i) $36.\overline{432} \times 10$

3. a) $\dfrac{1}{9} = \underline{\quad 0.111\ldots \quad}$

So $\dfrac{1}{90} = \underline{\quad 0.0111\ldots \quad}$

b) $\dfrac{4}{9} = \underline{\qquad\qquad}$

So $\dfrac{4}{900} = \underline{\qquad\qquad}$

c) $\dfrac{2}{3} = \underline{\qquad\qquad}$

So $\dfrac{2}{3000} = \underline{\qquad\qquad}$

4. $\dfrac{137}{999} = 0.\overline{137}$. What is $\dfrac{137}{9990}$? $\underline{\qquad\qquad}$

5. a) $13 \times 0.01 = \underline{\qquad\qquad}$ $13 \times 0.011 = \underline{\qquad\qquad}$ $13 \times 0.0111 = \underline{\qquad\qquad}$

b) Predict: $13 \times 0.0111\ldots = \underline{\qquad\qquad}$

c) Why should $\dfrac{13}{90}$ be equal to your answer to part b)? Check using a calculator.

d) Use $\dfrac{13}{9} = 1\dfrac{4}{9}$ to find $\dfrac{13}{90}$ in a different way.

6. Write each decimal as a fraction.

a) $0.\overline{1} = \underline{\quad}$ $0.\overline{8} = \underline{\quad}$ $0.0\overline{8} = \underline{\quad}$

$0.5\overline{8} = 0.5 + 0.0\overline{8} = \underline{\quad} + \underline{\quad} = \underline{\quad}$

b) $0.\overline{01} = \underline{\quad}$ $0.\overline{27} = \underline{\quad}$ $0.0\overline{27} = \underline{\quad}$

$0.4\overline{27} = 0.4 + 0.0\overline{27} = \underline{\quad} + \underline{\quad} = \underline{\quad}$

c) $0.\overline{001} = \underline{\quad}$ $0.\overline{253} = \underline{\quad}$ $0.0\overline{253} = \underline{\quad}$

$5.6\overline{253} = \underline{\quad} + \underline{\quad} = \underline{\quad} + \underline{\quad} = \underline{\quad}$

d) $0.\overline{5} = \underline{\quad}$ so $4.\overline{5} = \underline{\quad}$

$0.0\overline{5} = \underline{\quad}$ so $4.0\overline{5} = \underline{\quad}$

e) $0.1\overline{5}$

f) $1.\overline{7}$

g) $2.3\overline{5}$

h) $0.24\overline{361}$

i) $2.4\overline{361}$

NS8-82 Percents

> The words "per cent" mean "out of 100." A percent is a ratio that compares a number or amount to 100.
>
> The symbol for a percent is %. Example: $45\% = 45 : 100 = \dfrac{45}{100}$

1. a) 40 out of 100 squares are shaded. The ratio of shaded squares

   to all squares is _____ : 100.

   So, _____% of the grid is shaded.

   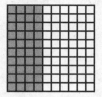

   b) 49 out of 100 letters are Bs. The ratio of Bs to all letters

   in the set is _____ : 100.

   So, _____% of the letters are Bs.

   BBBBCCBBAABBCABBBCCB
   AAABBBCCBBAABAAABBBC
   CBCABBBCCBBBCCBBAAAB
   BAAABBABCBBAABCCBBAB
   BCCBAABBAAAABBCCABAB

2. Write the ratio as a percent.

   a) $50 : 100 = $ _____%   b) $72 : 100 = $ _____%   c) $7 : 100 = $ _____%   d) $43 : 100 = $ _____%

3. Write the percent as a ratio.

   a) $70\% = $ _____ : _100_   b) $13\% = $ _____ : _____   c) $38\% = $ _____ : _____   d) $8\% = $ _____ : _____

4. Write the ratio as a fraction and as a percent.

   a) $60 : 100 = \dfrac{}{100} = $ _____%   b) $10 : 100 = \dfrac{}{100} = $ _____%

5. Write the fraction as a percent.

   a) $\dfrac{52}{100} = $ _____%   b) $\dfrac{39}{100} = $ _____%   c) $\dfrac{18}{100} = $ d) $\dfrac{2}{100} = $ e) $\dfrac{6}{100} = $

6. Write the percent as a fraction.

   a) $12\% = \dfrac{}{100}$ b) $7\% = \dfrac{}{100}$ c) $49\% = $ d) $3\% = $ e) $100\% = $

7. Complete the chart.

Drawing				
Fraction	$\dfrac{34}{100}$	$\dfrac{}{100}$	$\dfrac{67}{100}$	$\dfrac{}{100}$
Percent	34%	52%	_____ %	_____ %

NS8-83 Adding and Subtracting Percents

1. There are 100 squares on the grid.

   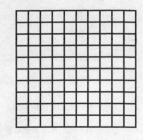

   Colour 10 out of 100 squares red. The red area is ____% of the grid.

   Colour 40 out of 100 squares blue. The blue area is ____% of the grid.

   There are now $10 + 40 =$ ____ coloured squares on the grid.

   So, ____% of the grid is coloured.

2. Write the percents as fractions. Add or subtract. Then write the sum or difference as a percent.

   a) $40\% + 30\% = \dfrac{}{100} + \dfrac{}{100} = \dfrac{}{100} =$ ____%
   b) $60\% + 10\% = \dfrac{}{100} + \dfrac{}{100} = \dfrac{}{100} =$ ____%

   c) $60\% - 35\% = \dfrac{}{100} - \dfrac{}{100} = \dfrac{}{100} =$ ____%
   d) $80\% - 40\% = \dfrac{}{100} - \dfrac{}{100} = \dfrac{}{100} =$ ____%

3. Calculate.

   a) $17\% + 30\% =$ ____%
   b) $22\% + 68\% =$ ____%
   c) $49\% - 16\% + 7\% =$ ____%

4. Determine the missing percent in the circle graph. The whole circle represents 100%.

   a) **Gases in Earth's Atmosphere**

   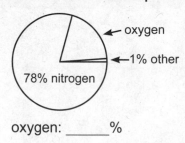

   oxygen: _____%

   b) **Composition of Earth's Water**

   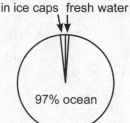

   2% frozen in ice caps   unfrozen fresh water

   97% ocean

   unfrozen fresh water: _____%

   c) **Land Cover in North America**

   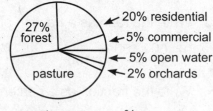

   27% forest

   pasture

   20% residential
   5% commercial
   5% open water
   2% orchards

   pasture: _____%

5. a) The ratio of cents in a penny to cents in a dollar is 1 : 100, so a penny is ____% of a dollar.

   The ratio of cents in a dime to cents in a dollar is ____ : 100, so a dime is ____% of a dollar.

   A quarter is ____ cents out of 100, so a quarter is ____% of a dollar.

   b) What percent of a dollar is 35 cents? _____%

   What percent of a dollar is two pennies and two quarters? ____%

   c) You have a dollar and you spend 26¢. What percent of the dollar do you

   have left? ____%

NS8-84 Tenths, Decimals, and Percents

1. Shade the percent.

    a) 60%

    b) 40%

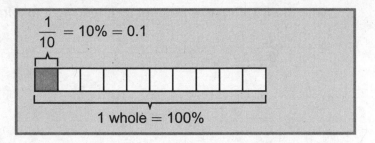

$\frac{1}{10} = 10\% = 0.1$

1 whole = 100%

2. ____% of the 10 dots are white.

    ____% of the 10 dots are grey.

3. a) Shade 70% of the 10 dots.

    b) What percent of the dots are not shaded? _____

4. 10% of 100 marbles are blue. How many of the marbles are not blue? _____

5. Write the percent as a fraction and then as a decimal.

    a) $80\% = \dfrac{}{100} = 0.\underline{\ \ }\,\underline{\ \ }$ b) $75\% = \dfrac{}{100} = 0.\underline{\ \ }\,\underline{\ \ }$ c) $21\% = \dfrac{}{100} = 0.\underline{\ \ }\,\underline{\ \ }$ d) $9\% = \dfrac{}{100} = 0.\underline{\ \ }\,\underline{\ \ }$

    e) $15\% = \underline{\ \ \ } = \underline{\ \ \ }$ f) $42\% = \underline{\ \ \ } = \underline{\ \ \ }$ g) $7\% = \underline{\ \ \ } = \underline{\ \ \ }$ h) $100\% = \underline{\ \ \ } = \underline{\ \ \ }$

6. Write the percent as a decimal.

    a) $25\% = 0.\underline{\ \ }\,\underline{\ \ }$ b) $75\% = 0.\underline{\ \ }\,\underline{\ \ }$ c) $13\% = \underline{\ \ \ \ }$ d) $40\% = \underline{\ \ \ \ }$
    e) $7\% = \underline{\ \ \ \ }$ f) $9\% = \underline{\ \ \ \ }$ g) $70\% = \underline{\ \ \ \ }$ h) $1\% = \underline{\ \ \ \ }$

7. Write the decimal as a percent.

    a) $0.2 = \dfrac{2}{10} = \dfrac{}{100} = \underline{\ \ \ }\%$ b) $0.3 = \dfrac{}{10} = \dfrac{}{100} = \underline{\ \ \ }\%$ c) $0.7 =$

    d) $0.23 = \dfrac{}{100} = \underline{\ \ \ }\%$ e) $0.57 =$ f) $0.08 =$

8. Write the decimal as a percent by moving the decimal point two places to the right.

    a) $0.5 = \underline{\ \ \ }\%$ b) $0.7 = \underline{\ \ \ }\%$ c) $0.4 =$ d) $0.1 =$ e) $0.9 =$

    f) $0.27 = \underline{\ \ \ }\%$ g) $0.60 = \underline{\ \ \ }\%$ h) $0.53 =$ i) $0.07 =$ j) $0.99 =$

9. Approximately what percent does the decimal represent? Example: $0.1234 \approx 0.12 = 12\%$.
    Hint: Remember to round to two decimal places.

    a) $0.382 \approx \underline{\ \ \ }\%$ b) $0.925 \approx \underline{\ \ \ }\%$ c) $0.3779 \approx$ d) $0.1036 \approx$

10. Ken bought 7 classical CDs and 3 jazz CDs. What fraction of the CDs are classical?
    What percent are jazz?

NS8-85 Fractions and Percents

1. Write the fraction as a percent by changing it to a fraction over 100.

   a) $\dfrac{3 \times 20}{5 \times 20} = \dfrac{60}{100} = 60\%$

   b) $\dfrac{4}{5}$

   c) $\dfrac{3}{20}$

   d) $\dfrac{8}{25}$

2. Two out of five friends, or $\dfrac{2}{5}$, ordered pizza. What percent ordered pizza? ____

3. Change the fraction to a percent. Reduce the fraction to lowest terms if necessary.

   a) $\dfrac{9}{15} = \dfrac{3}{5} = \dfrac{60}{100} = 60\%$

   b) $\dfrac{3}{15} =$

   c) $\dfrac{9}{18} =$

   d) $\dfrac{6}{24} =$

   e) $\dfrac{2}{5}$

   f) $\dfrac{7}{10}$

   g) $\dfrac{3}{15}$

   h) $\dfrac{17}{20}$

   i) $\dfrac{12}{48}$

4. Divide to change the fraction to a decimal. Then write the decimal as a percent.

   a) $\dfrac{3}{4} = 3 \div 4 = 0.\underline{}\,\underline{} = \underline{}\%$

   b) $\dfrac{4}{5}$

   c) $\dfrac{6}{15}$

   d) $\dfrac{15}{25}$

   e) $\dfrac{65}{500}$

5. Write the percent as a decimal, then as a fraction, then in lowest terms.

   a) 30%

   b) 84%

   c) 55%

   d) 4%

   e) 90%

6. Is the fraction closest to 10%, 25%, 50%, 75%, or 100%?

   a) $\dfrac{4}{5}$

   b) $\dfrac{2}{10}$

   c) $\dfrac{2}{5}$

   d) $\dfrac{9}{10}$

   e) $\dfrac{11}{20}$

   f) $\dfrac{16}{20}$

   g) $\dfrac{4}{25}$

7. Estimate what percent the fraction is. Say what fraction you used to make your estimate. Then divide to change the fraction to a decimal. Was your estimate close?

   a) $\dfrac{11}{40}$

   b) $\dfrac{23}{49}$

   c) $\dfrac{60}{84}$

   d) $\dfrac{14}{24}$

   e) $\dfrac{4}{42}$

   f) $\dfrac{21}{31}$

8. Write the fraction as a decimal. Round to two decimal places. Write the approximate percent.

   a) $\dfrac{5}{12} = 5 \div 12 = 0.41\overline{6} \approx 0.42 = \underline{}\%$

   b) $\dfrac{1}{3}$

   c) $\dfrac{2}{3}$

   d) $\dfrac{2}{9}$

   e) $\dfrac{5}{6}$

   f) $\dfrac{1}{7}$

1. What percent of the figure is shaded?

a) 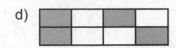 ____%

b) ____%

c) ____%

d)  ____%

e) ____%

f) ____%

g) ____%

2. Shade 50% of each figure.

a)

b)

3. Write different expressions for the shaded area.

$$\frac{}{20} = \frac{}{100} = 0.\underline{\quad} = \underline{\quad}\%$$

4. Write the percents that are equivalent to the fractions.

$$\frac{0}{10} \qquad \frac{2}{5} \quad \frac{1}{2} \qquad \frac{7}{10} \qquad \frac{10}{10}$$

____% ____% ____% ____% ____%

5. Measure the line segment. Extend the segment to show 100%.

a) |——50%——|

b) |—20%—|

c) |———75%———|

6. Estimate the percent of the line segment to the left of the mark.

a)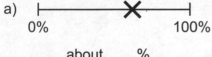
0%   100%

about ____%

b)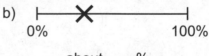
0%   100%

about ____%

7. 25 out of 50 squares in a grid are shaded. What fraction and percent of the squares are shaded?

8. Alice must do 40 hours of community service. She has completed 10 hours. What fraction and percent of the hours has she completed? What percent of the hours must still be completed?

9. When would you use the measurement to describe the amount, and when would you use the percent (if ever)? Write a sentence using each expression.

a) 3 h of the school day or 50% of the school day

b) 12 kg of berries or 40% of the berries

NS8-87 Comparing Fractions, Decimals, and Percents

1. Complete the chart.

Fraction	$\frac{1}{4}$		$\frac{3}{20}$			$\frac{6}{15}$	$\frac{23}{25}$		
Decimal		0.35			0.60				0.55
Percent				40%				75%	

2. Write $<$ or $>$ or $=$ between each pair of numbers. First change the numbers to a pair of decimal fractions with the same denominator.

a) $\frac{1}{2}$ 47%

$\frac{1 \times 50}{2 \times 50}$ $\frac{47}{100}$

$\frac{50}{100}$ $\boxed{>}$ $\frac{47}{100}$

b) $\frac{1}{2}$ 57% $\square$

c) $\frac{1}{5}$ 22 % $\square$

d) $\frac{3}{5}$ 80% $\square$

e) $\frac{3}{4}$ 67% $\square$

f) 0.26   42% $\square$

g) 0.05   7% $\square$

h) $\frac{3}{10}$ 30% $\square$

i) $\frac{21}{25}$ 18% $\square$

j) $\frac{39}{50}$ 76% $\square$

k) 0.8   15% $\square$

l) $\frac{16}{20}$ 32% $\square$

3. Change the numbers in each set to decimals. Then order the decimals from least to greatest.

a) $\frac{3}{5}$, 42%, 0.73

b) $\frac{1}{2}$, 0.73, 80%

c) $\frac{1}{4}$, 0.09, 15%

4. a) In Abeed's school, $\frac{3}{5}$ of students like gym and 65% like drama. Which class is more popular?

b) In Rachel's class, 0.45 of the students like pepperoni pizza best, 35% like cheese, and $\frac{1}{5}$ like vegetarian. Which type of pizza do the most students like best?

NS8-88 Finding Percents

If you use a thousands cube to represent 1 whole, you can see that taking $\frac{1}{10}$ of a number is the same as dividing by 10 (the decimal shifts one place left):

$\frac{1}{10}$ of ▦ = ▦ $\frac{1}{10}$ of ▦ = | $\frac{1}{10}$ of | = ▫

$\frac{1}{10}$ of 1 = 0.1 $\frac{1}{10}$ of 0.1 = 0.01 $\frac{1}{10}$ of 0.01 = 0.001

1. Find $\frac{1}{10}$ of each number by shifting the decimal. Write your answers in the boxes provided.

   a) 7   b) 10   c) 35   d) 210   e) 6.4   f) 50.6

2. 10% is short for $\frac{10}{100}$ or $\frac{1}{10}$. Find 10% of each number.

   a) 1   b) 3.9   c) 4.05   d) 6.74   e) 0.09   f) 60.08

How to Find Percents That Are Multiples of 10

Step 1: Find 10% of the number.

Step 2: Multiply the result by the number of tens in the percent.

Example: Find 30% of 21.

10% of 21 = $\boxed{2.1}$

There are 3 tens in 30 (30 = 3 × 10).

3 × $\boxed{2.1}$ = 6.3

So 30% of 21 = 6.3.

---

3. Find the percent using the method above.

   a) 30% of 15

      10% of _15_ = ☐

      3 × ☐ = ___

   b) 40% of 35

      10% of ___ = ☐

      ___ × ☐ = ___

   c) 20% of 2.7

      10% of ___ = ☐

      ___ × ☐ = ___

   d) 50% of 62

      10% of ___ = ☐

      ___ × ☐ = ___

   e) 80% of 17

      10% of ___ = ☐

      ___ × ☐ = ___

   f) 30% of 0.7

      10% of ___ = ☐

      ___ × ☐ = ___

4. If you know 10% of a number *n*, then 5% of *n* is 10% divided by 2. Complete the chart.

5%	3			
10%	6	20	42	1
100%	60			

Use these steps to find 1% of a number:

Step 1: Change the percent to a decimal and replace "of" with "×."

Step 2: Multiply by 0.01 by shifting the decimal two places left.

5. Fill in the blanks.

   a) 1% of 300 = __0.01__ × __300__ = _____   b) 1% of 2000 = _____ × _____ = _____

   c) 1% of 15 = _____ × _____ = _____   d) 1% of 60 = _____ × _____ = _____

6. Find 1% of 200 and use your answer to calculate each percent.

   a) 2% of 200 = _____   b) 3% of 200 = _____   c) 12% of 200 = _____

7. Use the method of Question 6 to calculate…

   a) 4% of 800   b) 2% of 50   c) 11% of 60   d) 2% of 4   e) 7% of 45

8. Fill in the missing numbers. (Hint: 8% = 4% + 4%.)

2%	4%	8%	10%	20%	50%	25%	100%
	20						
	30						
					60		
			50				

9. a) If 45% is 9, what is 90%?   b) If 3% is 12, what is 1%?
   c) If 40% is 64, what is 100%?   d) If 20% is 13, what is 100%?

10. Arti wants to leave a 15% tip on a meal that cost $60. How much tip should she leave? (Hint: 15% = 10% + 5%.)

11. a) A shirt that usually costs $40 is on sale for 25% off. What is 25% of $40? What is $40 − (25% of $40)? What is the sale price of the shirt?

   b) How would you estimate the price if a shirt that usually costs $32.99 is on sale for 25% off?

NS8-89 Further Percents

35% is short for $\dfrac{35}{100}$. To find 35% of 27, Sadie finds $\dfrac{35}{100}$ of 27.

Step 1: She multiplies 27 by 35.	**Step 2:** She divides the result by 100.
$\begin{array}{r} 27 \\ \times\,35 \\ \hline 135 \\ 810 \\ \hline 945 \end{array}$	$945 \div 100 = 9.45$ So 35% of 27 is 9.45.

1. Find the percent using Sadie's method.

   a) 23% of 34

   Step 1: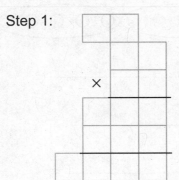

   Step 2: _____ $\div$ 100 = _____

   So _____ of _____ is _____ .

   b) 17% of 85

   Step 1: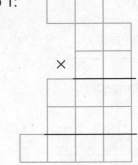

   Step 2: _____ $\div$ 100 = _____

   So _____ of _____ is _____ .

2. Find the percent using Sadie's method.

   a) 22% of 33   b) 14% of 48   c) 22% of 90   d) 69% of 44

   e) 83% of 75   f) 40% of 18   g) 31% of 52   h) 17% of 90

3. a) Find 35% of 40 in two ways. Do you get the same answer both ways?

   i) Use Sadie's method.

   ii) Use $35\% = 25\% + 10\%$.

   b) 35% is less than $50\% = \dfrac{1}{2}$. Is your answer to part a) less than half of 40?

   c) Is 35% closer to 0 or $\dfrac{1}{2}$? _____

   Was your answer to part a) closer to 0 or to half of 40? _____

   Is your answer to part a) reasonable? Explain.

4. Find 30% of 50 and 50% of 30. What do you notice? Why is this the case?

NS8-90 Writing Equivalent Statements for Proportions

These are equivalent statements:

$\frac{6}{9}$ of the circles are shaded.

$\frac{2}{3}$ of the circles are shaded.

6 is $\frac{2}{3}$ of 9.

$6 : 9 = 2 : 3$

part   whole

1. Write four equivalent statements for each picture.

a)

$\frac{4}{6}$ are shaded

_____

$\frac{2}{3}$ are shaded

_____

4 is $\frac{2}{3}$ of 6

_____

$4 : 6 = 2 : 3$

_____

b)

_____

_____

_____

_____

_____

c)

_____

_____

_____

_____

d)

_____

_____

_____

_____

2. For each picture, write a pair of equivalent ratios.

a)

4 is $\frac{1}{2}$ of 8

$\underset{\text{part}}{4} : \underset{\text{whole}}{8} = 1 : 2$

b)

6 is $\frac{3}{5}$ of 10

$\underset{\text{part}}{\quad} : \underset{\text{whole}}{\quad} = \_\_ : \_\_$

c)

2 is $\frac{1}{4}$ of 8

$\underset{\text{part}}{\quad} : \underset{\text{whole}}{\quad} = \_\_ : \_\_$

3. For each statement, write a pair of equivalent ratios and equivalent fractions.

a) 15 is $\frac{3}{4}$ of 20 $\underset{\text{part}}{\quad} : \underset{\text{whole}}{\quad} = \_\_ : \_\_$ $\dfrac{\text{part}}{\text{whole}}$ $\_\_ = \_\_$

b) 18 is $\frac{9}{10}$ of 20 $\underset{\text{part}}{\quad} : \underset{\text{whole}}{\quad} = \_\_ : \_\_$ $\dfrac{\text{part}}{\text{whole}}$ $\_\_ = \_\_$

4. Write a question mark where you are missing a piece of information.

a) 12 is $\frac{4}{5}$ of what number? $\underset{\text{part}}{\underline{12}} : \underset{\text{whole}}{\underline{?}} = \underline{4} : \underline{5}$ $\dfrac{\text{part}}{\text{whole}}$ $\dfrac{12}{?} = \dfrac{4}{5}$

b) 6 is how many quarters of 8? $\underset{\text{part}}{\underline{6}} : \underset{\text{whole}}{\underline{8}} = \underline{?} : \underline{4}$ $\dfrac{\text{part}}{\text{whole}}$ $\dfrac{}{} = \dfrac{}{}$

c) What is $\frac{3}{4}$ of 16? $\underset{\text{part}}{\underline{}} : \underset{\text{whole}}{\underline{}} = \underline{} : \underline{}$ $\dfrac{\text{part}}{\text{whole}}$ $\dfrac{}{} = \dfrac{}{}$

d) 20 is how many thirds of 30? $\underset{\text{part}}{\underline{}} : \underset{\text{whole}}{\underline{}} = \underline{} : \underline{}$ $\dfrac{\text{part}}{\text{whole}}$ $\dfrac{}{} = \dfrac{}{}$

5. For each statement, write a pair of equivalent ratios and a pair of equivalent fractions.

a) 15 is what percent of 20? $\underset{\text{part}}{\underline{15}} : \underset{\text{whole}}{\underline{20}} = \underline{?} : \underline{100}$ $\dfrac{\text{part}}{\text{whole}}$ $\dfrac{15}{20} = \dfrac{?}{100}$

b) What is 25% of 80? $\underset{\text{part}}{\underline{}} : \underset{\text{whole}}{\underline{}} = \underline{} : \underline{}$ $\dfrac{\text{part}}{\text{whole}}$ $\dfrac{}{} = \dfrac{}{}$

c) 9 is what percent of 12? $\underset{\text{part}}{\underline{}} : \underset{\text{whole}}{\underline{}} = \underline{} : \underline{}$ $\dfrac{\text{part}}{\text{whole}}$ $\dfrac{}{} = \dfrac{}{}$

d) 18 is 3% of what number? $\underset{\text{part}}{\underline{}} : \underset{\text{whole}}{\underline{}} = \underline{} : \underline{}$ $\dfrac{\text{part}}{\text{whole}}$ $\dfrac{}{} = \dfrac{}{}$

6. Write the two pieces of information you are given and what you need to find (?). Then write an equation for the problem.

a) What percent of 30 is 5?   part $\underline{5}$ whole $\underline{30}$ percent $\underline{?}$ $\dfrac{5}{30} = \dfrac{?}{100}$

b) If 7 is 20%, what is 100%?   part $\underline{}$ whole $\underline{?}$ percent $\underline{}$ $\dfrac{}{?} = \dfrac{}{100}$

c) What is 6% of 24?   part $\underline{?}$ whole $\underline{}$ percent $\underline{}$ $\dfrac{?}{} = \dfrac{}{100}$

d) If 3 is 12%, what is 100%?   part $\underline{}$ whole $\underline{}$ percent $\underline{}$ $\dfrac{}{} = \dfrac{}{100}$

e) What percent of 90 is 4?   part $\underline{}$ whole $\underline{}$ percent $\underline{}$ $\dfrac{}{} = \dfrac{}{100}$

f) What is 52% of 18?   part $\underline{}$ whole $\underline{}$ percent $\underline{}$ $\dfrac{}{} = \dfrac{}{100}$

g) 7 is what percent of 25?   part $\underline{}$ whole $\underline{}$ percent $\underline{}$ $\dfrac{}{} = \dfrac{}{100}$

If 5 subway tickets cost $4, how much do 20 tickets cost? Write the ratio of tickets to dollars as a fraction, then find an equivalent fraction by multiplying.

Step 1: $\dfrac{4}{5} = \dfrac{?}{20}$	Step 2: $\dfrac{4}{5} \xrightarrow[\times 4]{\times 4} \dfrac{}{20}$	Step 3: $\dfrac{4}{5} \xrightarrow[\times 4]{\times 4} \dfrac{16}{20}$

1. Solve the ratio. Draw arrows and show what you multiply by.

   a) $\dfrac{3}{4} = \dfrac{}{20}$ b) $\dfrac{1}{5} = \dfrac{}{15}$ c) $\dfrac{3}{5} = \dfrac{}{35}$ d) $\dfrac{4}{7} = \dfrac{}{49}$

   e) $\dfrac{3}{8} = \dfrac{}{24}$ f) $\dfrac{2}{3} = \dfrac{}{18}$ g) $\dfrac{13}{20} = \dfrac{}{100}$ h) $\dfrac{5}{9} = \dfrac{}{72}$

2. Solve the ratio as you did in Question 1. Note: The arrows will point from right to left.

   a) $\dfrac{15}{} = \dfrac{3}{4}$ b) $\dfrac{12}{} = \dfrac{2}{5}$ c) $\dfrac{15}{} = \dfrac{3}{7}$ d) $\dfrac{12}{18} = \dfrac{}{3}$

3. For each question, you will have to reduce the fraction given before you can find the equivalent fraction. The first one has been started for you.

   a) $\dfrac{8}{10} = \dfrac{4}{5} = \dfrac{}{15}$ b) $\dfrac{4}{6} = \dfrac{}{} = \dfrac{}{15}$ c) $\dfrac{40}{100} = \dfrac{}{} = \dfrac{}{45}$

   d) $\dfrac{15}{18} = \dfrac{}{} = \dfrac{}{30}$ e) $\dfrac{70}{100} = \dfrac{}{} = \dfrac{}{90}$ f) $\dfrac{50}{75} = \dfrac{}{} = \dfrac{}{36}$

4. Write a proportion to represent the percent problem. Solve the proportion.

   a) What percent of 20 is 4?   part ____   whole ____   percent ____ $\dfrac{}{} = \dfrac{}{100}$

   b) If 6 is 25%, what is 100%?   part ____   whole ____   percent ____ $\dfrac{}{} = \dfrac{}{100}$

   c) What is 17% of 10?   part ____   whole ____   percent ____ $\dfrac{}{} = \dfrac{}{100}$

   d) What is 17% of 50?   part ____   whole ____   percent ____ $\dfrac{}{} = \dfrac{}{100}$

   e) 4 is what percent of 5?

   f) 6 is 25% of what number?

   g) 24 is 80% of what number?

5. Explain why the proportion $\frac{3}{25} = \frac{x}{100}$ will be easy to solve.

6. Write a proportion $\frac{a}{b} = \frac{x}{100}$ to represent each problem. Solve by first writing $\frac{a}{b}$ in lowest terms.

   a) What percent of 15 is 3?   b) What percent of 24 is 6?   c) What percent of 30 is 12?

7. Write a proportion to represent the percent problem. Find an equivalent ratio to rewrite the proportion.

   a) If 6 is 40%, what is 100%?   part __6__   whole __?__   percent __40__ $\frac{6}{?} = \frac{40}{100}$ $\frac{6}{?} = \frac{2}{5}$

   Hint: Start by writing $\frac{40}{100}$ as an equivalent ratio with numerator 2.

   b) What is 75% of 48?   part ____   whole ____   percent ____ $\frac{\ \ }{\ \ } = \frac{\ \ }{100}$ $\frac{\ \ }{\ \ } = \frac{\ \ }{\ \ }$

   Hint: Start by writing 75% as an equivalent ratio with denominator 4.

   c) What percent of 60 is 45?   part ____   whole ____   percent ____ $\frac{\ \ }{\ \ } = \frac{\ \ }{100}$ $\frac{\ \ }{\ \ } = \frac{\ \ }{\ \ }$

   Hint: Start by writing $\frac{45}{60}$ as an equivalent ratio with denominator 20.

   d) What is 64% of 15?   part ____   whole ____   percent ____ $\frac{\ \ }{\ \ } = \frac{\ \ }{100}$ $\frac{\ \ }{\ \ } = \frac{\ \ }{\ \ }$

   Hint: Start by writing $\frac{64}{100}$ as an equivalent ratio with denominator 5.

8. Solve the proportions in Question 7. Explain why the proportions in Question 7 were more challenging to solve than those in Question 4.

9. Solve.

   a) 8 is 40% of what number?   b) What is 60% of 30?

   c) 15 is 75% of what number?   d) What percent of 240 is 60?

10. If 4 of 25 fish are blue, what percent of the fish are blue? What percent are not blue?

11. If 45% of 180 students voted for Kendra for student council, how many of the students voted for Kendra?

12. 12 students in a class (60% of the class) are fluent in French. How many students are in the class?

$\dfrac{3}{4} = 0.75$ means the same thing as $3 \div 4 = 0.75$.

1. a) Write $\dfrac{a}{b} = c$ as a division statement. _____ $\div$ _____ = _____

b) Use the information from part a) to write a as a product. $a =$ _____ $\times$ _____

2. Change the equation to a multiplication statement.

a) $\dfrac{9}{x} = 2$ b) $7 = \dfrac{x}{5}$ c) $\dfrac{x}{3} = 11$ d) $3 = \dfrac{21}{x}$

    $\underline{\quad 9 = 2x \quad}$ $\underline{\quad 7 \times 5 = x \quad}$ $\underline{\qquad\qquad}$ $\underline{\qquad\qquad}$

e) $\dfrac{12}{x} = 11$ f) $\dfrac{x}{9} = 7$ g) $\dfrac{24}{x} = 8$ h) $6 = \dfrac{x}{7}$

3. Write the equation as a multiplication statement. Then solve for x.

a) $\dfrac{7}{x} = 3$ b) $8 = \dfrac{x}{5}$ c) $2 = \dfrac{5}{x}$ d) $\dfrac{x}{3} = 10$

$7 = 3x$

$\dfrac{7}{3} = \dfrac{3x}{3}$

$\dfrac{7}{3} = x$

e) $5 = \dfrac{20}{x}$ f) $9 = \dfrac{x}{8}$ g) $\dfrac{x}{5} = 11$ h) $\dfrac{36}{x} = 4$

$\dfrac{3}{4} = \dfrac{9}{12}$ so $3 \div 4 = 9 \div 12$

                 $12 \times 3 \div 4 = 12 \times 9 \div 12$ Multiply both sides by 12.

                 $12 \times 3 \div 4 = 9$ Rewrite the right side.

         $12 \times 3 \div 4 \times 4 = 9 \times 4$ Multiply both sides by 4.

                 $12 \times 3 = 9 \times 4$ Rewrite the left side.

To rewrite $\dfrac{3}{4} = \dfrac{9}{12}$ as $12 \times 3 = 9 \times 4$ is called **cross-multiplying** because the products can be obtained from an "X": $\dfrac{3}{4} \bowtie \dfrac{9}{12}$

4. Check that cross-multiplying works for these equivalent fractions.

a) $\dfrac{2}{5} = \dfrac{6}{15}$ b) $\dfrac{3}{4} = \dfrac{6}{8}$ c) $\dfrac{1}{2} = \dfrac{5}{10}$ d) $\dfrac{2}{3} = \dfrac{8}{12}$ e) make your own

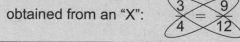

     $2 \times 15 = 5 \times 6$

       $30 = 30 \checkmark$

5. Cross-multiply and write = (equal) or ≠ (not equal) in the box. Then decide if the fractions are equivalent.

a) $\frac{3}{4}$ and $\frac{10}{13}$

____3____ × ___13___ ☐ ___4___ × ___10___

Are $\frac{3}{4}$ and $\frac{10}{13}$ equivalent? _____

b) $\frac{2}{5}$ and $\frac{10}{25}$

_____ × _____ ☐ _____ × _____

Are $\frac{2}{5}$ and $\frac{10}{25}$ equivalent? _____

c) $\frac{9}{10}$ and $\frac{81}{100}$

_____ × _____ ☐ _____ × _____

Are $\frac{9}{10}$ and $\frac{81}{100}$ equivalent? _____

d) $\frac{5}{7}$ and $\frac{28}{35}$

_____ × _____ ☐ _____ × _____

Are $\frac{5}{7}$ and $\frac{28}{35}$ equivalent? _____

e) $\frac{3}{4}$ and $\frac{15}{20}$

f) $\frac{5}{6}$ and $\frac{35}{42}$

g) $\frac{91}{105}$ and $\frac{104}{120}$

h) $\frac{14}{21}$ and $\frac{30}{48}$

6. Cross-multiply to write an equation for x. (Do not solve.)

a) $\frac{7}{x} = \frac{3}{5}$

____$7 \times 5 = 3x$____

b) $\frac{x}{9} = \frac{2}{5}$

____$5x = 2 \times 9$____

c) $\frac{11}{x} = \frac{5}{2}$

_____

d) $\frac{4}{9} = \frac{x}{3}$

e) $\frac{5}{21} = \frac{3}{x}$

f) $\frac{x}{52} = \frac{4}{8}$

g) $\frac{20}{x} = \frac{12}{25}$

h) $\frac{12}{x} = \frac{3}{10}$

7. Solve for x.

a) $\frac{9}{6} = \frac{x}{3}$

b) $\frac{4}{x} = \frac{2}{3}$

c) $\frac{3}{4} = \frac{6}{x}$

d) $\frac{100}{7} = \frac{9}{x}$

e) $\frac{2}{x} = \frac{10}{4}$

You can solve percent problems by first writing a proportion and then cross-multiplying.

Example: What is 70% of 9? $\frac{x}{9} = \frac{70}{100}$ so $100x = 70 \times 9$

$100x = 630$

$\frac{100x}{100} = \frac{630}{100}$

$x = 6.3$

---

8. Solve the problem by first writing a proportion.

a) What is 90% of 6?

b) 9 is 2% of what number?

c) 5 is what percent of 8?

Write an equation for each of the problems below and solve the equation. Use a calculator.

9. a) What percent of 32 is 8? b) What percent of 125 is 5?
c) What percent of 128 is 32? d) What percent of 15 is 0.6?

10. Round the solution to the nearest one.

a) 5 is about what percent of 24? b) About what percent of 17 is 9?
c) 4 is about what percent of 9? d) About what percent of 7 560 is 3 000?
e) 1.3 is about what percent of 27?

11. If Yvonne has read 54 of the 297 pages in her library book, about what percent of the book has she read so far?

12. Find the amounts. Include units in your answers.

a) 26% of 130 g b) 11% of 407 m
c) 32% of 11 mL d) 99% of 8 m²
e) 40% of 2 222 min

13. About 3% of 592 students are vegans. About how many of the students are vegans?

14. A basketball team won 60% of the 25 games it played this year.

a) What percent of the games played did the team lose?
b) How many games did the team lose?

15. Find 100% if…

a) 25% is 30 b) 15% is 30 c) 3% is 12

16. Round the solution to the nearest one.

a) 10 is 7%. About what is 100%? b) 74 is 32%. About what is 100%?
c) 2 is 9%. About what is 100%?

17. In a Grade 8 class, 6 students, or about 27%, were on the honour roll. How many students were in the class?

18. Kai bought a new computer at a 15% discount. He paid $1 020.

a) What percent of the original price did he pay?
b) What was the original price?
c) How many dollars did Kai save by buying the computer at a discount?

19. A computer costs $1 000 plus 15% tax. Which of these is the best deal?

A: The store offers a 15% discount on the $1 000 purchase price, then adds the tax onto the sale price.

B: The store will pay the tax.

C: The store offers a 15% discount, calculated after the tax is added.

NS8-93 Percents Less Than 1%

1. $100\% = 1$, $10\% = \dfrac{1}{10}$, 1% is $\dfrac{1}{100}$. What fraction is equivalent to 0.1%? _____

2. Circle the two numbers in the set that are equal.

   a) 0.3%   0.03   0.003   b) $\dfrac{9}{10}$ 0.9% $\dfrac{9}{1000}$ c) 0.25 25% 0.25%

> To write the decimal 0.235 as a percent, multiply by 100:
>
> If $0.235 = x\,\%$, then $0.235 = \dfrac{x}{100}$, so $x = 0.235 \times 100 = 23.5$
>
> So $0.235 = 23.5\%$.

3. Write the decimal as a percent.

   a) 0.273 = _____.___%   b) 0.848 = _____   c) 0.369 = _____   d) 0.405 = _____

   e) 0.005 = _____   f) 0.125 = _____   g) 0.077 = _____   h) 6.242 = _____

4. Each small rectangle on the grid is one thousandth of the whole grid.

   a) Shade 21.5% of the grid.   b) Shade 45.3% of the grid.

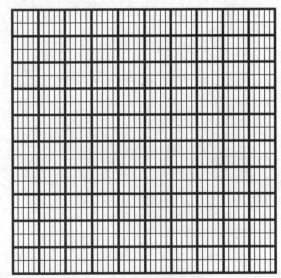 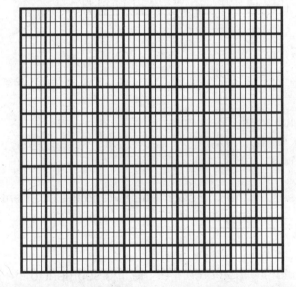

> Grasslands make up $2\dfrac{1}{2}\%$ of the habitat of birds in North America. $2\dfrac{1}{2}\% = 2.5\% = \dfrac{2.5}{100}$.
>
> To get a proper fraction, multiply the numerator and denominator by 10. $\dfrac{2.5 \times 10}{100 \times 10} = \dfrac{25}{1000} = \dfrac{1}{40}$

5. Express the percent as a proper fraction and rewrite the fraction in lowest terms.

   a) 17.5%   b) 0.7%   c) 6.4%   d) 0.04%

   e) $33\dfrac{1}{3}\%$ f) $12\dfrac{1}{2}\%$ g) $3\dfrac{1}{8}\%$ h) $66\dfrac{2}{3}\%$

NS8-94 Percents Greater Than 100%

1. Determine the total percent of the grids that is shaded as a fraction, decimal, and percent.

a)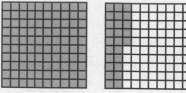

Fraction: $\dfrac{}{100} + \dfrac{}{100} = 1\dfrac{}{100}$

Decimal: _____ + 0._____ = _____

Percent: _____% + _____% = _____%

b)

Fraction: _____ + _____ + _____ = _____

Decimal: _____ + _____ + _____ = _____

Percent: _____% + _____% + _____% = _____%

2. a) Shade the grids to represent 134%.

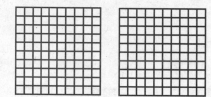

b) Shade the grids to represent 273%.

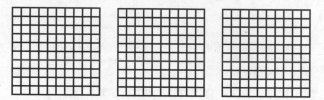

3. Add the percents.

a) 125% + 240% = _____%   b) 80% + 60% = _____%   c) 150% + 75% = _____%

4. Subtract the percents.

a) 117% − 17% = _____%   b) 125% − 40% = _____%   c) 675% − 50% = _____%

5. Measure the line segment. Extend the segment to show 150%.

a) 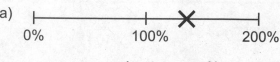 50%

b) 75%

6. Estimate the percent of the line segment to the left of the mark.

a)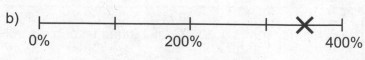

0%   100%   200%

about _____%

b)

0%   200%   400%

about _____%

7. Write the ratio as an improper fraction and as a percent.

a) $110 : 100 = \dfrac{}{100} = $ _____%   b) $350 : 100 = \dfrac{}{100} = $ _____%   c) $261 : 100 = \dfrac{}{100} = $ _____%

8. Write the percent as a mixed number with the fractional part in lowest terms.

a) 130%   b) 275%   c) 308%   d) 1505%   e) 785%

9. Complete the chart. Hint: If a decimal with one decimal place is given, add a zero to make two decimal places.

Percent			190%	535%			
Mixed Number						$1\frac{76}{100}$	$1\frac{8}{100}$
Decimal	9.2 = _9.20_	2.32			3.4 = _____		

10. About what percent does the decimal represent? Example: $4.715 \approx 4.72 = 472\%$

   a) $4.382 \approx$ _____%   b) $5.925 \approx$ _____%   c) $5.007 \approx$ d) $2.999 \approx$

11. Write the percent as a decimal, then as a mixed number, then in lowest terms.

   a) 350%   b) 540%   c) 275%   d) 360%   e) 515%

12. Write the mixed number as a percent.

   a) $2\frac{1}{2}$ b) $3\frac{3}{4}$ c) $8\frac{3}{10}$ d) $1\frac{1}{5}$ e) $20\frac{3}{20}$ f) $17\frac{9}{25}$

13. Write the mixed number as a decimal. Round the decimal to two places. Then write the approximate percent.

   a) $3\frac{5}{12} = 3 + 0.41\overline{6} \approx 3.42 =$ _____%   b) $3\frac{1}{3}$ c) $4\frac{2}{3}$ d) $1\frac{2}{9}$ e) $2\frac{1}{7}$

14. Change the numbers in each set to decimals. Then order the numbers from greatest to least.

   a) $1\frac{1}{2}$ 1.73   180%   b) $1\frac{6}{10}$ 157%   1.62   c) $6\frac{1}{4}$ 6.09   615%

15. Determine the amount mentally.

   a) 300% of 20 = _____   b) 250% of 50 = _____   c) 110% of 6 = _____   d) 330% of 2 = _____

16. If 30% = 150, what is 10%? _____   What is 100%? _____

17. Determine 100% mentally.

   a) If 40% = 200, then 100% = _____.   b) If 5% = 20, then 100% = _____.

   c) If 150% = 12, then 100% = _____.   d) If 300% = 18, then 100% = _____.

18. Estimate the solution. Use a calculator to check your estimate. Was your estimate close?

   a) What percent of 20 is 30?   b) What percent of 45 is 87?   c) What percent of 2 is 17?
   d) What percent of 7 is 13?   e) What percent of 1.5 is 4.4?   f) What percent of 1.1 is 59.3?

NS8-95 Percent Problems

1. Calculate.

   a) 80% − 65% + 22% = _____   b) 41% + _____ = 100%   c) 96% − _____ = 25%

2. What is the sales tax where you live? _____

   Calculate the amount of tax you would pay on each price.

   a) $15 _____   b) $40 _____   c) $67.25 _____   d) $82.52 _____

3. In the school elections, $\frac{2}{5}$ of the students voted for Anne and 17% voted for Ravi.

   The rest voted for Yen. What percent voted for Yen?

4. A builder spent $400.00 on equipment. Complete the chart.

Item	Money spent		
	Fraction	Percent	$ Amount
Drywall			$220.00
Paint	$\frac{2}{5}$		
Wallpaper		30%	

5. A student hopes to raise $500 for his favourite charity. He has already raised $100 by having a garage sale. What percent of the $500 does he still need to raise?

6. Complete the chart.

Item	Regular Price	Discount (percent)	Discount ($ amount)	Sale Price
Gloves	$36.00	10%	$3.60	$36.00 − $3.60 = $32.40
Shoes	$49.92	25%		
CD	$14.90	30%		

7. Clare bought a computer at a 40% discount. She paid $800. How many dollars did she save by buying the computer at a discount?

8. John spent $720 on furniture. He spent 25% on a chair, $327.60 on a table, and the rest on a sofa. What fraction and what percent of the $720 did he spend on each item?

9. Erik had 1 400 stamps. 20% of the stamps were Canadian. Recently he bought 300 new Canadian stamps. How many Canadian stamps does he have now? What percent and what fraction of his stamps are Canadian?

NS8-96 Relating Fractions, Ratios, and Percents

1. Write the number of boys (**b**), girls (**g**), and children (**c**) in each class.

   a) There are 7 boys and 6 girls in a class.   **b** _____   **g** _____   **c** _____

   b) There are 5 boys and 9 girls in a class.   **b** _____   **g** _____   **c** _____

   c) There are 18 boys and 22 girls in a class.   **b** _____   **g** _____   **c** _____

   d) There are 15 girls in a class of 27 children. **b** _____   **g** _____   **c** _____

2. Write the number of boys, girls, and children in each class. Then write the fraction of children who are boys and the fraction who are girls in the boxes provided.

   a) There are 6 boys and 9 girls in a class.   **b** ___ ▢   **g** ___ ▢   **c** ___

   b) There are 17 children in the class and 9 are boys.   **b** ___ ▢   **g** ___ ▢   **c** ___

3. Fill in the missing numbers for each classroom.

	Ratio of boys to girls	Fraction of boys	Fraction of girls	Percentage of boys	Percentage of girls
a)	3 : 2	$\dfrac{3}{5}$	$\dfrac{2}{5}$	$\dfrac{3}{5} = \dfrac{60}{100} = 60\%$	40%
b)	1 : 5				
c)		$\dfrac{11}{20}$			
d)				30%	
e)		$\dfrac{12}{25}$			
f)	32 : 18				
g)			$\dfrac{27}{50}$		
h)					45%
i)				19%	

4. Fill in the missing numbers for each classroom.

	Number of students	Fraction of boys	Fraction of girls	Number of boys	Number of girls
a)	20	$\frac{4}{5}$	$\frac{1}{5}$	$\frac{4}{5} \times 20 = 16$	4
b)	40	$\frac{1}{5}$			
c)	24		$\frac{1}{4}$		
d)	38	$\frac{5}{19}$			

5. Determine the number of girls and boys in each class.

a) There are 20 children and $\frac{2}{5}$ are boys.

b) There are 42 children and $\frac{3}{7}$ are girls.

c) There are 15 children.
The ratio of girls to boys is 3 : 2.

d) There are 24 children.
The ratio of girls to boys is 3 : 5.

e) There are 25 children and 60% are girls.

f) There are 28 children and 25% are boys.

6. For each question, say which classroom has more girls.

a) In classroom A, there are 40 children and 60% are girls.
In classroom B, there are 36 children. The ratio of boys to girls is 5 : 4.

b) In classroom A, there are 28 children. The ratio of boys to girls is 5 : 2.

In classroom B, there are 30 children and $\frac{3}{5}$ of the children are boys.

7. Ron and Ella shared $35 in the ratio 4 : 3. What fraction of the money did each person receive? What amount of money did each person receive?

8. Students in a class each chose one sport to participate in for a sports day. Complete the chart. How did you find the number of students who chose swimming?

Chosen sport	Fraction of the class that chose the sport	Percent	Decimal	Number of students who chose the sport
Soccer	$\frac{1}{5}$			4
Swimming		40%		
Baseball				
Gymnastics			.15	

NS8-97 Finding the Whole from the Part

$\dfrac{2}{3}$ of a number is 100. What is the number?

$\dfrac{2}{3} = \dfrac{100}{?}$ part whole $\dfrac{2}{3} \overset{\times 50}{\underset{\times 50}{\rightrightarrows}} \dfrac{100}{?}$ $\dfrac{2}{3} = \dfrac{100}{150}$ The number is 150.

1. Find the number.

   a) $\dfrac{2}{5}$ of a number is 4.

   b) $\dfrac{3}{7}$ of a number is 9.

   c) $\dfrac{5}{11}$ of a number is 25.

2. A box holds red and blue beads. Find the total number of beads in the box.

   a) $\dfrac{3}{4}$ of the beads are red. Six beads are red.

   b) $\dfrac{3}{5}$ of the beads are blue. Twelve beads are blue.

   c) 60% of the beads are red. Fifteen beads are red.

   d) The ratio of red to blue beads is 4 : 5. There are 20 red beads.

3. Ron and Lisa share a sum of money. Ron receives $\dfrac{2}{5}$ of the money. Lisa receives $24.

   a) What fraction of the sum does Lisa receive?   b) How much money do Ron and Lisa share?

4. At Franklin Middle School, $\dfrac{3}{8}$ of the students take a bus to school, $\dfrac{3}{5}$ walk, and

   the rest bike. There are 20 students who bike to school. How many students are

   in the school?

5. In a fish tank, $\dfrac{2}{3}$ of the fish are red, $\dfrac{1}{4}$ are yellow, and the rest are green. There are

   42 more red fish than green fish.

   a) What fraction of the fish are green?

   b) What fraction of the total number of fish does 42 represent? Hint: 42 is the
      difference between the number of red and green fish.

   c) How many fish are in the tank?

6. In Tina's stamp collection, 70% of the stamps are Canadian and the rest are
   international. Tina has 500 more Canadian stamps than international stamps.
   How many stamps does she have?

7. On a neon sign, $\dfrac{1}{5}$ of the lights are yellow and the rest are blue and red. There are

   twice as many blue lights as yellow lights, and there are 200 red lights on the sign.

   How many lights of all colours are on the sign?

NS8-98 Further Percent Problems

1. A pair of jeans costs $80. Now the jeans are 20% off. Find the new cost of the jeans in two ways:

   a) Find 20% of 80. Then subtract this amount from 80.
   b) 100% − 20% = 80%. Find 80% of 80.

2. A daily planner cost $12.50 last year. The price has increased 20%. What is the new price?

3. A game sells for $25 plus 14% tax. Is $28 enough to buy the game?

4. a) 115% = 46. What is 100%?   b) 120% = 80. What is 100%?   c) 150% = 45. What is 100%?

   $115\% \div 115 = 46 \div 115$

   $1\% = 46 \div 115 = 0.4$

   $100\% = 1\% \times 100$

   $ = 0.4 \times 100$

   $ = 40$

5. The total cost of a T-shirt, including 14% tax, is $23.00. The total cost is 114% of the price before taxes. What is the price of the T-shirt before taxes?

6. A grocery buys organic apples at 80 cents each and sells them for $1 each. What percent does the store mark up the price of each apple?

7. This year, 20 more students joined the band than last year. That is a 10% increase.
   a) How many students were in the band last year?
   b) How many students are in the band this year?

8. The tax on a purchase of $20 is $2.80. How much tax will there be on a purchase of $45.50?

9. Suppose you bought something that was priced at $6.95, and the total bill was $7.61. What is the sales tax rate in this city? (Round your answer to one decimal place.)

10. Calculate the percent. Round to one decimal place if necessary.

    a) 25% of 50% $= 0.25 \times 0.50$ b) 10% of 60% = _____   c) 80% of 30% = _____

    $ = 0.125$

    $ = 12.5\%$

11. Ravi gave 60% of his stamp collection to his brother. He sold 20% of the remaining amount. What percent of his collection did he sell?

NS8-99 Word Problems

1. An 8-slice pizza is shared among 3 people. Mayah eats 2 pieces, Tegan eats 3 pieces, and Matias eats 3 pieces. The pizza costs $12.99 plus 14% tax. How much should each person pay?

2. Two hockey goalies, Dillon and Melissa, are comparing their records. Dillon saved 53 out of 60 shots in 3 games. Melissa saved 65 out of 70 shots in 2 games. Find…

   a) the percentage of shots each person saved (to one decimal place).

   b) the average number of goals allowed per game by each person (to one decimal place).

   c) Who do you think is the better goalie? Why?

3. Philip gave away 45% of his hockey cards.

   a) What fraction of his cards did Philip keep?

   b) Philip put his remaining cards in a scrapbook. Each page held 18 cards and he filled $23\frac{5}{6}$ pages. How many cards did he put in the book?

   c) How many cards did Philip have before he gave part of his collection away?

4. Pure gold is 24 karat, so 12-karat gold is 50% pure and 18-karat gold is 75% pure.

   a) What percentage of pure gold is in 15-karat gold?

   b) Rita has a gold bracelet weighing 50 g. It is 15-karat gold. If pure gold costs $23.64/g, what is a fair price for the bracelet?

5. Kevin gave $\frac{2}{7}$ of his savings to charity and spent $\frac{3}{5}$ of the remainder on holiday gifts.

   a) What fraction of Kevin's money was left?

   b) If Kevin had $300 left, how much money did he have to start with?

6. A book costs $17.50. The salesperson tells you that the total price, including taxes, is $21.43. How can you tell if the total price is reasonable without using a calculator?

7. You invest $4 000 in a fund that earns 10% interest each year. If you leave the money in the fund and do not touch it, how much money will you have after two years?

8. Two years ago, a calculator cost $120. The price increased by 10% last year. This year, last year's price increased by 12%. What is this year's price? What percent did the price increase over the two years?

9. A population increased by 10% one year and then increased by 15% the next year. Explain why there was not a 25% increase in population over the two years.

NS8-100 Three-Term Ratios

There can be more than two terms in a ratio.

1 : 2 : 3
white to black to grey triangles
This is a part-part-part ratio.

1 : 2 : 6
white to black to all triangles
This is a part-part-whole ratio.

1. Write the ratios.

   a) white to grey to striped squares

   ____ : ____ : ____

   striped to white to all squares

   ____ : ____ : ____

   b) white to grey to black blocks

   ____ : ____ : ____

   black to all to white blocks

   ____ : ____ : ____

2. The ratio of red to blue to green marbles is 3 : 4 : 5.

   a) What is the ratio of…

i) red to green marbles?	ii) green to blue marbles?	iii) blue to red marbles?
iv) green to red marbles?	v) blue to green marbles?	vi) red to blue marbles?

   b) If there are 12 red marbles, how many green marbles are there?

   c) If there are 12 blue marbles, how many red marbles are there?

   d) If there are 60 marbles altogether, how many marbles of each colour are there?

   e) Ron counts 9 red marbles, 12 blue marbles, and 14 green marbles. His teacher told him there should be one more marble. What colour is the missing marble?

3. Fill in the blanks using the ratios in the equation 2 : 7 : 5 = 6 : 21 : 15.

   a) 2 : 7 = ____ : ____

   b) 7 : 5 = ____ : ____

   c) 2 : 5 = ____ : ____

   d) 5 : 7 = ____ : ____

   e) 5 : 2 = ____ : ____

   f) 7 : 2 = ____ : ____

How to solve the 3-term proportion 2 : : 4 = ▨ : 9 : 12

Step 1: Write three 2-term proportions.

2 : ▦ = ▨ : 9   2 : 4 = ▨ : 12   ▦ : 4 = 9 : 12

Step 2: Solve the 2-term proportions that have only one unknown.

2 : 4 = ▨ : 12   ▦ : 4 = 9 : 12

2 × 3 : 4 × 3 = ▨ : 12   ▦ × 3 : 4 × 3 = 9 : 12

▨ = 2 × 3 = 6   ▦ × 3 = 9, so ▦ = 3

Step 3: Write the 3-term proportion. 2 : 3 : 4 = 6 : 9 : 12.

---

4. Solve the 3-term proportions. Do the rough work in your notebook.

   a) 3 : 1 : 2 = 12 : ____ : ____

   b) 8 : 6 : ____ = 12 : ____ : 24

   c) ____ : 5 : 7 = 9 : ____ : 21

   d) 4 : ____ : 3 = ____ : 14 : 6

   e) ____ : 8 : 6 = 55 : 40 : ____

   f) 45 : ____ : 54 = 5 : 8 : ____

NS8-101 Rates

A **rate** is a ratio of two quantities measured in different units. Rates are written with a slash instead of a colon or as a fraction. Example: $2 / 3 min (we read this as "$2 **per** 3 minutes")

1. Find the equivalent rate.

   a) $\dfrac{10 \text{ km}}{2 \text{ h}} = \dfrac{5 \text{ km}}{1 \text{ h}}$ b) $\dfrac{18 \text{ km}}{3 \text{ h}} = \dfrac{\text{km}}{1 \text{ h}}$ c) $\dfrac{20 \text{ km}}{8 \text{ s}} = \dfrac{\text{m}}{2 \text{ s}}$ d) $\dfrac{42 \text{ km}}{3 \text{ L}} = \dfrac{\text{km}}{1 \text{ L}}$

   e) $\dfrac{\$35}{7 \text{ kg}} = \dfrac{\$5}{\text{kg}}$ f) $\dfrac{\$96}{6 \text{ h}} = \dfrac{\$32}{\text{h}}$ g) $\dfrac{\$1.05}{10 \text{ min}} = \dfrac{\$}{2 \text{ min}}$ h) $\dfrac{8 \text{ m}^2}{0.5 \text{ L}} = \dfrac{\text{m}^2}{1 \text{ L}}$

In a **unit rate**, the second term is equal to 1. The 1 is often left out. Example: 60 km / 1 h = 60 km/h

2. Find the unit rate for each rate (include the units).

   a) 20 km / 5 h = _4 km_ / 1 h   b) $12 / 2 boxes = _____ / 1 box   c) $70 / 2 h = _____ / 1 h

   d) 96 m / 12 s = _____ / 1 s   e) $45 / 9 jars = _____ / 1 jar   f) $32 / 4 kg = _____ / 1 kg

3. Change both prices to a unit rate to find out which offer is a better buy.

   a) 6 golf balls for $10 or 12 golf balls for $24?
   b) $112 for 7 CDs or $68 for 4 CDs?
   c) $36.52 for 2 cans of paint or $46.20 for 3 cans?

4. Density is the ratio of mass to volume measured in grams per cubic centimetre (g/cm^3).

   a) 500 cm^3 of human blood weigh 612 g. What is the density of human blood?

   b) One litre of milk weighs 1.003 kg. Is milk denser than human blood?

   c) The density of gasoline is 0.737 g/cm^3. Which is heavier: 500 mL of gasoline or 400 mL of milk?

5. Anne donates blood at a rate of 200 mL in 3 minutes. How long will it take Anne to donate 500 mL of blood?

6. A space shuttle flies at a speed of 11 km/s. The Moon is 380 000 km from Earth. How long will it take for the space shuttle to get from Earth to the Moon?

7. Jade is sick. She needs to take 0.5 mL of antibiotic per kilogram of her body weight each day. Jade weighs 42 kg.

   a) How much antibiotic does she need each day?

   b) Jade takes the antibiotic 3 times per day. How much antibiotic does she need to take each time?

   c) Jade will take the antibiotic for 10 days. How much antibiotic will she get in total?

8. Estimate to the nearest half hour how long it would take to drive each distance at 100 km/h.

   a) 254 km   b) 723 km   c) 1 425 km

NS8-102 Using Unit Rates

> **REMINDER ▶** Often a unit rate is written with the 1 left out. Example: 100 km / 1 h is written 100 km/h.

1. Use the unit rates in the chart to convert the measurements.

Example: Convert 25 mm to centimetres.

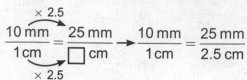

$$\frac{10 \text{ mm}}{1 \text{ cm}} = \frac{25 \text{ mm}}{\square \text{ cm}} \rightarrow \frac{10 \text{ mm}}{1 \text{ cm}} = \frac{25 \text{ mm}}{2.5 \text{ cm}}$$

10 mm/cm	1 000 mL/L	60 s/min
100 cm/m	1 000 mg/g	60 min/h
1 000 m/km	1 000 g/kg	24 h/day

So, 25 mm = 2.5 cm.

a) 50 mm to cm   b) 25 cm to m   c) 3 200 m to km   d) 4 500 mL to L
e) 6 900 mg to g   f) 240 s to min   g) 4 200 min to h   h) 120 h to days

2. The scale on this map is 120 km/1 cm. Measure the distance between Edmonton and each other place on the map in centimetres. Use the scale to determine the distances in real life.

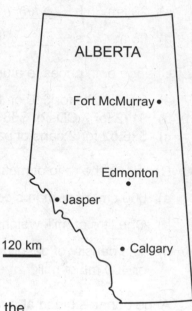

	Distance on map	Distance in real life
Edmonton and Calgary		
Edmonton and Jasper		
Edmonton and Fort McMurray		

3. On a map, 2.5 cm represents 40 km. How many kilometres do 17.5 cm on the map represent?

4. Cars are rated according to their fuel efficiency. David's car gets 11.45 km/L, Felicity's gets 12.76 km/L, and Jack's gets 38 km/L. How many kilometres can they each travel on 50 L of gas?

5. A spacecraft accelerates from the speed of 7 793 m/s to the speed of 10 822 m/s. It adds 9.52 m/s to its speed every second. How long will the acceleration take?

6. Connor is using paint that covers 12 square metres per can of paint. He needs to cover 160 m². How many cans of paint will he need? Explain your answer.

7. Grapes cost $2.80/kg, watermelon costs $1.50/kg, and peaches cost $1.80/kg. Julie made a fruit salad for a party with grapes, watermelon, and peaches in a ratio of 1 : 2 : 3. She made 18 kg of fruit salad. How much did she spend on fruit?

NS8-103 Ratio and Rates with Fractional Terms

Problem: A granola recipe uses $\frac{1}{2}$ cup of raisins for every 3 cups of oats. How many cups of oats are needed for 2 cups of raisins?

Solution: Write the names of the quantities being compared.

Write the given quantities under their names, as a ratio.

Find an equivalent ratio so that both terms are whole numbers.

Write the given and unknown quantities under their names.

cups of raisins		cups of oats
$\frac{1}{2}$	:	3
1	:	6
2	:	?

Solve the two ratios that consist of whole numbers only. **1 : 6 = 2 : ?**
In this case, ? = 12, so 12 cups of oats are needed.

1. Make both terms a whole number without changing the ratio.

   a) 3 km walked / $\frac{1}{2}$ h =

   b) 5 km rowed / $\frac{1}{3}$ h =

   c) $\frac{1}{4}$ cup of flour : 5 cups of flour =

   In parts d) and e), multiply each term by 10.

   d) 0.7 km / 3 L of gas =

   e) 1.7 mL of ginger ale : 0.3 mL of orange juice =

2. Solve the proportions.

   a) $\dfrac{2.4}{4} = \dfrac{24}{40} = \dfrac{}{20}$

   b) $\dfrac{5}{0.9} = \dfrac{}{} = \dfrac{}{45}$

   c) $\dfrac{3.9}{0.2} = \dfrac{}{} = \dfrac{}{1}$

   d) $\dfrac{6}{2.1} = \dfrac{}{} = \dfrac{20}{}$

   e) $\dfrac{7.2}{3.2} = \dfrac{}{} = \dfrac{}{4}$

   f) $\dfrac{5.4}{0.6} = \dfrac{}{} = \dfrac{18}{}$

3. Solve the problem by changing the ratio into a more convenient form.

   a) Rhonda can ride her bike 6 km in $\frac{1}{4}$ of an hour. How far can she ride in 3 hours?

   b) A plant grows 0.5 cm in 4 days. How many days will it take to grow 9 cm?

   c) On a map, 0.3 cm equals 50 m. How many metres does 7 cm on the map represent?

   d) A recipe uses $\frac{1}{3}$ cup milk to 2 cups flour. How much milk do you need if you use 3 cups of flour?

PDM8-6 Relative Frequency Tables

A **frequency table** shows how many times a data value occurs in a set.

A **relative frequency table** shows the percent of time each data value occurs.

Sometimes a table can show both frequency and relative frequency.

1. Look at the table below.

    a) How many people were surveyed? _____

    b) How many people chose Action as their favourite type of movie? _____

    c) If 100 people were surveyed instead, predict the number of people who would choose Action as their favourite type of movie: _____ Explain your prediction.

    d) Write the frequencies and relative frequencies (percents) for the tallies in the table.

Favourite Types of Movies			
Type	Tally	Frequency	Percent
Comedy	⫘ ⫘ ⫘ /	16	
Horror	⫘ ///		
Action	⫘ ⫘ ⫘		
Other	⫘ ⫘ /		

2. Tally the marks, then complete the table.

    A   B   D   C   B   B   B   A   B   B   A   B   B   C   C   B   A   B   D   B   B

Mark	Tally	Frequency	Percent
A			
B			
C			
D			

REMINDER ▶ To calculate 15% of 60,

change 15% to a fraction ($15\% = \dfrac{15}{100}$),

replace "of" with a multiplication sign ($\times$), and multiply:

$$15\% \text{ of } 60 = \frac{15}{100} \times 60$$
$$= \frac{3}{20} \times 60$$
$$= \frac{180}{20} = 9$$

---

3. a) Miki surveyed the 20 students in his class about their favourite type of music. Use the relative frequencies to complete the frequency table.

    b) Would you use the frequency or the relative frequency to decide…

    i) how many tickets the class should buy for each type of concert?

    ii) how many of each type of song to play at a class party? Explain.

Favourite Type of Music		
Type	Frequency	Percent
Pop		35%
Hip Hop		45%
Rock		15%
Other		5%

PDM8-7 Circle Graphs

> Use a circle divided into 100 equal parts to show percents. This is called a **circle graph**.

1. a) What percent of Grade 8 students prefer each type of movie in each school? Complete the chart.

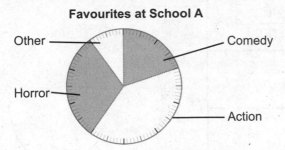

Favourites at School A

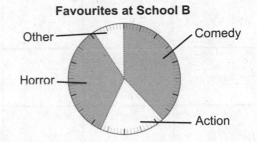

Favourites at School B

	Comedy	Action	Horror	Other	Total
School A	20%				
School B					

b) What is the total percent for each school? Why does this make sense?

2. Which of these statements can be deduced from the circle graphs in Question 1?

   a) At School A, more people prefer Action movies than Horror movies.
   b) More people prefer Action movies at School A than at School B.
   c) Most people at School A prefer Action movies.
   d) A greater percentage of people prefer Action movies at School A than at School B.

   Explain why the other statements cannot be deduced from the circle graphs.

3. Gisela copied the following percents from a circle graph she saw on the Internet.

Favourite Type of Movie			
Comedy	Action	Horror	Other
48%	21%	26%	9%

How can you tell that she made a mistake?

4. Lina says that School A is better at Science than School B because the "A" section in School A's graph looks bigger.

   a) Explain Lina's mistake.

   b) How are the graphs misleading?

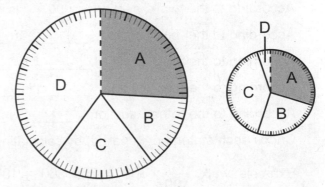

Science Marks at School A Science Marks at School B

PDM8-8 Drawing Circle Graphs

1. Complete the relative frequency table, then draw a circle graph.

Favourite Type of Book	Frequency	Fraction	Percent
Mystery	16	$\dfrac{16}{40} = \dfrac{2}{5}$	$\dfrac{2 \times 20}{5 \times 20} = \dfrac{40}{100} = 40\%$
Fantasy	4		
Romance	12		
Other	8		

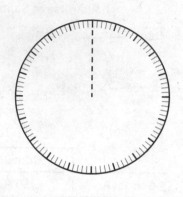

2. a) Find the percent of students who use each mode of transportation to get to school. Then use a protractor to find the angle of each section in the circle.

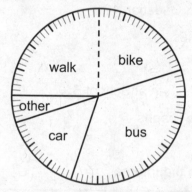

	Percent	Angle in circle
walk	25%	90°
bike		
bus		
car		
other		

b) Add the percents in your chart. _____ + _____ + _____ + _____ = _____

Do you get a total of 100%? If not, find your mistake.

c) Add the angles in your chart. _____ + _____ + _____ + _____ = _____

Do you get a total of 360°? If not, find your mistake.

d) Look at the chart above.

According to the "walk" section, ___90___ ° is ___25___ % of 360°.

According to the "bike" section, _____ ° is _____ % of 360°.

According to the "bus" section, _____ ° is _____ % of 360°.

According to the "car" section, _____ ° is _____ % of 360°.

According to the "other" section, _____ ° is _____ % of 360°.

e) Check each statement in part d) by calculating the percent.

Example: walk $\dfrac{25}{100} \times 360° = 25 \times 360° \div 100 = 90°$

Probability and Data Management 8-8

3. Complete each chart and then use your protractor to draw a circle graph. Use labels to make it clear what each part of the circle represents. Make sure all your percents total 100% and all your angles total 360°.

a) Survey results: Daily newspaper habit

Title: _____

	Percent	Angle in circle
delivered to home	40%	
buy occasionally		180°
never look at	10%	

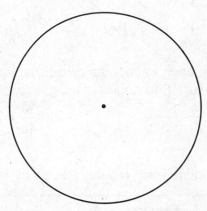

b) Survey results: How students spend money

Title: _____

	Percent	Angle in circle
entertainment (movies, CDs, etc.)		162°
clothes and personal care	30%	
snacks		36°
savings	15%	

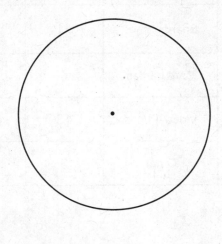

c) Survey results: Favourite kind of pie

Title: _____

	Percent	Angle in circle
apple	20%	
blueberry		54°
cherry		
other	55%	

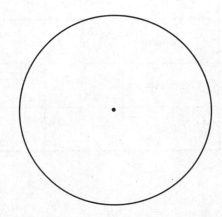

4. Write each fraction as an equivalent fraction over 100 and then as a percent.

a) $\dfrac{3}{10} = \dfrac{}{100} = \underline{}$ %

b) $\dfrac{7}{25} = \dfrac{}{100} = \underline{}$ %

c) $\dfrac{9}{20} = \dfrac{}{100} = \underline{}$ %

d) $\dfrac{33}{75} = \dfrac{}{25} = \dfrac{}{100} = \underline{}$ %

e) $\dfrac{12}{30} = \dfrac{}{10} = \dfrac{}{100} = \underline{}$ %

f) $\dfrac{52}{80} = \dfrac{}{20} = \dfrac{}{100} = \underline{}$ %

5. Write each fraction as an equivalent fraction over 360 to determine the degree measure (the angle) in a circle graph.

a) $\dfrac{9}{20} = \dfrac{}{360}$

b) $\dfrac{13}{40} = \dfrac{}{360}$

c) $\dfrac{70}{400} = \dfrac{}{40} = \dfrac{}{360}$

d) $\dfrac{21}{108} = \dfrac{}{36} = \dfrac{}{360}$

6. Complete each relative frequency table. Then draw a circle graph.

a)

Favourite Indoor Games	Frequency	Fraction of total	Angle in circle
Board games	11	$\dfrac{11}{36}$	110°
Card games	4		
Video games	18		
Other	3		

Title: _____

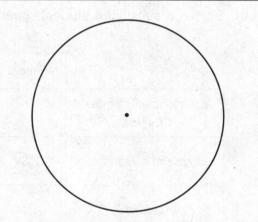

b)

Favourite Sport	Frequency	Fraction of total	Angle in circle
Hockey	8		144°
Swimming	7		
Running	3		
Other	2		

Title: _____

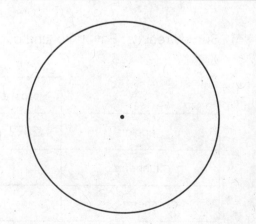

PDM8-9 Reading Circle Graphs

How to find the percentages from a circle graph

Step 1: Write each angle degree as a fraction of 360.

Example: $\dfrac{72}{360}$

Step 2: Change each fraction to a percent. (See p. 12)

Example: $\dfrac{72}{360} = 20\%$

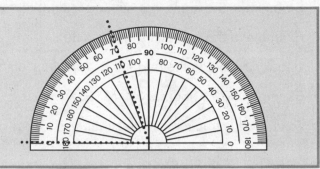

1. Calculate the percent.

a) 90° is _____% of 360°   b) 36° is _____% of 360°   c) 280° is _____% of 360°

2. a) Use a protractor to determine the angle of the "part-time" section in each circle graph. Then find the percent of people in each company who work part-time.

 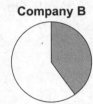 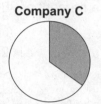

Company A   Company B   Company C

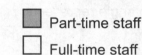
■ Part-time staff
□ Full-time staff

b) Company A has 300 employees, Company B has 30 employees, and Company C has 60 employees. Calculate the number of full-time and part-time employees in each company.

c) Which company has the greatest number of part-time staff? Why did the circle graphs not show this?

3. Company A and Company B draw circle graphs to show the distribution of their employees' ages.

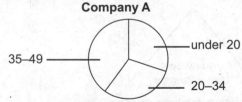

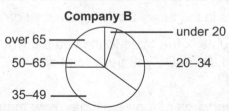

a) Company A has 40 employees and Company B has 200 employees. Draw a double bar graph for Companies A and B with these categories: under 20, 20–34, 35–49, 50–65, over 65.

b) Answer each question and write which graph helped you most—bar, circle, or both.

   i)   Which company has more employees under 20? _____   Which graph? _____

   ii)   Which company has the greater percentage of employees under 20? _____ Which graph? _____

   iii) Which company has more employees under 20 than over 65? _____   Which graph? _____

   iv) Which company has more employees 35 and over than under 35? _____   Which graph? _____

Sometimes the angle in a circle does not correspond to a whole number percent of 360°.

Example: If the angle in a circle is 30°, $\frac{30}{360} = \frac{1}{12} = 0.08\overline{3} = 8.\overline{3}\%$, so 30° is $8.\overline{3}\%$ of 360°.

Usually, rounding the percent to 1 decimal place is enough accuracy.

Example: 30° is about 8.3% of 360°.

To change a fraction to a decimal, use long division or a calculator.

4. Change each fraction to a decimal (rounded to 3 decimal places) and then to a percent (rounded to 1 decimal place).

a) $\frac{7}{12} \approx 0.$ _ _ _ = _____ %

b) $\frac{11}{36} \approx 0.$ _ _ _ = _____ %

c) $\frac{5}{18} \approx 0.$ _ _ _ = _____ %

d) $\frac{4}{15} \approx 0.$ _ _ _ = _____ %

5. Write each angle as a fraction of 360°. Then find the percent of 360° (rounded to 1 decimal place) that each angle represents.

a) 60°   b) 200°   c) 40°   d) 210°   e) 13°

6. Lina keeps track of how many servings of each type of food she eats in a month. She draws a circle graph to show her results.

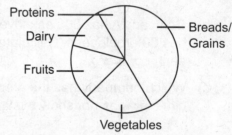

a) Use a protractor to find the angle in the circle for each type of food.

b) Find the percent of 360° (rounded to 1 decimal place) that each angle represents. Complete the relative frequency table.

	Breads/Grains	Vegetables	Fruits	Dairy	Proteins
Percent					

c) Add the percents in the table. Do you get a total of 100%?

d) Round the percents in the table to the nearest whole number and add them. Do you get a total of 100%? What happened?

e) If Lina eats 24 servings of food each day, how many servings of each type of food does she have each day?

f) Lina finds the pyramid at right on the Internet. The pyramid shows the recommended number of servings per day of each type of food. Compare what Lina eats to these recommendations. Are Lina's eating habits healthy?

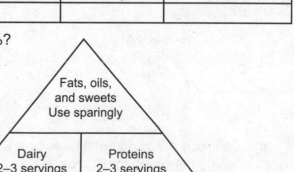
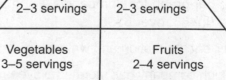

Probability and Data Management 8-9

PDM8-10 Scatter Plots

> Use a **scatter plot** when you have two sets of data measurements associated with a single person, object, or event. To draw a scatter plot, plot the ordered pairs on a coordinate grid. Each dot represents one individual person, object, or event.

1. Five students recorded their ages and their heights and then made a scatter plot.

	Age (years)	Height (cm)
Tanya	13	160
Jomar	14	157
Kevin	13	166
Melanie	13	166
Mona	14	170

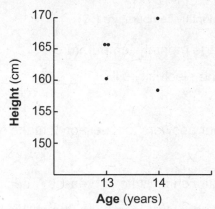

Each dot shows the height and age of one person.

a) Circle Mona's dot.

b) Which two people are the same age and height? _____

How is this shown on the scatter plot? _____

> **Scatter plots** are used to show whether there is a relationship between two sets of data.

INVESTIGATION ▶ How are age and height related?

A. Look at the scatter plot for ages 1 to 10.

a) How many 5-year-olds are part of the data?

b) Do 10-year-olds tend to be taller or shorter than 9-year-olds?

c) Was every 10-year-old taller than every 9-year-old?

d) As age increases from 1 to 10, does height tend to increase or decrease?

e) How does the scatter plot show your answer to part d)?

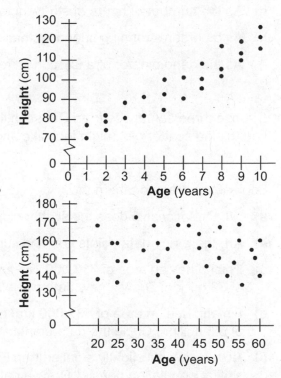

B. Look at the scatter plot for ages 20 to 60.

a) As age increases from 20 to 60, does height increase too? Does it decrease? Or is it not affected by age?

b) How does the scatter plot show your answer to part a)?

2. Based on the scatter plot, write "increases," "decreases," or "is not affected."

a)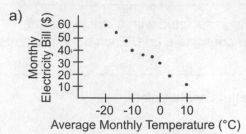

As the average monthly temperature

increases, the electricity bill _____.

b)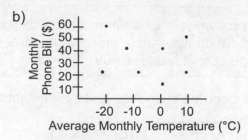

As the average monthly temperature

increases, the phone bill _____.

3. Explain why your answers to Question 2 make sense.

4. Predict the relationship. Write "increases," "decreases," or "is not affected."

a) As a child's shoe size increases, the child's height _____.

b) As an adult's shoe size increases, the adult's monthly cable bill _____.

c) As the length of a rectangle increases, the rectangle's perimeter _____.

d) As a person's age increases, the length of the person's given name _____.

e) As the number of test questions left unanswered increases, the test score _____.

f) As the distance from the US border increases, a Canadian city's population _____.

g) As the number of hours of study increases, the test score _____.

h) As a person's running speed increases, the person's heart rate _____.

i) As the denominator of a fraction increases, the value of the fraction _____.

5. Choose three sentences from Question 4 with different answers. Sketch what you think a scatter plot might look like. Include titles and labels, but not scales.

6. Look at the graph on the right.

a) What relationship does the scatter plot show? Explain.

b) Are there any data points you find surprising?

c) Poland has an area of 313 000 km² and a population of 39 million. Draw a new data point for Poland.

d) Finland has an area of 338 000 km² and a population of 5.3 million. Circle the data point for Finland.

e) Norway is only slightly smaller than Finland and has similar population density. Draw a data point where you would expect to find it for Norway.

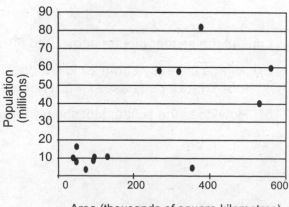

Relationship between population and area for 13 countries in western Europe

Probability and Data Management 8-10

7. Draw three scatter plots based on the following data about a soccer team.

Age (years)	12	13	14	14	15	15	13	14	15	12	15	14
Height (cm)	141	162	174	154	166	174	150	168	182	156	160	152
Gender	F	M	M	F	F	M	F	M	M	M	F	F

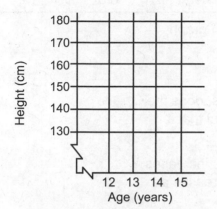 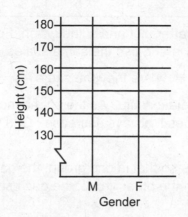 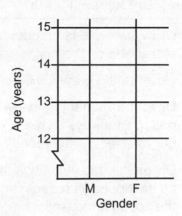

Which of the following statements do you agree with? Explain your answers.

a) Males on the soccer team are likely to be taller.
b) Older people on the soccer team are likely to be taller.
c) Males on the soccer team are likely to be older.

8. Tasfia and Ahmed both did projects about housing prices in Toronto.

Tasfia's data

# of bedrooms	0	1	1	0	2	3	1	2
Price ($10 000)	18	23	34	19	47	96	52	41

Ahmed's data

Distance from subway line (km)	1	4	7	15	8	9	6	2
Price ($10 000)	120	62	43	21	15	32	31	89

a) How much does the most expensive house listed here cost? _____

b) Draw the scatter plot to show Tasfia's data.

c) Describe the relationship Tasfia's data shows.

d) Draw the scatter plot to show Ahmed's data.

e) Describe the relationship Ahmed's data shows.

f) Ahmed looks at both scatter plots. He thinks that houses closer to the subway will have more bedrooms. How strongly does the data support Ahmed's thinking? Explain. Hint: Use your answers in Question 7 to help you explain.

PDM8-11 Comparing Scatter Plots and Line Graphs

1. Sara tested her car to find out how much gas it used (L/100 km) at different speeds (km/h). Here is her data.

Speed (km/h)	30	45	60	75	90	105	120
Gas used (L/100 km)	9.7	8	7.5	7.5	7.1	8.3	10

a) Draw Sara's data on both a scatter plot and a line graph. For each graph, plot speed on the horizontal axis and use the same scales.

b) How are the graphs different? How are they the same?

c) Does the scatter plot show a relationship? As the speed increases, does the gas used always increase? Does it always decrease? Can you say that it is not affected by the speed?

d) Divide the data into two groups so that in one group, the gas used increases as the speed increases, and in the other group, the gas used decreases as the speed increases.

e) Does the line graph show a trend? If so, describe it.

f) When is the line graph the steepest? What does this tell you?

g) Which graph tells you more — the line graph or the scatter plot? Explain.

2. Several people tested their cars the way Sara did (see Question 1). Here is the speed at which each car was tested and the gas it used:

Speed (km/h)	30	30	50	65	70	75	90	100	100
Gas used (L/100 km)	9.7	11.4	7.5	8.2	7.1	8.3	10	12.3	9.8

a) Draw the data on both a scatter plot and a line graph. Use the same scales for each.

b) Explain why this data is more difficult to draw as a line graph than the data from Question 1.

c) Explain the advantage of a scatter plot over a line graph in this situation.

d) Split the data to draw two scatter plots — one that shows that the gas used increases as speed increases, and the other that shows that the gas used decreases as speed increases.

3. Decide whether to use a line graph or a scatter plot to graph each set of data, then use a computer to draw the graph. Explain your choice of graph and what you learned from the graph. Did you find a trend or a relationship?

a)

Sara's foot length (inches)	5	5.8	6.6	7	7.4	7.8	8.2	8.6	9.1
Sara's height (cm)	80	90	100	110	120	130	140	150	160

b)

Foot length (inches)	6	10	9	9.2	8.6	8.5	10.4	9.6	8.5	10.6	11.2	11.1
Height (cm)	150	158	163	163	165	168	168	171	172	174	174	178

Probability and Data Management 8-11

PDM8-12 Histograms

1. The data set shows the weekly salaries (in dollars) of 20 employees at a company.

| 200 | 225 | 250 | 300 | 300 | 310 | 330 | 450 | 550 | 620 |

| 630 | 640 | 710 | 850 | 875 | 900 | 1000 | 1100 | 1200 | 1450 |

To draw a bar graph, divide the data into categories and draw one bar for each category. Use intervals as the categories and ask how many data values are in each interval.

a) Tara uses intervals that have the same number of data values. Finish Tara's bar graph.

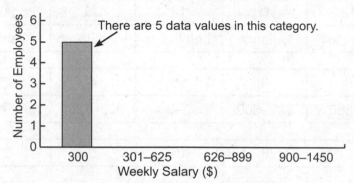

Tara's Frequency Table	
Interval	Frequency
0–300	5
301–625	5
626–899	5
900–1450	5

b) Margaret uses intervals of the same size. Finish Margaret's frequency table and bar graph.

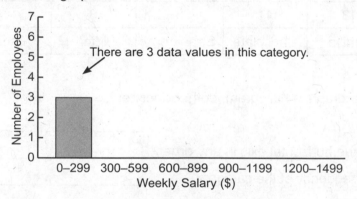

Margaret's Frequency Table	
Interval	Frequency
0–299	3
300–599	
600–899	
900–1199	
1200–1499	

c) Whose graph provides more information about the data?

d) The company hires a new employee at a weekly salary of $899.50. Margaret wants to plot the new data on her graph. Why does she run into trouble?

e) What title would you give Margaret's graph?

A histogram is like a bar graph, but the categories are numerical intervals of the same size. The next interval begins exactly where the previous interval ends, so there are no spaces between the bars. A number on the border of an interval is always put in the higher interval.

---

f) Finish drawing the histogram based on Margaret's graph. Include the new employee from part d) in the data, as well as a title, labels, and scale.

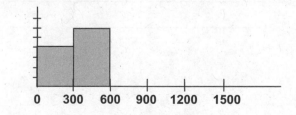

g) Another new employee earns $600.00 a week. In which interval does the new data belong?

A histogram is used when the data on the horizontal axis is **continuous**. There are no spaces between the bars.

A bar graph is used when the categories are **discrete** (Examples: colours, movie types, book types). There are spaces between the bars.

2. Draw a bar graph or a histogram for each set of data. Explain your choice of graph.

a)

Number trying out	12	11	14	10	20
Position	Goalie	Defence	Left Wing	Right Wing	Centre

b)

Number of employees	6	8	15	5	2
Weekly salary ($)	0–300	300–600	600–900	900–1200	1200–1500

c)

Number of students	6	8	15	5	2
Hours spent on homework each week	0–2	2–4	4–6	6–8	8–10

d)

Number of students	13	11	8	3	4
Favourite ice cream	Vanilla	Chocolate	Strawberry	Mint	Other

3. Are each of these statements true for a bar graph, a histogram, both, or neither?

a) The bars touch each other. _____

b) The category labels can be written on the horizontal axis in any order. _____

c) The heights of the bars represent the frequency of the category. _____

d) The graph has a title, labels, and a scale. _____

e) The categories are numeric intervals of the same size. _____

f) All the bars have equal width. _____

4. Explain how a bar graph and a histogram are the same and how they are different.

_____

_____

_____

_____

Probability and Data Management 8-12

5. a) How many students live…

    i) between 4 km and 6 km from school? _____

    ii) 6 km or more from school? _____

    iii) within 2 km of the school? _____

b) Can you tell…

    i) how many students live between 3 km and 5 km from school? _____

    ii) how far from school the closest student lives? _____

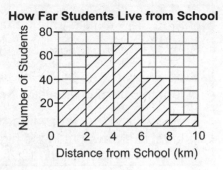

How Far Students Live from School

c) How could you choose the intervals differently so that you can tell how many students live between 3 km and 5 km from school? Remember that the intervals all have to be the same length.

BONUS ▶ What type of graph could you draw that would make it easy to tell how far from school the closest student lives? Hint: We have not seen this graph yet (see page 192), but you might know it from last year.

6. a) Use the graph to complete the frequency table.

Average Mark	Frequency
20–39	
40–59	
60–79	
80–99	

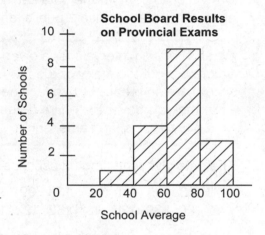

School Board Results on Provincial Exams

b) How many schools were included in this data? _____

c) A passing mark is 60. How many schools' averages were below the passing mark? _____

7. Here are the class results on a test: ~~56~~ ~~68~~ ~~70~~ ~~95~~ 75 41 66 82 89 77 73 60 79 81

a) Complete the table. The first four tally marks have been added for you.

Grouping of Marks	Tally	Frequency
40–50		
50–60	/	
60–70	/	
70–80	/	
80–90		
90–100	/	

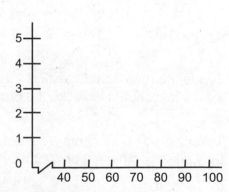

b) Why was the mark 70 placed in the 70–80 group instead of the 60–70 group?

c) Complete the histogram.

PDM8-13 Drawing Histograms

How to draw a histogram from this data set: 29 35 35 41 13 21 24 12 30 32 18 34

Step 1: Find the range of the data. In this case, the range is 41 − 12 = 29.

Step 2: Divide the range into intervals of the same length. For a range of 29 (almost 30), 6 intervals of length 5, or 5 intervals of length 6, would be suitable. Interval borders: 12, 18, 24, 30, 36, 42

Step 3: Place the data values in the correct intervals. Remember: A number on the **border** of an interval is always put in the higher interval.

Interval	12–18	18–24	24–30	30–36	36–42
Frequency	2	2	2	5	1

Step 4: Draw the histogram. The height of each bar represents the frequency for the interval. Include an appropriate title, labels, and scale.

1. Draw a histogram for the data set in the box above. The numbers represent the ages of people who use a public tennis court.

When choosing intervals for a given data set, be sure that
• there are not too many or too few intervals,
• there are no breaks or overlaps between the intervals,
• the intervals cover the entire range of the data,
• every interval is the same length.

2. The data gives the time (in seconds) for students competing in the 100 m backstroke.

121 118 135 149 145 133 99 123 108 117 103 137 146 114 100
142 120 139 126 114 132 122 139 124 116 111 90 148 96 102

What is wrong with each group of intervals for the data?

a) 100–110   110–120   120–130   130–140   140–150

b) 90–100   100–110   100–120   120–140   140–160

c) 90–95   95–100   100–105   105–110   110–115   115–120
   120–125   125–130   130–135   135–140   140–145   145–150

d) 90–140   140–190

3. Divide the data from Question 2 into intervals and make a histogram. Your scale should look like the one at right.

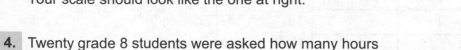

4. Twenty grade 8 students were asked how many hours they spend on homework per week. Here is the data.

5	6	4	3	3	3.5	5	6	4.5	4
9	5	8	1	0	2	7	7.5	3.5	4

Draw a histogram for the data set. Include a title, a scale, and labels.

Probability and Data Management 8-13

The height of the bars in a bar graph or histogram can represent percents instead of frequencies. In this case, draw a relative frequency table instead of a frequency table.

5. Here is a relative frequency table for the time it takes students to get to school.

Time to get to school (minutes)	0–10	10–20	20–30	30–40	40–50	50–60
Number of students	7	6	5	4	2	1
Percent of students	28	24	20	16	8	4

a) Draw two histograms, one based on the frequency and the other based on the relative frequency. Be sure to label the axes.

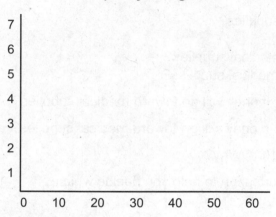

Frequency Histogram

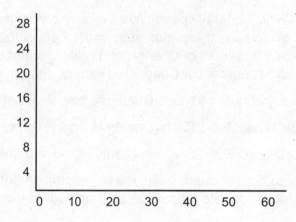

Relative Frequency Histogram

b) How are the two graphs the same? How are they different?

_____

_____

_____

c) Use the relative frequency table to draw a circle graph from the same data.

Title: _____

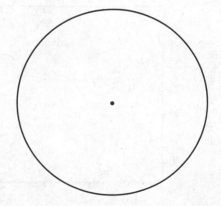

d) Answer these questions and say which graph you used and why.

i) Do more people take more than 20 minutes or less than 20 minutes to get to school?

ii) Does the number of students increase or decrease as the amount of time increases?

iii) The teacher notices that people who take either 0–10 minutes or 50–60 minutes to get to school tend to arrive the latest. Is that more or less than half the students?

iv) What percentage of students take either 0–10 minutes or 50–60 minutes to get to school?

PDM8-14 Comparing Graphs

1. Sally wants to donate money to a charity that sends medical supplies to developing countries. The chart below shows how two charities spend their money.

Money spent (millions of $)				
	Fundraising	Shipping	Administration	Medical Supplies
Charity A	60	40	30	70
Charity B	25	25	10	40

a) Draw a double bar graph to show the data. Include a key, a title, labels, and a scale.

b) Draw two circle graphs to show the percentage of each charity's spending in each area.

c) Answer the questions and say which graph was most helpful in each case.

   i) Which charity spends more money on medical supplies?
   ii) Which charity spends more money altogether?
   iii) What percent of Charity A's money is spent on medical supplies?
   iv) What percent of Charity B's money is spent on medical supplies?

d) If Sally donates $100 to Charity A, how much of her money will go toward medical supplies?

e) If Sally donates $100 to Charity B, how much of her money will go toward medical supplies?

f) If you were Sally, to which charity would you give $100? Why?

g) Which type of graph gave you the most relevant information to help you decide which charity to donate money to? Explain your answer.

2. Draw two bar graphs (using the scales provided) to show the data given below.

Province	Percent of households reporting "gifts of money and contributions"
British Columbia	74
Alberta	76
Saskatchewan	83
Manitoba	80
Ontario	80

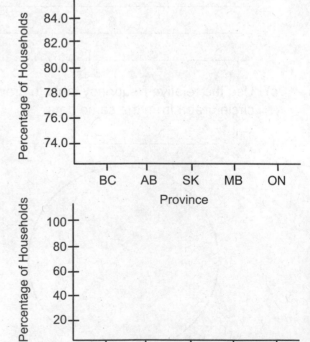

a) Which graph makes it look as though the percentage of households giving money in Saskatchewan is almost 10 times the percentage of households giving money in British Columbia?

b) In which graph is it harder to see the difference between the households in each province?

c) Which graph is the better representation of the data?

d) Would a histogram be a good choice of graph for this data? Explain.

                                             Probability and Data Management 8-14

3. Match each type of graph with its purpose. The first one has been done for you.

a) Line Graph — Compares two sets of data of similar range

b) Circle Graph — Shows a trend in data or makes a prediction (usually used when graphing change over time)

c) Histogram — Visually displays the frequency of results

d) Double Bar Graph — Shows whether one type of data increases, decreases, or neither when another type of data increases

e) Bar Graph — Shows how data is divided into fractions of a whole

f) Scatter Plot — Visually displays the frequency of results for continuous data

4. Match the data with its graph.

a)

Favourite Sport	Frequency	Percent
Hockey	42	30
Soccer	35	25
Baseball	28	20
Volleyball	28	20
Other	7	5

b)

Time to get to school (minutes)	0–10	10–20	20–30	30–40	40–50	50–60
Number of students	6	7	7	4	2	1

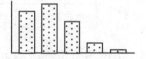

c) Martha's math test scores (out of 10):

Test#	1	2	3	4	5	6	7	8	9	10
Score	3	4	6	5	6	6	7	7	8	8

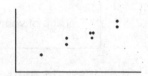

d)

Month	Jan	Feb	Mar	Apr	May	Jun
Company A's home sales	3	4	5	6	5	5
Company B's home sales	10	8	6	7	6	6

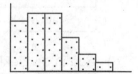

e) Families are surveyed about how many cars they have:

Number of cars	0	1	2	3	4
Frequency	12	15	11	5	2

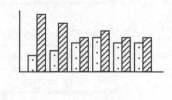

f)

Number of hours of studying	1	4	2	4	3	2	3	3
Score on math test	3	9	6	8	7	5	7	6

5. Using each type of graph (line, bar, double bar, circle, histogram, scatter plot) only once, select which type of graph you would use if you wanted to…

a) know how many hours a night people in your class study (0 hours, 1 hour, 2 hours, etc.)

_____

b) compare the number of tickets sold at a hockey arena and a movie theatre each month

_____

c) know whether vocabulary increases with age

_____

d) know how much of your $100 donation a charity will spend on building a shelter for homeless people

_____

e) know how the temperature of a glass of ice water changes over time

_____

f) group students in the school according to height

_____

6. In your notebook or on a computer, choose and draw an appropriate graph to represent each set of data and then explain your choice. Use each type of graph (line, circle, bar, double bar, histogram, scatter plot) only once. Include a title, labels, and a scale.

a) Ages of people at a tennis club:

Age	10–20	20–30	30–40	40–50	50–60	60–70	70–80
Frequency	14	56	48	35	36	20	3

b) Fraction of votes given to each candidate in a school election:

Candidates	Katie	John	Rita	Melanie	Paul
Fraction of votes	$\frac{2}{5}$	$\frac{1}{4}$	$\frac{1}{5}$	$\frac{1}{10}$	$\frac{1}{20}$

c) Jessica's marks on five science and math tests (each out of 100):

Test	1	2	3	4	5
Science Marks	70	84	85	80	82
Math Marks	68	78	81	72	76

d) Age and weekly allowance of different people:

Age	10	12	11	8	12	9	8	10	13	13	9	12	11	8	13
Weekly Allowance ($)	40	80	50	10	100	75	20	30	60	70	30	20	60	30	90

e) A class survey showing how many pets the students have:

Number of Pets	0	1	2	3	4	5+
Frequency	8	7	6	1	2	20

f) Number of times Friday the 13th occurred (or will occur) in each year:

Year	2002	2003	2004	2005	2006	2007	2008	2009	2010	2011	2012	2013
# of Occurrences	2	1	2	1	2	2	1	3	1	1	3	2

Probability and Data Management 8-14

G8-15 Points and Lines

Object	point	line	line segment	ray
Diagram	A •	A ←•————•→ B no endpoints	A •————• B 2 endpoints	A •————•→ B 1 endpoint
Name	A	AB (or BA)	AB (or BA)	AB (**not** BA)

1. Draw two points on the line. Name the line.

a)

line _____

b)

line _____

2. Name the line in two ways.

a)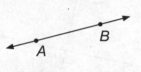

line __AB__ or _____

b)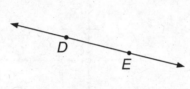

line _____ or _____

c)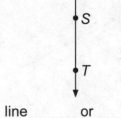

line _____ or _____

3. a) Connect *P* and *Q* with a straight line.

b) Is *PQ* a line, line segment, or ray? _____

P
•

Q
•

4. Measure line segment *EF*.

length of *EF* = _____

E ————————————————— *F*

5. Draw a line segment *PQ* of length 5 cm.

6. a) Circle the endpoint on the ray.

b) Name the ray. The endpoint always goes first.

i)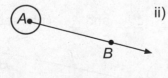

ray __AB__

ii)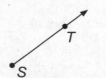

ray _____

iii)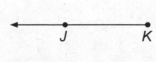

ray _____

iv)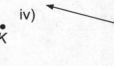

ray _____

7. Name the rays.

a)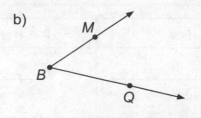

_____RA_____ and _____

b)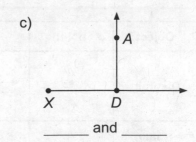

_____ and _____

c)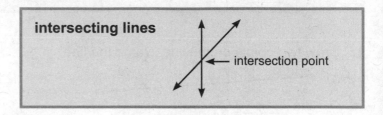

_____ and _____

8. Give an example of intersecting lines in your classroom.

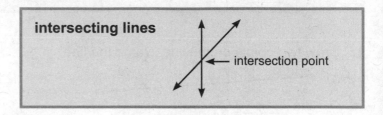

9. Name the intersecting lines, line segments, or rays and the intersection point.

a)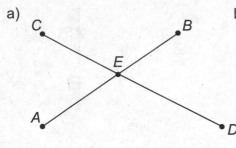

_____CD_____ and _____ intersect at _____

b)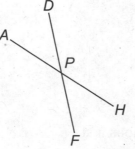

_____ and _____ intersect at _____

c)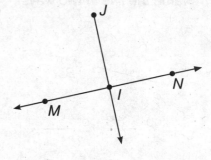

_____ and _____ intersect at _____

You do not need to draw arrows and/or dots at the ends of lines, rays, or line segments, unless you want to show that what you are drawing is a line, ray, or line segment.

10. Name the intersecting lines and the intersection point.

a)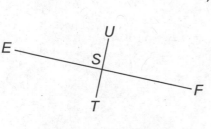

_____ and _____ intersect at _____

b)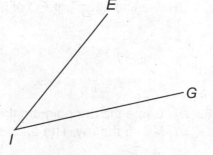

_____ and _____ intersect at _____

c)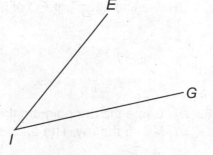

_____ and _____ intersect at _____

11. a) Draw any point *P* on *AB*.
b) Draw a line segment *XY* that intersects *AB* at point *P*.

Geometry 8-15

G8-16 Angles and Shapes

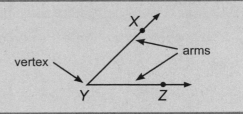

1. Circle the vertex on the angle.

a)   b)   c)   d)   e)

2. Circle the vertex. Then name the angle in two ways.

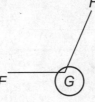 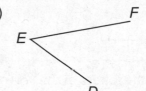 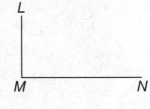

  ∠FGH or ∠HGF   ∠__V__ or ∠__V__   ∠____ or ∠____   ∠____ or ∠____

3. Name the angle.

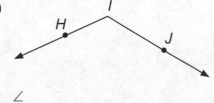 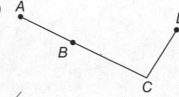 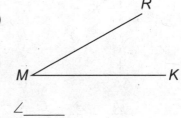

a) ∠____   b) ∠____   c) ∠____

BONUS ▶ Name all the angles you can see.

_____

_____

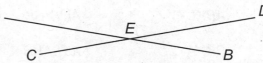

4. Circle all the possible names for the angle.

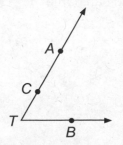

∠ACT or ∠TCA   ∠CTB or ∠BTC

∠ATB or ∠BTA   ∠BCA or ∠ACB

∠CBT or ∠TBC   ∠CTA or ∠ATC

The vertex letter alone can name an angle when there is no chance of confusion.

5. Circle each vertex. Write the names of the angles.

a)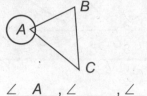

∠ _A_ , ∠ ____ , ∠ ____

b)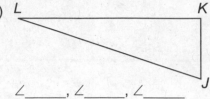

∠ ____ , ∠ ____ , ∠ ____

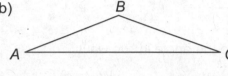

Triangle

side →

angle

vertex

6. Name the sides of the triangle.

a)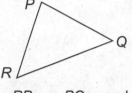

__RP__ , __PQ__ , and ____

b)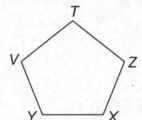

____ , ____ , and ____

c)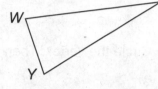

____ , ____ , and ____

To name a polygon, write the letters at the vertices in order (clockwise or counter-clockwise).
You may start with any letter.

7. Name the polygon.

a)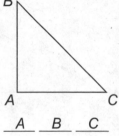

_A_ _B_ _C_

b)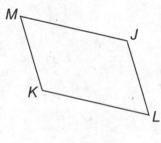

____ ____ ____ ____

c)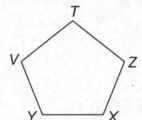

____ ____ ____ ____ ____

d)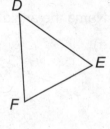

____ ____ ____

8. a) Circle the correct names for this polygon.

ABKLXY   ALYXBK   BKALYX

BKXAYL   XYLAKB   LYBKAX

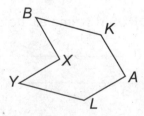

b) Write another correct name for this polygon. _____

BONUS ▶ Label the vertices, then name the
line segments that form the shape.

a)

b)

BONUS ▶ Circle the angles you can name
(if any) using only the vertex letter.

a)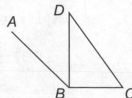

b)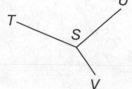

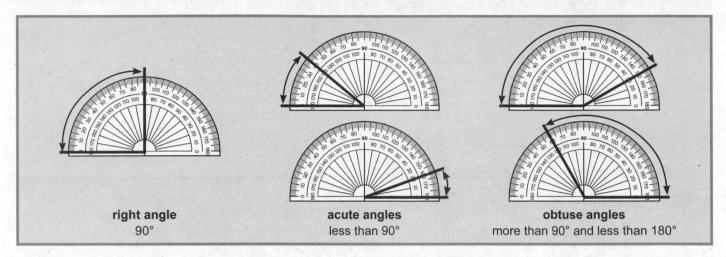

right angle	acute angles	obtuse angles
90°	less than 90°	more than 90° and less than 180°

1. Without using a protractor, identify the angle as **acute** or **obtuse**.

a)

b)

c)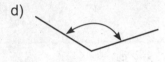

d)

_____   _____   _____   _____

2. Practise choosing the correct scale to measure an angle.

i)   Identify the angle as acute or obtuse.

ii) Circle the 2 numbers that the arm of the angle passes through.

iii) Choose the correct angle measure. Example: if the angle is acute, the measure
is less than 90°.

a)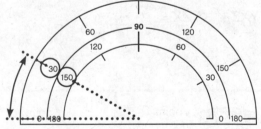

The angle is acute / obtuse. (circle one)

The angle measures _____°.

b)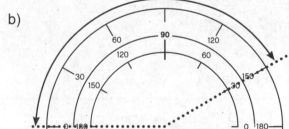

The angle is acute / obtuse. (circle one)

The angle measures _____°.

c)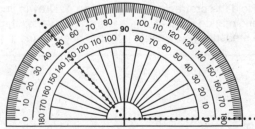

The angle is acute / obtuse. (circle one)

The angle measures _____°.

d)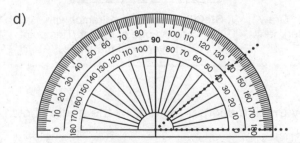

The angle is acute / obtuse. (circle one)

The angle measures _____°.

3. Measure the angle. Record your measurement inside the angle. You will need to extend the arms in part c).

a) 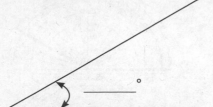   _____ °

b) 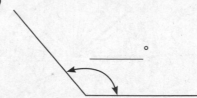   _____ °

c) 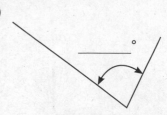   _____ °

Remember to place the protractor so that the vertex of the angle is exactly at the origin of the protractor.

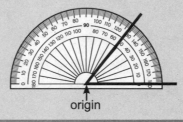
origin

4. In each triangle, $\angle XYZ = 90°$. Measure the other angles and find their sum. What do you notice?

a)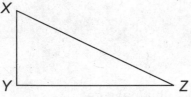

$\angle YXZ =$ _____ $\angle YZX =$ _____

$\angle YXZ + \angle YZX =$ _____

b)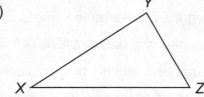

$\angle YXZ =$ _____ $\angle YZX =$ _____

$\angle YXZ + \angle YZX =$ _____

Drawing an angle

Step 1: Draw a line segment.

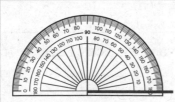

Step 2: Place the protractor with the origin on one endpoint. This point will be the vertex of the angle.

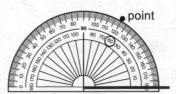

Step 3: Hold the protractor in place and mark a point at the angle measure you want.

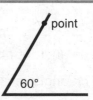

Step 4: Draw a line from the vertex through the angle mark.

5. Copy the line segment and draw the angle shown.

a) 30°

_____

b) 120°

_____

G8-18 Making a Sketch

▶ **Work quickly — a sketch is not supposed to be perfect.**

1. Sketch the figure.

    a) a rectangle divided into 2 triangles
    b) line segment *AB* intersecting line *CD*
    c) a right triangle

▶ **Draw sides and angles roughly to scale.**

2. Circle the sketch that is more to scale.

a)
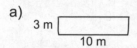

b)
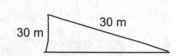

3. Circle the sketch that looks more like…

    a) a 90° angle   b) a 45° angle   c) an 135° angle

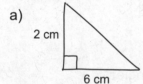
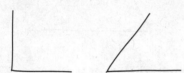

4. Make a better sketch.

a)

b)

5. Sketch the figures. Add all necessary labels and side and angle markings.

    a) Line segment *AB* is twice as long as line segment *CD*.
    b) △*ABC* has all sides equal. △*TUV* has all sides twice as long as △*ABC*.
    c) △*PQR* is a right triangle with two 45° angles.

▶ **Include all the important information you have been given.**

6. Circle the sketch that includes all the important information given.

    a) Information: △*ABC* has all sides equal.   b) Information: △*TUV* is isosceles.

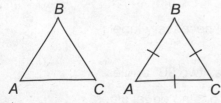
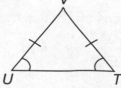
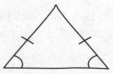

▶ **Leave out any information you are sure you do not need.**

7. Cross out any information you do not need to solve the problem. Then sketch the problem.

	Problem	Sketch
a)	~~A strut on a bridge over a highway is shaped like~~ a triangle with two equal sides. The angle between them is 70°. What are the other two angles?	
b)	A rectangular gift box is 15 cm long and 10 cm wide. It has a transparent lid decorated with a paper flower 5 cm in diameter. What is the area of the bottom of the box?	

▶ **Be careful not to accidentally add any information you do not know for sure.**

8. Circle the sketch that has accidentally added information not known.

a) A quadrilateral has an 8 cm side.

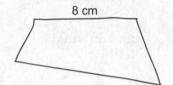

b) One angle of a triangle is 45°.

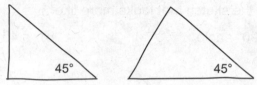

▶ **Sometimes you will want to make a few sketches to see the problem in different ways.**

9. One side of an isosceles triangle is 3 cm. The perimeter of the triangle is 11 cm. What are the lengths of the sides of the triangle?

Make two sketches to show that where you put the 3 cm side on your sketch will make a difference to the answer.

10. One angle of an isosceles triangle is 40°. What are the measures of the other angles?

Make two sketches to show that where you put the 40° angle will make a difference to the answer.

▶ **Use symbols instead of words to keep your sketch clear and uncluttered.**

11. Circle the better sketch.

a)

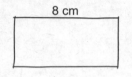

b)

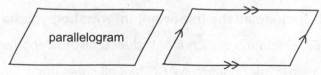

12. Sketch two different polygons that match the description. Add all necessary labels and side and angle markings.

a) *ABCD* has all equal sides.

b) *JKLM* has two 90° angles.

c) *PQRS* has exactly 2 equal sides.

d) *ABCDE* has no equal sides.

▶ **Add other information you can deduce.**

13. These sketches show the information given in a problem. What other information can you deduce? Mark this additional information on the sketch.

a)

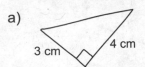

3 cm   4 cm

b)

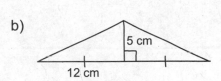

5 cm

12 cm

> **The Pythagorean Theorem**
>
> In a right triangle with sides a, b, c, with c opposite the right angle, $c^2 = a^2 + b^2$.

14. Problem: A 13 m ladder is propped against a vertical wall. The foot of the ladder is 5 m from the wall. The top of the ladder is 0.5 m below a window. The ground is horizontal. How high above the ground is the window?

Sketch A

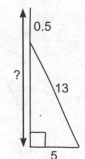

0.5

?

13

5

a) Do both of these sketches include all the important information given in

the problem? _____

b) Sketch A shows that the triangle is a right triangle. How did the student who drew the sketch know that the angle between the wall and the ground is a right angle?

_____

c) Which sketch would it be easier for you to draw?

_____

Sketch B

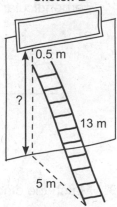

0.5 m

?

13 m

5 m

d) Which sketch is more convenient to work with? Explain.

e) Solve the problem: Label the missing side of the triangle x. What does the Pythagorean theorem say about the sides of the triangle?

_____

Solve the equation for x.

_____

f) Is x the value you are asked to find in the problem? _____

What is the height of the window above the ground? _____

> **Some Sketching Tips**
>
> • When you first start working on a problem, you might know only part of what you need to know to solve the problem. You have to use what you are given to figure out more information. You do not know what you might find out, so do simple sketches that do not lock you in to one way of thinking about the problem.
>
> • If you start a sketch and it does not seem to be helping, try doing a different sketch — or try another problem-solving strategy.

G8-19 Perpendicular Lines

Perpendicular lines meet at a right angle (90°). The ⊥ symbol means "is perpendicular to."

$EG \perp FZ$

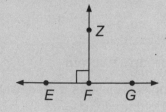

$AB \perp ST$

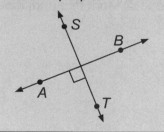

1. Name the perpendicular lines.

a)

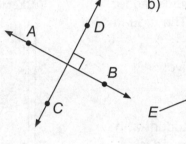

b)

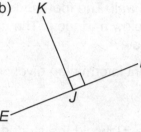

c)

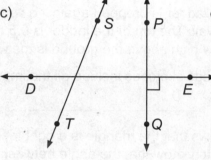

d)

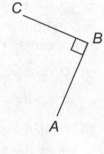

____ AB ____ ⊥ _____

_____ ⊥ _____

_____ ⊥ _____

_____ ⊥ _____

2. Use a protractor to find any right angles. Draw a square corner () to show any perpendicular lines.

a)

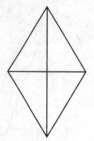

b)

c)

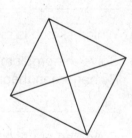

3. Match the diagrams to the descriptions.

A

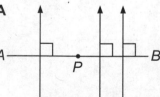

B

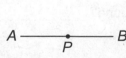

C

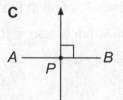

D

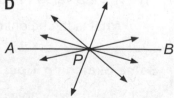

_____ point P on line segment AB

_____ lines that pass through point P on AB

_____ lines perpendicular to AB

_____ the line perpendicular to AB that passes through point P

Drawing a line segment perpendicular to *AB* through point *P* using a set square or a protractor

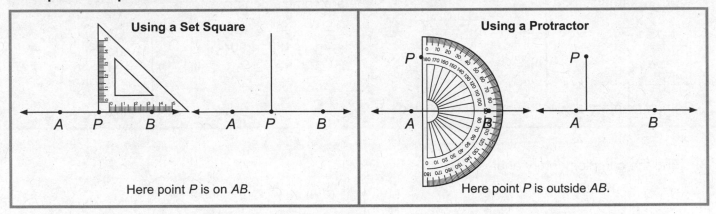

Using a Set Square	Using a Protractor
Here point *P* is on *AB*.	Here point *P* is outside *AB*.

4. Use a set square. Draw a line segment perpendicular to *AB* that passes through *P*.

a)

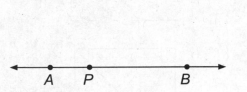

b)

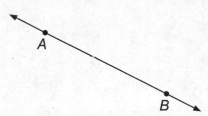

5. Use a set square or a protractor.

a) Draw a line segment *AB*.

Draw a line segment *CD* perpendicular to *AB*.

Explain how you know the two lines are perpendicular.

b) Draw any line *CD*.

Draw a point *P* **not** on *CD*.

Draw any line *LM* that is perpendicular to *CD* and passes through *P*.

6. A rectangle has 4 right angles.

a) Draw the missing sides to complete rectangle *ABCD*.

b) Name all the pairs of sides of *ABCD* that are perpendicular to one another.

_____ ⊥ _____   _____ ⊥ _____

_____ ⊥ _____   _____ ⊥ _____

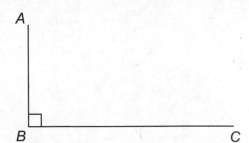

c) **Adjacent** sides share a vertex. In a rectangle, are any two adjacent sides perpendicular? Explain.

7. ∠*ABC* is 90°. ∠*ABD* is 50°.

a) What is the measure of ∠*DBC*? _____

How do you know? _____

b) Measure ∠*DBC* with a protractor to check your answer in a).

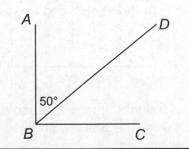

<table>
<tr>
<td>

Complementary angles are angles whose sum is 90°. Example:

Complementary angles: ∠1 and ∠2   ∠A and ∠B

</td>
<td>

Note: The two acute angles in a right triangle are complementary angles:

$x + y + 90° = 180°$
$x + y = 180° - 90°$
$x + y = 90°$

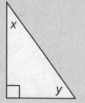

</td>
</tr>
</table>

8. Find the complementary angles.

a)

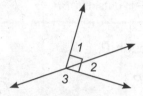

_____ and _____

b)

_____ and _____

c)

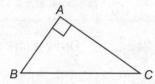

_____ and _____

d)

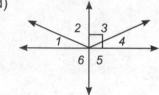

_____ and _____

_____ and _____

e)

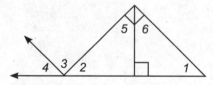

∠2 and _____, ∠2 and _____

∠6 and _____, ∠6 and _____

f)

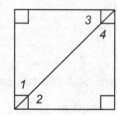

∠1 and _____, ∠1 and _____

∠4 and _____, ∠4 and _____

9. Find the value of x.

a)

∠x = _____

b)

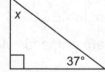

∠x = _____

c)

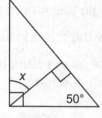

∠x = _____

10. In a right triangle, one acute angle is 4 times larger than the other acute angle. Finish the sketch and use equations to find both angles.

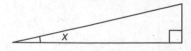

11. In a right triangle, one acute angle is 20° more than the other acute angle. Sketch the triangle and use equations to find both angles.

G8-20 Supplementary and Opposite Angles

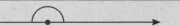

A **straight angle** measures 180°.

Supplementary angles are pairs of angles whose sum is 180°. Examples:

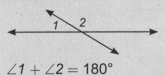

$\angle 1 + \angle 2 = 180°$

$\angle 3 + \angle 4 = 180°$

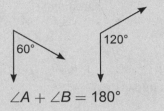

$\angle A + \angle B = 180°$

1. Find the supplementary angles in the graph.

a)
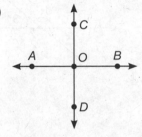

$\angle AOC + \underline{\quad} = 180°$

$\angle AOC + \underline{\quad} = 180°$

$\angle AOD + \underline{\quad} = 180°$

$\angle BOD + \underline{\quad} = 180°$

b)
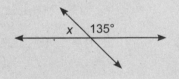

$\angle 2 + \underline{\quad} = 180°, \angle 6 + \underline{\quad} = 180°$

$\angle 2 + \underline{\quad} = 180°, \angle 6 + \underline{\quad} = 180°$

$\angle 4 + \underline{\quad} = 180°, \angle 8 + \underline{\quad} = 180°$

$\angle 4 + \underline{\quad} = 180°, \angle 8 + \underline{\quad} = 180°$

c)
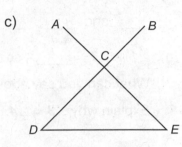

$\angle ACD + \underline{\quad} = 180°$

$\underline{\quad} + \underline{\quad} = 180°$

$\underline{\quad} + \underline{\quad} = 180°$

$\underline{\quad} + \underline{\quad} = 180°$

Find $\angle x$:

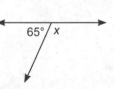

Solution:

$\angle x + 135° = 180°$ (Supplementary angles)
$\angle x = 180° - 135°$
$\angle x = 45°$

2. Find $\angle x$ and $\angle y$, or $\angle x + \angle y$.

a)
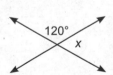

$\angle x = \underline{\quad}$

b)
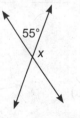

$\angle x = \underline{\quad}$

c)

$\angle x = \underline{\quad}$

d)
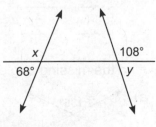

$\angle x = \underline{\quad}, \angle y = \underline{\quad}$

e)
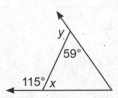

$\angle x = \underline{\quad}, \angle y = \underline{\quad}$

f)
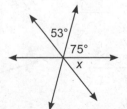

$\angle x = \underline{\quad}$

g)
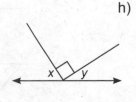

$\angle x + \angle y = \underline{\quad}$

h)
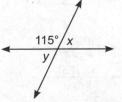

$\angle x = \underline{\quad}, \angle y = \underline{\quad}$

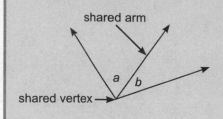

Adjacent angles share a vertex and an arm.

shared arm

a *b*

shared vertex

Opposite angles are the non-adjacent angles formed by two intersecting lines.

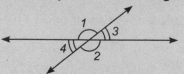

∠1 and ∠2 are opposite angles
∠3 and ∠4 are also opposite angles

3. a) Which angles in this picture are supplementary angles?

_____ and _____, _____ and _____, _____ and _____, _____ and _____

b) ∠1 + ∠3 = _____°, so ∠1 = _____.   ∠2 + ∠3 = _____°, so ∠1 = _____.

What can you say about opposite angles and ∠1 and ∠2? _____

c) Explain why ∠3 = ∠4.

4. Find angles that are opposite (and equal).

a)

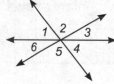

∠AOC = _____

∠AOD = _____

b)

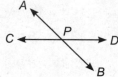

_____ = _____

_____ = _____

c)

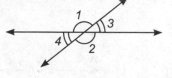

∠1 = _____, ∠2 = _____

∠5 = _____, ∠6 = _____

d)

_____ = _____,   _____ = _____

_____ = _____

e)

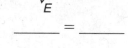

_____ = _____

_____ = _____

f)

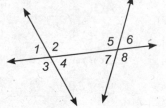

_____ = _____

_____ = _____

5. Find the missing angles.

a)

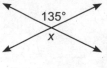

∠x = _____

b)

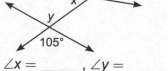

∠x = _____, ∠y = _____

c)

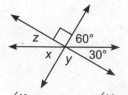

∠x = _____, ∠y = _____, ∠z = _____

d)

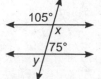

∠x = _____, ∠y = _____

e)

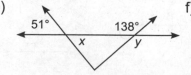

∠x = _____, ∠y = _____

f)

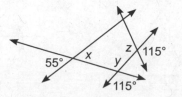

∠x = _____, ∠y = _____, ∠z = _____

Geometry 8-20

G8-21 Parallel Lines

> **Parallel lines** never intersect, no matter how far they are extended in either direction.
>
>

1. Extend both lines. Use a ruler. Do the lines intersect or are they parallel? _____

2. Match the lines below to the descriptions.

   A The lines intersect.
   B If the lines were extended far enough, they would intersect.
   C The lines are parallel.

   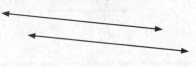   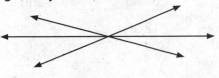   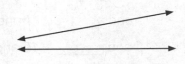

   _____   _____   _____

3. Give two examples of parallel lines in the world around you.

> We mark parallel lines using arrow symbols
> ($>$, $>>$, and so on). The ‖ symbol means "is parallel to."
>
> For example, $AB \parallel CD$ or $AB \parallel DC$.

4. Use arrow symbols to mark the sides or edges of these shapes that look like they are parallel.

   a) 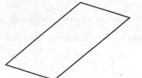   b) 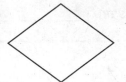   c) 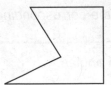   d)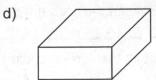

5. State which lines are parallel.

   a) 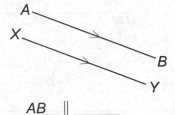   b) 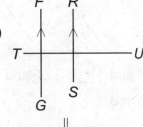   c)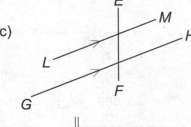

   ___AB___ ‖ _____   _____ ‖ _____   _____ ‖ _____

6. The lines AB and DE are parallel. Measure the line segments.

   $AD =$ _____ $BE =$ _____ $CF =$ _____

   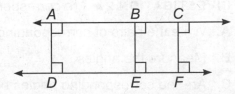

   What do you notice? _____

G8-22 Corresponding Angles and Parallel Lines

Corresponding angles create a pattern like in the letter F:

These pairs of angles are corresponding angles:

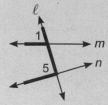 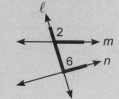 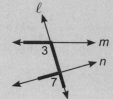 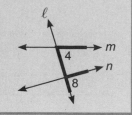

1. List the corresponding angles.

∠1 and _____, ∠1 and _____   ∠2 and _____, ∠2 and _____

∠5 and _____, ∠5 and _____   ∠6 and _____, ∠6 and _____

∠11 and _____, ∠11 and _____   ∠12 and _____, ∠12 and _____

∠15 and _____, ∠15 and _____   ∠16 and _____, ∠16 and _____

INVESTIGATION 1 ▶ What are the measures of corresponding angles for two parallel lines?

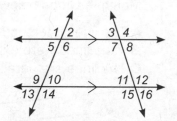

A. Write the pairs of corresponding angles.

∠1 and _____, ∠2 and _____, ∠5 and _____, ∠6 and _____

B. Measure the angles.

∠1 = _____, ∠2 = _____.   ∠3 = _____, ∠4 = _____.

∠5 = _____, ∠6 = _____.   ∠7 = _____, ∠8 = _____.

C. What can you say about the measures of the corresponding angles when the lines are parallel?

When the lines are parallel, the corresponding angles are _____.

---

1. List the corresponding equal angles.

a)
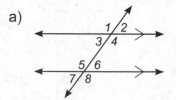

b)
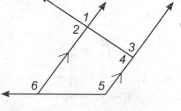

c)

∠1 and _____, ∠3 and _____   ∠1 and _____, ∠2 and _____   ∠3 and _____, ∠5 and _____

∠2 and _____, ∠4 and _____   ∠5 and _____   ∠4 and _____, ∠10 and _____

INVESTIGATION 2 ▶ Are corresponding angles always equal?

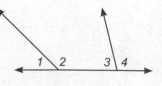

A. Write the pairs of corresponding angles. ∠1 and _____, ∠2 and _____

B. Measure the angles. ∠1 = _____, ∠2 = _____, ∠3 = _____, ∠4 = _____

C. Are the corresponding angles equal? _____

2. Find the measure of the corresponding angles.

a)
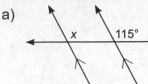
∠x = _____

b)
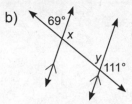
∠x = _____, ∠y = _____

c)
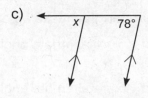
∠x = _____

d)
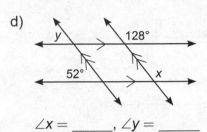
∠x = _____, ∠y = _____

e)
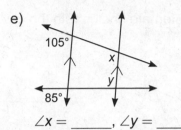
∠x = _____, ∠y = _____

f)
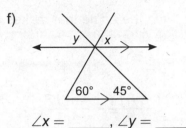
∠x = _____, ∠y = _____

When corresponding angles are equal, the lines are parallel.
We can use this to prove that lines are parallel.

REMINDER ▶ Opposite angles are equal. Supplementary angles
add to 180° (a + b = 180°).

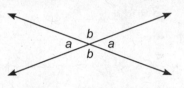

---

3. Find x. Then decide if the lines are parallel.

a)
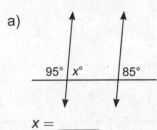
x = _____

parallel   not parallel

b)
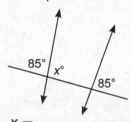
x = _____

parallel   not parallel

c)
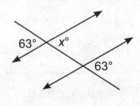
x = _____

parallel   not parallel

d)
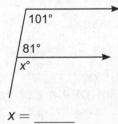
x = _____

parallel   not parallel

---

4. Mark any parallel lines. State which lines are parallel. If no lines are parallel, write "none".

a)
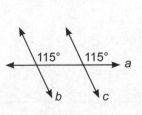
b ∥ c

b)
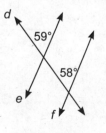
_____

c)
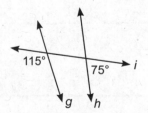
_____

d)
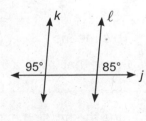
_____

e)
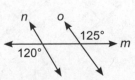
_____

f)
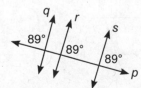
_____

g)
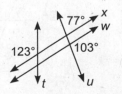
_____

h)
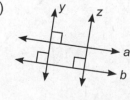
_____

G8-23 Alternate Angles and Parallel Lines

Alternate angles make a pattern like the letter Z: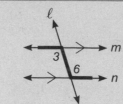

∠3 and ∠6 are alternate angles for parallel lines
m and *n*.

∠4 and ∠5 are alternate angles for lines *p* and *r*.

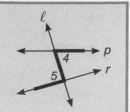

1. Find the angle that makes a pair of alternate angles with the given angle. All pairs are different!

a)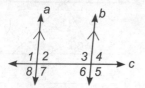

∠2 and _____

∠3 and _____

b)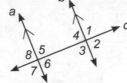

∠3 and _____

∠4 and _____

c)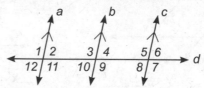

∠4 and _____, ∠9 and _____

∠5 and _____, ∠8 and _____

∠11 and _____, ∠2 and _____

INVESTIGATION ▶ What can be said about alternate angles when the lines are parallel?

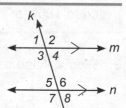

A. Write two pairs of alternate angles. ∠3 and _____, ∠4 and _____

B. Measure the four angles. ∠3 = _____, ∠4 = _____, ∠5 = _____, ∠6 = _____

Make a conjecture: *If the lines are parallel, than the alternate angles are* _____.

REMINDER ▶ Corresponding angles: see p. 72. Opposite angles: see p. 70.

C. Fill in the blanks to prove your conjecture.

Lines *m* and *n* are _____.

∠3 and ∠7 are _____ angles, so ∠3 = ∠7.

∠6 and ∠7 are _____ angles, so ∠6 = _____.

This means ∠3 = _____.

D. Prove that ∠4 = ∠5.

---

2. Find the missing angles.

a)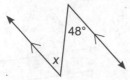

∠x = _____

b)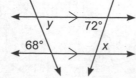

∠x = _____, ∠y = _____

c)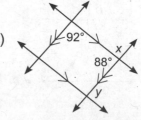

∠x = _____, ∠y = _____

3. Fill in *all* the missing angles using what you know about opposite, supplementary, corresponding, and alternate angles.

a)

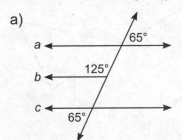

b)

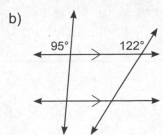

c)

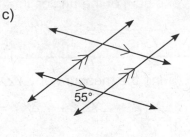

4. Do the opposite of what you did in the Investigation to prove this statement:
If alternate angles are equal, then the lines are parallel.

$\angle KPQ = \angle PQN = x°$

$\angle KPQ$ and _____ are opposite angles, so $\angle$_____ $= x°$.

$\angle PQN$ and _____ are corresponding angles and they both measure $x°$.

If corresponding angles are equal, then the lines are _____,

so MN _____.

5. Fill in all the missing angles. Then decide which lines are parallel.

a)

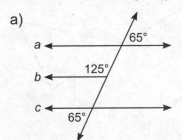

b)

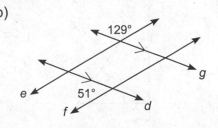

c)

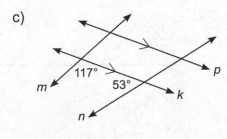

_____   _____   _____

6. Lines *a* and *b* are parallel. Use what you know about corresponding, alternate, and opposite angles to explain why $\angle 3 + \angle 5 = 180°$.

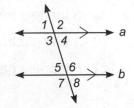

7. All the angles in a rectangle are right angles.

a) Mark the right angles on this rectangle.

b) $AD \perp AB$ and $AD \perp$ _____, so $AB \parallel$ _____

$DC \perp AD$ and $DC \perp$ _____, so $AD \parallel$ _____

c) Use the angle measures to explain how you know that these pairs of sides are parallel.

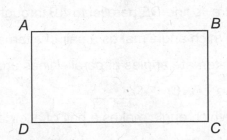

G8-24 Angles and Triangles

The sum of the angles in a triangle is always 180°.

$\angle A + \angle B + \angle C = 180°$

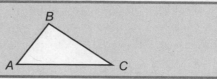

1. Find the measure of $\angle YZX$.

   $\angle XYZ + \angle YZX + \angle ZXY = $ ___, so $\angle YZX = $ ___° $- (60° + 90°)$

   $= $ ___° $- $ ___°

   $= $ ___°

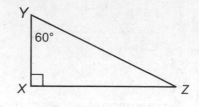

2. Find the missing angle measure.

   a)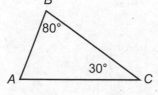

   $\angle A = 180° - (80° + 30°)$

   $= $ ___

   b)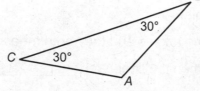

   $\angle A = 180° - ($ ___° $+$ ___°$)$

   $= $ ___

   c)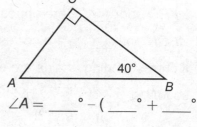

   $\angle A = $ ___° $- ($ ___° $+$ ___°$)$

   $= $ ___

   d)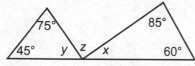

   $\angle x = $ ___

   $\angle y = $ ___

   $\angle z = $ ___

   e)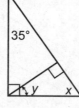

   $\angle x = $ ___

   $\angle y = $ ___

   f)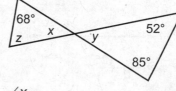

   $\angle x = $ ___

   $\angle y = $ ___

   $\angle z = $ ___

3. a) A triangle has a 30° angle and a 60° angle. What is the third angle in the triangle? _____

   b) A triangle has two 45° angles. What is the third angle in the triangle? _____

   c) A triangle has all angles equal. What is the measure of each angle? _____

4. Marco wants to prove (using logic) that the sum of the angles in $\angle ABC$ is 180°.
   He draws line DE parallel to AB through C.

   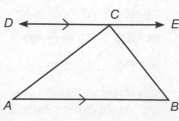

   a) Which angle makes a pair of alternate angles with $\angle BAC$? _____

      Alternate angles at parallel lines are _____,

      so $\angle BAC = \angle$ _____.

   b) Which angle makes a pair of alternate angles with $\angle ABC$? $\angle$ _____

      Alternate angles at parallel lines are _____, so $\angle ABC = \angle$ ___.

   c) $\angle BAC + \angle ACB + \angle ABC = \angle$ _____ $+ \angle ABC + \angle$ _____ $= $ ___°

An **exterior angle** is formed by extending a side of a triangle. Angle x is an exterior angle:

Exterior Angle Theorem (EAT)
An exterior angle of a triangle is equal to the sum of the two
opposite angles in the triangle ($x = a + b$).

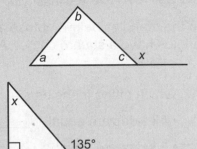

Example 1:
$x = 88° + 45°$
$\quad = 133°$

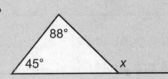

Example 2:
$x + 90° = 135°$
$\quad\quad x = 135° - 90°$
$\quad\quad x = 45°$

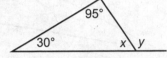

5. Find the missing angles. Show your work in your notebook.

a)

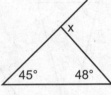

$\angle x =$ ___

b)

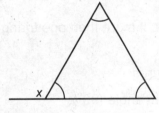

$\angle x =$ ___, $\angle y =$ ___

c)

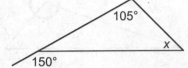

$\angle x =$ ___

d)

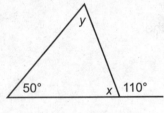

$\angle x =$ ___, $\angle y =$ ___

e)

$\angle x =$ ___

f)

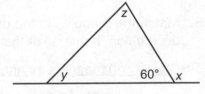

$\angle x =$ ___, $\angle y + \angle z =$ ___

g)

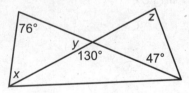

$\angle x =$ ___, $\angle y =$ ___, $\angle z =$ ___

h)

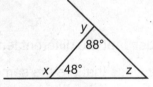

$\angle x =$ ___, $\angle y =$ ___, $\angle z =$ ___

i)

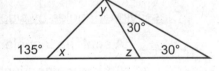

$\angle x =$ ___, $\angle y =$ ___, $\angle z =$ ___

6. Prove the Exterior Angle Theorem (EAT) using logic.

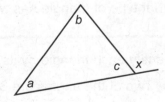

a) What does the EAT say about $\angle x$? $\angle x =$ _____

b) What do you know about the measures of $\angle a$, $\angle b$, $\angle c$? Explain.

_____

c) What do you know about the measures of $\angle x$ and $\angle c$? Explain.

_____

d) Write an equation connecting the measures of $\angle a$, $\angle b$, $\angle c$, and $\angle x$. _____

Solve your equation for x. _____

G8-25 Properties of Triangles

INVESTIGATION ▶ Classifying triangles

In the triangles below, obtuse angles are circled and right
angles have a square corner. All the other angles are acute.

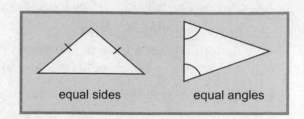

equal sides   equal angles

A. Which of the triangles match each description?

• All sides are equal. _____

• 2 sides are equal. _____

• No sides are equal. _____

• 1 angle is a right angle. _____

• All angles are acute. _____

• 1 angle is obtuse. _____

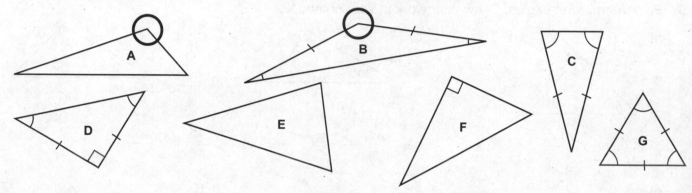

B. Match the triangles to the definitions. If more than one triangle matches the
description, name all of them.

Classifying triangles by angle measures

_____ A **right** triangle has one right angle (90°).

_____ An **acute** triangle has all angles less than 90° (all acute angles).

_____ An **obtuse** triangle has one angle greater than 90° (1 obtuse angle).

Classifying triangles by side lengths

_____ A **scalene** triangle has 3 sides that are different lengths.

_____ An **isosceles** triangle has 2 sides that are the same length.

_____ An **equilateral** triangle has 3 sides that are the same length.

C. What type of triangle has two equal angles? Three equal angles?

---

1. Identify each triangle by its angle measures.

   a) Two of the angles are 30°. The other angle is $180° - (30° + 30°) = $ ____°.

   This is an _____ triangle.

   b) Two of the angles are 50° and 40°. The other angle is $180° - (50° + 40°) = $ ____°.

   This is a _____ triangle.

   c) Two of the angles are 75° and 25°. The other angle is $180° - (75° + 25°) = $ ____°.

   This is an _____ triangle.

2. Identify each triangle by its side lengths (equilateral, isosceles, or scalene).

   a) The sides are 5 cm, 6 cm, and 7 cm. There are ____ equal sides. This triangle is _____.

   b) The sides are 8 cm, 7 cm, and 8 cm. There are ____ equal sides. This triangle is _____.

   c) The sides are 5 m, 5 m, and 5 m. There are ____ equal sides. This triangle is _____.

3. An isosceles triangle has sides 4 m and 7 m. What are the two possible lengths

   for the third side? _____

4. Draw an example of each of the six types of triangle. Use isometric grid or dot paper. Mark equal sides and angles. Label each triangle. Your triangles can have any measurements as long as they match the definitions.

5. a) Check off the combinations that are possible triangles (e.g., a right scalene triangle is possible).

   b) Which two combinations are not possible? Explain why they are impossible.

	right	acute	obtuse
scalene	✓		
isosceles			
equilateral			

6. Classify all the triangles by side lengths and angles.

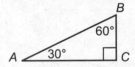 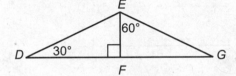 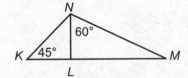

7. a) Draw and label a triangle satisfying each of the conditions below. Mark any equal sides and angles. Use a ruler and a protractor or compass to make sure that your triangle satisfies the conditions stated.

   i) △XYZ, an isosceles triangle with sides 3 cm and 6 cm
   ii) △JKL, a right triangle with ∠J = 60°
   iii) △ABC, a right triangle with ∠A = 90° and AC = 5 cm

   b) For each triangle in part a), predict whether you can use the same instructions to draw a different triangle. Explain your prediction. Try to draw a different triangle to check your prediction.

8. a) Could a triangle ever have more than one obtuse angle? Use a sketch to help you explain.

   b) Could a triangle ever have more than one right angle? Use a sketch to help you explain.

9. a) A triangle has two equal angles. One of the angles in this triangle measures 30°. What are the other angles? (Hint: There are two solutions. Try sketching the possibilities.)

   b) A triangle has two equal angles. One of the angles in this triangle measures 110°. What are the other angles?

   c) How are problems a) and b) different? Why do they have a different number of solutions?

G8-26 Solving Problems Using Angle Properties

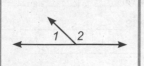 Supplementary Angle Theorem (SAT) $\angle 1 + \angle 2 = 180°$	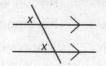 Corresponding Angle Theorem (CAT)	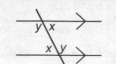 Alternate Angle Theorem (AAT)	Opposite Angle Theorem (OAT)	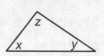 Sum of Angles in a Triangle Theorem (SATT) $x + y + z = 180°$

1. Use the theorems above to find the missing angles. List the theorem you used to find each angle.

2. a)

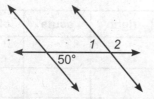

∠1 = ___50° (AAT)___

∠2 = ___130° (SAT)___

b)

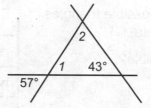

∠1 = _____ ( )

∠2 = _____ ( )

c)

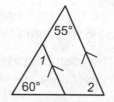

∠1 = _____ ( )

∠2 = _____ ( )

d)

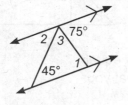

∠1 = _____ ( )

∠2 = _____ ( )

∠3 = _____ ( )

e)

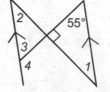

∠1 = _____ ( )

∠2 = _____ ( )

∠3 = _____ ( )

f)

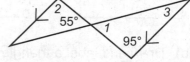

∠1 = _____ ( )

∠2 = _____ ( )

∠3 = _____ ( )

g)

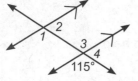

∠1 = _____ ( )

∠2 = _____ ( )

∠3 = _____ ( )

∠4 = _____ ( )

h)

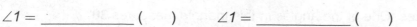

∠1 = _____ ( )

∠2 = _____ ( )

∠3 = _____ ( )

∠4 = _____ ( )

i)

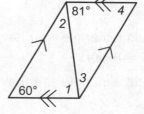

∠1 = _____ ( )

∠2 = _____ ( )

∠3 = _____ ( )

∠4 = _____ ( )

Isosceles Triangle Theorem (ITT)	Exterior Angle Theorem (EAT)

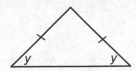 The **base angles** in an isosceles triangle are **equal**.

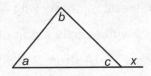 $\angle x = \angle a + \angle b$

3. To find the missing angles, you will need to find some angles that are not marked. Use numbers to label these angles on the diagrams. Say what theorem you used to find each angle.

a)
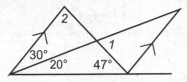

_____
_____
_____

b)
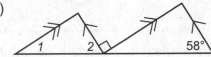

_____
_____
_____

c)
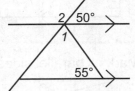

_____
_____
_____

4. Find the missing angles. Say what theorem you used to find each angle.

a)
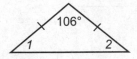

b)
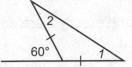

c)

d)
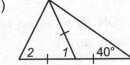

5. Write an equation for each figure. Write the abbreviation for the theorem you used beside your equation. Then solve the equation and find the angles of the triangle.
Note: You might need to use more than one equation and theorem.

a)
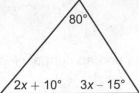

$(2x + 10°) + (3x − 15°) + 80° = 180°$ (SATT)
$2x + 10° + 3x − 15° + 80° = 180°$
$2x + 3x = 180° − 10° + 15° − 80°$
$5x = 105°$
$x = 21°$

$2x + 10° = 2(21) + 10 = 52°$ $3x − 15° = 3(21) − 15 = 63 − 15 = 48°$

b)
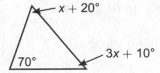

c)
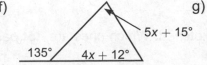

d)
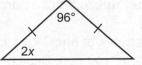

e)
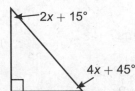

f)
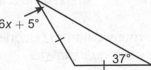

g)
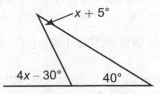

G8-27 Special Quadrilaterals

A **parallelogram** is a quadrilateral (a shape with 4 straight sides) with 2 pairs of parallel sides.

A **trapezoid** is a quadrilateral with exactly 1 pair of parallel sides.

A **rectangle** is a parallelogram with 4 right angles.

A **rhombus** is a parallelogram with all sides equal.

A **square** is a parallelogram with all sides and all angles equal.

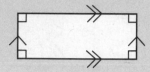 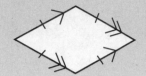 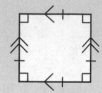

1. Mark all parallel sides and right angles, then identify the quadrilateral.

   a)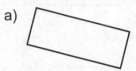

   b)

   c)

   d)

   _____ _____ _____ _____

2. a) I have 4 equal sides, but no right angles. What am I? _____

   b) I have 4 right angles, but my sides are not all equal. What am I? _____

   BONUS ▶ I am a special quadrilateral with 4 sides, and exactly 3 are equal.
   What am I? _____

3. Use the words "all," "some," or "no" to complete each statement.

   a) _____ squares are rectangles.   b) _____ trapezoids are parallelograms.

   c) _____ parallelograms are trapezoids.   d) _____ parallelograms are rectangles.

4. On grid paper draw a quadrilateral with…

   a) no right angles   b) 1 right angle   c) 2 right angles
   d) no parallel sides   e) 1 pair of parallel sides   f) 2 pairs of parallel sides and no right angles

5. Describe any similarities or differences between a trapezoid and a parallelogram.

6. a) Why is a square a rectangle?   b) Why are some rectangles not squares?
   c) Why is a trapezoid not a parallelogram?   d) Why is a square also a rhombus?

7. a) Take 4 straws of equal length. Make as many different quadrilaterals using these
      4 straws as you can. Sketch and name each quadrilateral.

   b) Repeat part a) using 2 straws of one length and 2 straws of another length. Try
      placing the sides in different orders.

   c) Look at the quadrilaterals you sketched. Which ones are **not** parallelograms?

8. Draw three different quadrilaterals with two angles of 45° and two angles of 135°. Try
   placing angles in different Qrders. Which types of quadrilaterals have you drawn?

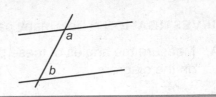

REMINDER ▶
∠*a* + ∠*b* = 180° when the lines are parallel.
The reverse is also true: when the lines are parallel, ∠*a* + ∠*b* = 180°.
We can use this fact to prove that lines are parallel.

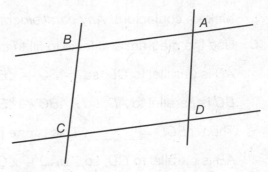

9. a) Name two angles you need to check add to 180° to show
   that the lines *AB* and *CD* are parallel. _____ and _____

   b) Measure both angles from a). Do they add to 180°? _____
   Are the lines *AB* and *CD* parallel?_____

   c) Which angles do you need to measure to check if the
   lines *BC* and *AD* are parallel? _____ and _____

   d) Measure both angles from c). Do they add to 180°?_____
   Are the lines *AD* and *BC* parallel?_____

   e) Is *ABCD* a parallelogram, a trapezoid, or neither? _____

10. a) Use the angles marked to check if there are any parallel lines. Mark any parallel
    sides you find.

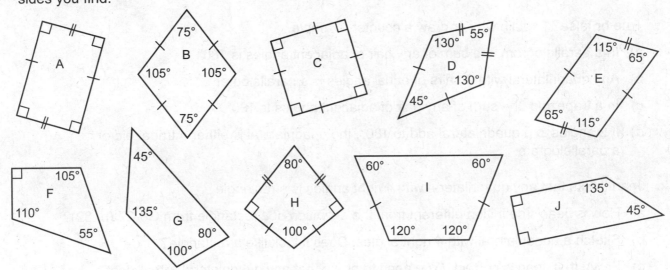

   b) Sort the quadrilaterals from part a) by their properties.

Property	Shapes		Property	Shapes
No equal sides			No right angles	
1 pair of equal sides			1 right angle	
2 pairs of equal sides			2 right angles	
4 equal sides			4 right angles	
No parallel sides			No equal angles	
1 pair of parallel sides			1 pair of equal angles	
2 pairs of parallel sides			2 pairs of equal angles	
			4 equal angles	

G8-28 Properties of Quadrilaterals

INVESTIGATION ▶ How many pairs of equal angles does a parallelogram have?

A. Measure the angles of these parallelograms. Write the measurements on the diagrams.

B. How many pairs of equal angles does each parallelogram have? _____

Make a conjecture: *Any parallelogram has* _____ *pairs of equal angles*.

C. Use the diagram and logic to fill in the blanks and prove your conjecture.

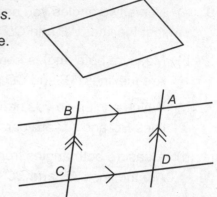

AB is parallel to CD, so ∠ABC + ∠BCD = _____°.

BC is parallel to AD, so ∠ABC + ∠BAD = _____°.

Then ∠BCD = _____. This is one pair of equal angles.

AB is parallel to CD, so ∠BAD + ∠CDA = _____° and

∠ABC = _____. This is the second pair of equal angles.

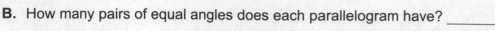

Two angles that share a side in a polygon are called **adjacent** angles.

1. True or false? Explain why or draw a counter-example.

a) In a parallelogram, the sum of any pair of adjacent angles is 180°.

b) Any quadrilateral with 2 pairs of equal angles is a parallelogram.

c) In a trapezoid, the sum of any pair of adjacent angles is 180°.

d) If 2 angles in a quadrilateral add to 180°, the quadrilateral is either a trapezoid or a parallelogram.

2. Jean thinks that any quadrilateral with 4 right angles is a rectangle.

a) How is Jean's definition different from the definition of a rectangle from G8-27 (p. 82)?

b) Sketch a quadrilateral with 4 right angles. Does it look like a rectangle?

c) Prove that Jean is correct. (You need to prove that any quadrilateral with 4 right angles is a parallelogram.)

3. A line that joins the opposite vertices in a quadrilateral is called a diagonal. Measure the diagonals in these quadrilaterals. Which quadrilaterals have equal diagonals? _____

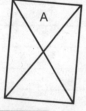
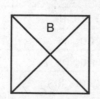
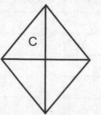
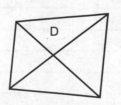
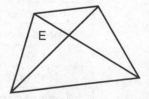

BONUS ▶ The sum of the angles in any quadrilateral is 360°. Use the sum of adjacent angles to explain why any quadrilateral with two pairs of equal angles is either a parallelogram or a trapezoid.

A **kite** is a quadrilateral with 2 pairs of equal adjacent sides and no indentation.

The **Pythagorean Theorem**: In a right triangle with sides a, b, c, where c is opposite the right angle, $a^2 + b^2 = c^2$.

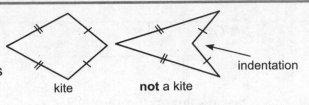

kite   **not** a kite   indentation

4. Use the Pythagorean Theorem to find the equal sides in the shapes. Which shapes are kites?

Example:

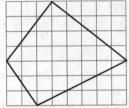

$a = 5$

$b = \sqrt{3^2 + 4^2} = \sqrt{25} = 5$, so $a = b$

$c = \sqrt{7^2 + 4^2} = \sqrt{49 + 16} = \sqrt{65}$

$d = \sqrt{2^2 + 7^2} = \sqrt{4 + 49} = \sqrt{53}$

This is not a kite.

a)

b)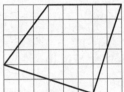

c)

5. Draw the diagonals of each shape in Question 4. Measure the angles between the diagonals you drew. What property do the kites have that the other shapes do not have?

6. a) Find the length of a, b, c, and d. Which two lengths are the same?

   b) Predict a general rule for the diagonals of all kites. Draw 2 more kites on grid or dot paper and test your prediction.

   c) Measure the angles of the kites you drew. What do you notice?

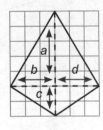

7. Sort these shapes into a Venn diagram with these properties:

   1. Diagonals meet at right angles.   2. Two or more pairs of equal adjacent sides.

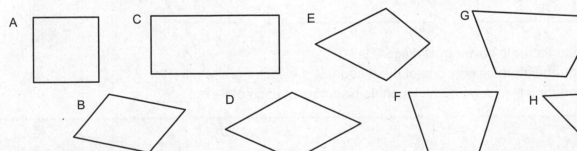

A   C   E   G

B   D   F   H

8. Find the name that fits best!

   a) A rhombus that is also a rectangle.   b) A parallelogram that is also a kite.
   c) A rectangle that is also a kite.   d) A kite that has equal opposite sides.

Geometry 8-28

G8-29 Perpendiculars and Bisectors

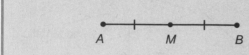

1. Length of segment *PQ*: _____ cm.
   Length ÷ 2 = _____ cm.
   Mark the midpoint of the line segment.

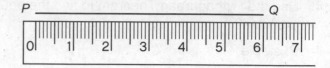

2. Draw a line segment 8 cm in length. Mark the midpoint.

3. a) Name each midpoint shown in the figure and the line segment it is the midpoint of.

   _____ is the midpoint of _____

   _____ is the midpoint of _____

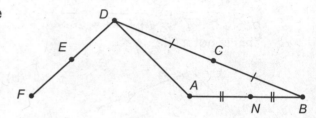

   b) Can you tell from the diagram whether *E* is the midpoint of *FD*? Why or why not?

BONUS ▶ Any line segment has a midpoint, but can a line have a midpoint? Explain.

4. Mark the midpoint of each line segment. Then draw 3 bisectors of the line segment.

   a)

   b)

5. a) Measure the diagonals of the special quadrilaterals. Find and mark the midpoint of each diagonal.

   A   B   C   D

   b) Which quadrilaterals have equal diagonals? _____
   c) In which quadrilateral is only one of the diagonals a bisector of the other? _____
   d) In which quadrilaterals are both diagonals bisectors of each other? _____

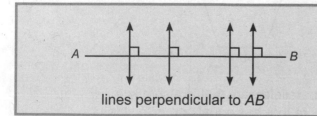

lines perpendicular to *AB*

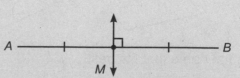

the **perpendicular bisector** of *AB*

Geometry 8-29

6. Draw the perpendicular bisector of each line segment. The midpoint is marked in a).

a)

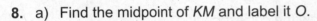

b)

7. a) Find the midpoint of *AC* and label it *O*.

   b) Draw the perpendicular bisector of *AC*. Construct two points, *B* and *D*, on the perpendicular bisector so that *OB* = *OD* is less than *OA*.

   c) Draw quadrilateral *ABCD*. What special quadrilateral have you constructed? _____

8. a) Find the midpoint of *KM* and label it *O*.

   b) Draw the perpendicular bisector of *KM*. Construct two points, *L* and *N*, on the perpendicular bisector so that *OK* = *OL* = *ON*.

   c) Draw quadrilateral *KLMN*. What special quadrilateral have you constructed? _____

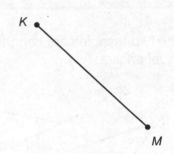

9. a) Find the midpoint of *PR* and label it *O*.

   b) Draw a bisector (but not a perpendicular bisector) of *PR*. Construct two points, Q and S, on the bisector so that *OP* = *OQ* = *OS*.

   c) Draw quadrilateral *PQRS*. What special quadrilateral have you constructed? _____

10. a) Draw a perpendicular to *WY* that does not bisect *WY*. Label the intersection point *O*. Construct two points, *X* and *Z* on the perpendicular, so that *OX* = *OZ*.

    b) Draw quadrilateral *WXYZ*. What special quadrilateral have you constructed? _____

The Pythagorean Theorem:
In a right triangle with sides *a*, *b*, *c*, where *c* is opposite the right angle, $a^2 + b^2 = c^2$.

BONUS ▶ Use the Pythagorean Theorem to explain why the adjacent sides of *WXYZ* are equal.

G8-30 Congruent Triangles

The corresponding sides and angles are marked in these triangles.

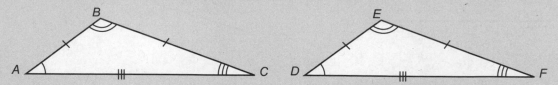

If the corresponding sides and angles in two polygons are equal, the two polygons are **congruent**.
In △ABC and △DEF above, all 3 pairs of sides and all 3 pairs of angles are equal.

AB = DE   BC = EF   AC = DF   and   ∠A = ∠D   ∠B = ∠E   ∠C = ∠F

So, △ABC is congruent to △DEF. You can also write this as △ABC ≅ △DEF.

The reverse is also true: If two polygons are congruent, all the corresponding sides and angles are equal.

---

1. The two triangles are congruent. Mark the triangles to show the corresponding equal angles.

   a)

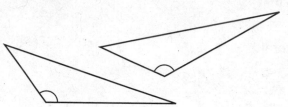

   b)
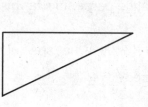

2. Which sides in each pair of triangles are corresponding equal sides?

   VW = ____   WX = ____   VX = ____

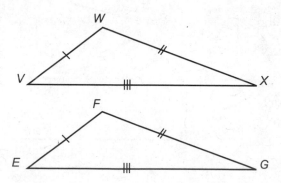

3. Which angles in each pair of triangles are corresponding equal angles?

   ∠M = ∠____   ∠N = ∠____   ∠O = ∠ ____

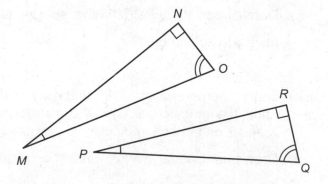

4. These triangles each have the same three angles. Which angles are corresponding equal angles?

   ∠A = ∠____ = ∠____   ∠B = ∠____ = ∠__   ∠C = ∠____ = ∠__

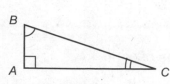
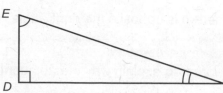
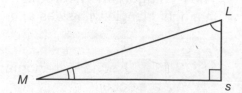

5. These triangles are congruent. Identify the pairs of corresponding equal sides and angles in the two triangles.

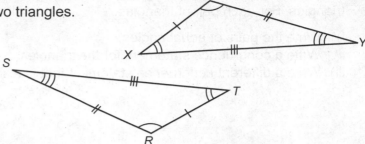

∠____ = ∠____   ∠____ = ∠____

∠____ = ∠____

____ = ____   ____ = ____

____ = ____

6. Kali notices that there are three equal angles in these two triangles. She decides that the triangles are congruent. Is she right? What did she forget to check?

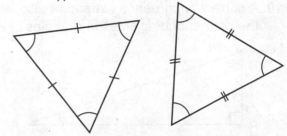

_____

_____

7. These two triangles are congruent. Why do you not have to mark the third pair of angles to know that they are equal? (Hint: If you know the measures of two angles in a triangle, then you know the measure of the third angle. Why?)

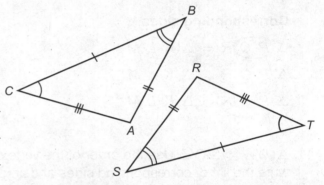

_____

_____

_____

Important: When two triangles are congruent, you have to write the letters that name the vertices in the proper order to show what is equal to what.

Example: The markings show that these two triangles are congruent. To write a correct congruence statement, follow these steps.

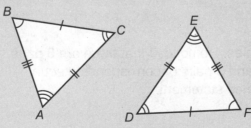

First triangle	Second triangle	Congruence statement
Choose any vertex on one of the triangles, e.g., vertex *A*.	Record the corresponding vertex on the other triangle, e.g., ∠*A* = ∠*E*	△*A* ≅ △*E*
Choose an adjacent vertex, e.g., vertex *B*.	Record the corresponding vertex on the other triangle.	△*AB* ≅ △*EF*
Write the letter of the third vertex.	Write the letter of the third vertex.	△*ABC* ≅ △*EFD*

8. Write a correct congruence statement for the pairs of triangles in Questions 5 and 7.

5. △ ____ ≅ △ ____   7. △ ____ ≅ △ ____

9. There are 2 or more equal angles in these congruent triangles. For each pair of triangles:

i) Write the pairs of equal angles.

ii) Write a congruence statement for the triangles.

iii) Write a different congruence statement that is also correct.

a)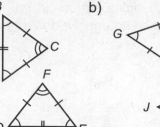

b)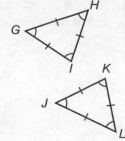

10. A correct congruence statement also tells you which sides are equal. Finish circling the corresponding sides and angles in congruent triangles *PQR* and *KLM*.

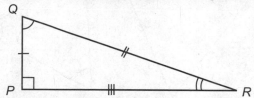 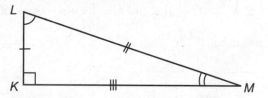

Corresponding sides

△ (P Q) R = △ (K L) M

△ P (Q R) = △ K L M

△ (P) Q (R) = △ K L M

Corresponding angles

△ (P) Q R = △ (K) L M

△ P (Q) R = △ K L M

△ P Q R = △ K L M

11. △*UVW* ≅ △*XYZ*. Use the order of the vertex names in the congruence statement to write the list of corresponding sides and angles for these two congruent triangles.

UV = XY   ∠ U = ∠ X

VW = YZ   ∠ ____ = ∠ ____

____ = ____   ∠ ____ = ∠ ____

12. Tom looked at these two triangles. He noticed that there are 3 pairs of corresponding equal sides and 3 pairs of corresponding equal angles. He wrote this congruence statement:

△*VWX* ≅ △*ABC*

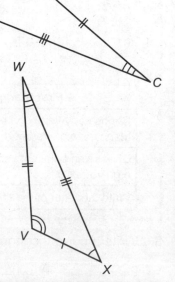

Then Tom lost his diagram, but he was not worried. He used his congruence statement to list the equal sides and angles. Here is his list:

VW = AB ∠V = ∠A
WX = BC ∠W = ∠B
XV = CA ∠X = ∠C

Compare Tom's list of equal sides and angles with the diagrams.
Is his list correct? Put an X beside any statements that are incorrect.

How should Tom have written the congruence statement?

△ _____ ≅ △ _____

G8-31 Congruence Rules

Congruence Rules for Triangles

Here are three rules for determining if two triangles are congruent:

SSS (side-side-side)   **SAS** (side-angle-side)   **ASA** (angle-side-angle)

  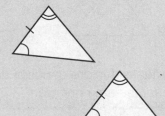

If two triangles have...

• three pairs of equal corresponding sides

• two pairs of equal corresponding sides and a pair of equal corresponding angles between these sides

• two pairs of equal corresponding angles and a pair of equal corresponding sides between them

...then the triangles are congruent.

1. Which congruence rule tells that the two triangles are congruent? Write the vertex letters in the names of the triangles in the correct order (the order that tells which corresponding parts are equal).

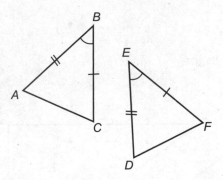   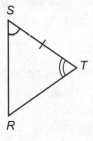   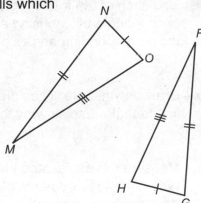

Congruence rule: _____   Congruence rule: _____   Congruence rule: _____

△ABC is congruent to △ _____.   △ _____ is congruent to △ _____.   △ _____ ≅ △ _____.

2. Are the two thick sides corresponding sides? Explain.

a)   b)   c)

      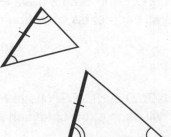

The fourth congruence rule for triangles is **AAS** (angle-angle-side):

If two triangles have two pairs of equal corresponding angles and one pair of equal corresponding sides that are opposite equal angles then the triangles are congruent.

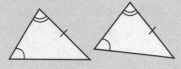   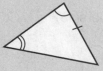

The equal sides are opposite equal angles —
the triangles are congruent.

The equal sides are opposite different angles —
the triangles are **not** congruent.

3. Are the two thick sides corresponding? Are they equal?

a) 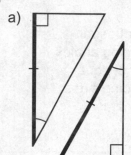   b) 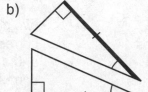   c) 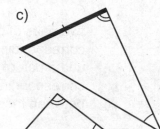   d)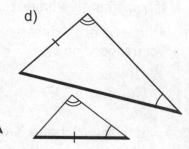

4. Use each of the four congruence rules to draw a pair of congruent triangles. Name each triangle by choosing a letter for each vertex. Mark each pair of triangles to show the corresponding angles and sides.

5. Draw any triangle. Then draw another triangle that is not congruent to the first triangle. Explain why the triangles are not congruent.

6. Measure the angles and the sides of these triangles.
Write the measurements on the diagram.
Which angles are equal? Which sides are equal?
Are the triangles congruent? Explain.

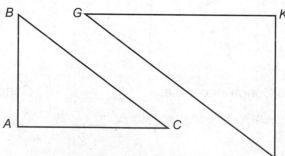

7. △PQR and △XYZ have PQ = XY = 5 cm and QR = YZ = 7 cm. Sketch the triangles. Will each extra condition make △PQR and △XYZ congruent? By which congruence rule?

a) ∠P = ∠Y   b) ∠Q = ∠Y   c) ∠P = ∠X   d) PR = XZ

8. △BCD and △FGH have PQ = XY = 5cm and QR = YZ = 7cm. Sketch the triangles. Will each extra condition make the triangles congruent? By which congruence rule?

a) ∠B = ∠F   b) CD = GH   c) BD = FH   d) BC = GH

Geometry 8-31

9. Sketch a counter-example to show why each statement is **false**.

   a) If two triangles have two corresponding sides that are equal, the triangles are congruent.

   b) If two triangles have three equal parts (sides or angles), then they are congruent.

10. $\triangle ABC$ and $\triangle DEF$ are both isosceles triangles. $\angle A = \angle D$ and $AB = DE$.
Are $\triangle ABC$ and $\triangle DEF$ always congruent? Explain.

   Hint: Start by making a sketch that includes all the information you have been given.
Try making more than one sketch using a different position for the equal angles.

INVESTIGATION ▶ Are two triangles that have two pairs of corresponding sides and one pair of corresponding angles **always** congruent?

A. What sides and angles in $\triangle ABC$ and $\triangle DEF$ are equal?

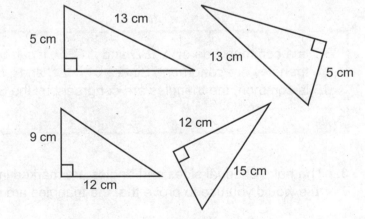

   _____

B. Can you use the SAS congruence rule? Why or why not?

   _____

C. Do triangles $\triangle ABC$ and $\triangle DEF$ look congruent? _____

D. Is **SSA** (side-side-angle) a congruence rule? What about **ASS** (angle-side-side)?
Explain.

---

11. Explain why these two triangles are congruent.
Which theorem will you use? Which congruence
rule? (SAS, ASA, SSS or AAS)

12. Explain why these two triangles are congruent.
Which theorem will you use? Which congruence
rule? (SAS, ASA, SSS or AAS)

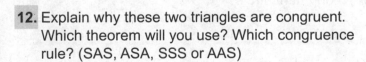

13. Are these two triangles congruent? How do you
know? Note: Triangles are not drawn to scale.

a)

b)

G8-32 Triangles and Quadrilaterals

An **angle bisector** divides an angle in half.

AD bisects ∠*BAC*, so ∠*BAD* = ∠*CAD*.

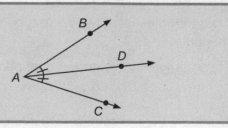

1. *AD* bisects ∠*CAB*. Determine the measure of ∠*BAD* and ∠*BAC*.

a)

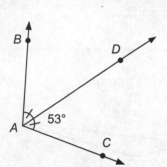

∠*BAD* = _____°

∠*BAC* = _____° + _____°

= _____°

b)

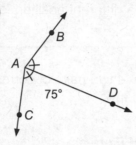

∠*BAD* = _____°

∠*BAC* = _____° + _____°

= _____°

c)

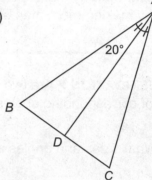

∠*BAD* = _____°

∠*BAC* = _____° + _____°

= _____°

2. a) Is a diagonal of a rectangle an angle bisector? Predict, then measure the angles to check.

   b) Is a diagonal of a square an angle bisector? Predict, then draw a square with a diagonal and check your prediction.

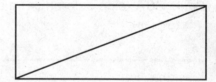

BD is a common side of △*ABD* and △*CBD*. It can be used to show that the triangles are congruent. Since ∠*A* = ∠*C* and ∠*BDA* = ∠*BDC*, and since *BD* is common, the triangles are congruent by the SAA congruence rule.

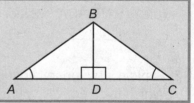

3. The pairs of equal sides and angles are marked in the diagram. Which congruence rule would you use to prove that the triangles are congruent?

a)

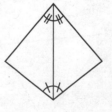

Rule _____

b)

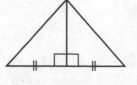

Rule _____

c)

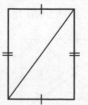

Rule _____

d)

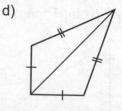

Rule _____

4. Use the diagram at right. Fill in the blanks to prove the
Isosceles Triangle Theorem:

*In an isosceles triangle, a median to the unequal side is
also the perpendicular bisector of the unequal side.*

Assume $\triangle ABC$ is isosceles, and BD is the median to the unequal side.

Then $AB =$ _____, $AD =$ _____, and BD is the common side

of $\triangle ABD$ and $\triangle$_____.

Then $\triangle ABD \cong \triangle$_____, by congruence rule _____.

This means $\angle ADB = \angle$ _____.

Since $\angle ADB$ and _____ together make a straight (180°) angle, they must each be _____.

This means $BD \perp$_____.

So the median BD is also a perpendicular bisector of the side _____.

5. The circles centred at A and C have equal radii.

a) Draw AB, AD, CB, CD, and BD.

b) There are many pairs of congruent triangles in the
diagram now. Which congruence rule would you use

to show that $\triangle ABD \cong \triangle CBD$? _____

c) Which angle in $\triangle ABD$ equals $\angle DBC$ in $\triangle CBD$? _____
Mark the angles as equal.

d) Label E the intersection point of AC and BD.
What can you tell about $\triangle ABE$ and $\triangle CBE$? Explain.

e) Explain why BD is the perpendicular bisector of AC.
What theorem have you used?

f) True or false?

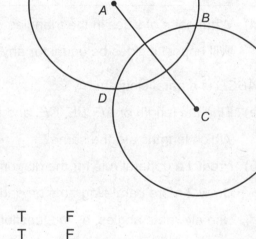

i) In a rhombus, both diagonals bisect each other.	T	F
ii) In a rhombus, the diagonals are equal.	T	F
iii) In a rhombus, the diagonals are perpendicular.	T	F
iv) In a rhombus, the diagonals are angle bisectors.	T	F

6. True or false? Check using the diagram at right.

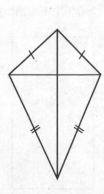

i) In a kite, both diagonals bisect each other.	T	F
ii) In a kite, one of the diagonals bisects the other.	T	F
iii) In a kite, the diagonals are equal.	T	F
iv) In a kite, the diagonals are perpendicular.	T	F
v) In a kite, one of the diagonals is an angle bisector.	T	F

BONUS ▶ Pick one of the statements you marked as true and explain why it is
true using logic.

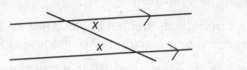

7. *ABCD* is a parallelogram.

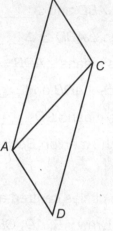

Measure the sides of *ABCD*. What do you notice about the opposite sides?

_____

Will this be true for any parallelogram? Consider:

a) *AC* intersects parallel lines *AB* and _____ .

Which two angles are alternate equal angles? _____ = _____
Mark them on the diagram.

b) *AC* intersects parallel lines *AD* and _____.

Which two angles are alternate equal angles? _____ = _____
Mark them on the diagram.

c) What can you say about △*ABC* and △*CDA*? How do you know? _____

_____

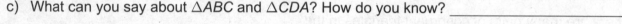

d) What pairs of sides in the triangles △*ABC* and △*CDA* are equal? _____

Will opposite sides be equal for any parallelogram? _____

8. *ABCD* is a parallelogram.

a) Find the length of *AE*, *BE*, *CE*, and *DE*.

Which lengths are the same? _____.

b) Predict a general rule for the diagonals of all parallelograms.

Draw 2 more parallelograms on grid or dot paper and test your prediction.

c) Use alternate angles, as in Question 7, to explain why △*ABE* ≅ △*CDE*.

d) Use the congruence statement from part c) to explain why your conjecture from
part b) is true for all parallelograms.

9. Sort the shapes into the Venn diagram.

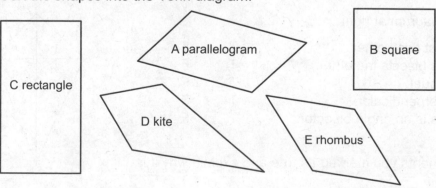

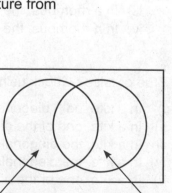

diagonals meet
at right angles

both diagonals
bisect each other

G8-33 Triangles and Circles

How to construct a perpendicular bisector of *AB* using a compass and straightedge:

Step 1: Put your compass point at one end of the line segment. Construct an arc as shown.

Step 2: With your compass at the same radius, construct a second arc centred at *B* as shown.

Step 3: Construct a line ℓ through the intersection points of the two arcs. This is the perpendicular bisector of *AB*.

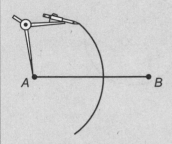

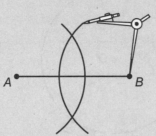

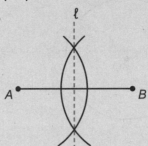

INVESTIGATION 1 ▶ What is special about the points on the perpendicular bisector of a line segment?

A. Line ℓ is a perpendicular bisector of the line segment *AB*. Choose a point *C* on the line ℓ. Draw the lines *AC* and *BC*. Measure *AC* and *BC*. What do you notice?

_____

B. Make a conjecture about the distances from a point on a perpendicular bisector to the endpoints of *AB*.

_____

_____

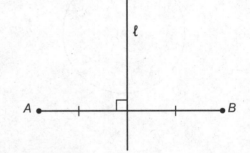

C. Prove your conjecture:
Label the midpoint of *AB* as *M*. What do you know about △*ACM* and △*BCM*?

How do you know? _____

_____

How does this help you to conclude that *AC* = *BC*? _____

A point that is at the same distance from points *A* and *B* is **equidistant** from those two points. You have just proved this:
Any point on the perpendicular bisector of a line segment is equidistant from the ends of the line segment.

INVESTIGATION 2 ▶ Are all points equidistant from *A* and *B* on the perpendicular bisector of *AB*? Could there be a point *C* that is not on the perpendicular bisector of *AB* and for which *AC* = *BC*?

A. The point *C* is equidistant from *A* and *B*. This means *AC* = _____

B. What type of triangle is △*ABC* ? _____

C. Find the middle of *AB* and label it *D*. Draw the median *CD*.

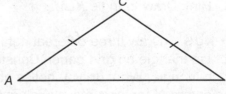

D. Can it be that *CD* bisects *AB*, but they are not perpendicular? Explain.

1. Point *O* is the centre of the circle. Draw the line segment *AB* and construct a perpendicular bisector of *AB*. What do you notice? Explain why this happens.

a)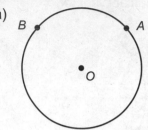

b)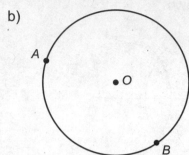

c)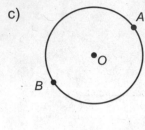

2. Point *O* is the centre of the circle. Draw the perpendicular bisectors of *AB*, *AC*, and *BC*. What do you notice? Explain why this happens.

a)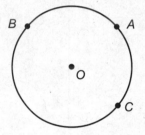

b)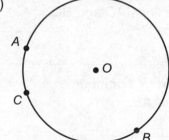

c)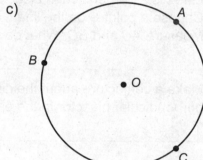

3. a) Draw perpendicular bisectors to the sides of △*ABC*. What do you notice?

_____

_____

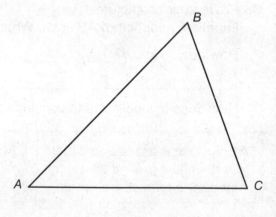

b) A circle that passes through all the vertices of a polygon is called a **circumcircle**. Sidra wants to construct a circumcircle of △*ABC*. Which point should she choose as the centre for her circle? _____

What should the radius of her circle be? _____

4. Construct a circle through the points *K*, *L*, *M*. Hint: Draw triangle *KLM*.

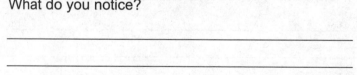

BONUS ▶ Draw three different right triangles and one obtuse triangle on grid paper. Construct a circumcircle for each triangle. What do you notice about the location of the centre of the circumcircle in right triangles?

M •

Geometry 8-33

G8-34 Similarity

Two shapes are similar if their corresponding sides are proportionate and their corresponding angles are equal.

In $\triangle ABC$ and $\triangle DEF$:
$AB : DE = BC : EF = AC : DF = 1 : 2$
$\angle A = \angle D, \angle B = \angle E, \angle C = \angle F$

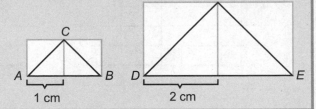

1. a) Find the ratio of the corresponding sides of the rectangles.

   $AB : EF$ = ___ : ___

   $BC : FG$ = ___ : ___

   $CD :$ ___ = ___ : ___

   $AD :$ ___ = ___ : ___

   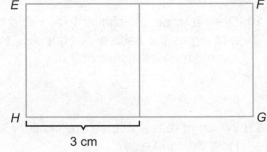

   b) Are these rectangles similar? _____

   c) Why is there no need to check equality between the angles to decide whether the rectangles are similar?

2. Rectangles A and B are similar. How can you find the length of B without a ruler?

   _____

   _____

   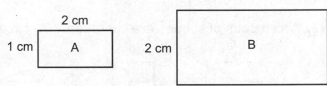

3. Rectangles A and B are similar. Find the length of B. (Do not forget to include the units!)

   a) width of A = 1 cm   width of B = 2 cm   length of A = 3 cm   length of B = _____

   b) width of A = 2 cm   width of B = 6 cm   length of A = 4 cm   length of B = _____

   c) width of A = 1 cm   width of B = 3 cm   length of A = 5 cm   length of B = _____

4. A square and a rectangle have the same angles. Are they similar? Explain.

5. Can a trapezoid and a square ever be similar? Explain.

6. Draw any triangle ABC. Draw a triangle that is congruent to $\triangle ABC$, and one that is similar to $\triangle ABC$.

7. All sides and all angles in an equilateral triangle are equal.

   a) $\triangle EFG$ and $\triangle QRS$ are both equilateral triangles. $EF = QR$. Are $\triangle EFG$ and $\triangle QRS$ congruent? Start by making a sketch. Explain your answer.

   b) $\triangle LMN$ and $\triangle TUV$ are both equilateral triangles. $\angle M = \angle U$. Is $\triangle LMN \cong \triangle TUV$? Explain.

8. Explain why congruent triangles are always similar, but similar triangles are not always congruent.

9. For each pair of rectangles, say how you know the rectangles are similar or not.

a)

b)
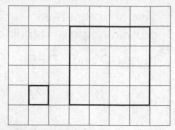
c)

d) 2 cm × 4 cm and 3 cm × 6 cm

e) 1 cm × 2 cm and 2.5 cm × 5.5 cm

10. Draw a trapezoid similar to A with a base that is two times as long as the base of A. Hint: A is 1 unit high. How high should the new figure be?

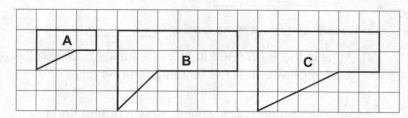

11. Which of these shapes are similar? How do you know?

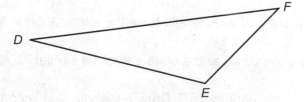

12. Which pairs of shapes are congruent? Which are similar? How do you know?

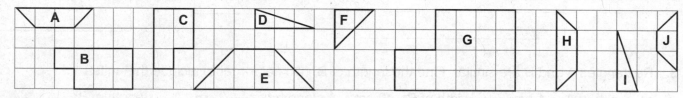

13. a) Measure all angles and all sides of these triangles.

b) Are △ABC and △DEF similar? Explain using both angle measurements and ratios of sides.

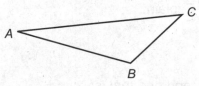
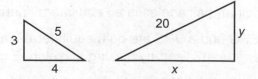

14. These triangles are similar. Find x and y.

a)

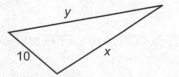

b)

15. a) △KLM has angles 30°, 60°, and 90°.
△POR has angles 35°, 55°, and 90°.
Are the triangles similar? Explain.

b) △GHI has sides 2 cm, 4 cm, and 5 cm.
△UVW has sides 3 cm, 8 cm, and 10 cm.
Are the triangles similar? Explain.

G8-35 Similar Triangles

If $\triangle ABC$ is similar to $\triangle A'B'C'$, then $\angle A = \angle A'$, $\angle B = \angle B'$, $\angle C = \angle C'$ and $\dfrac{A'B'}{AB} = \dfrac{A'C'}{AC} = \dfrac{B'C'}{BC}$

The ratio between the corresponding sides is often expressed as a number, and is called the **scale factor**.

INVESTIGATION ▶ Which information about a pair of triangles will ensure they are similar?

A. SSS (side-side-side)

  a) Draw a scalene triangle ABC. Measure the sides. $AB = $ _____ , $AC = $ _____ , $BC = $ _____

  b) Construct a triangle $A'B'C'$ with sides twice as large. $A'B' = $ _____ , $A'C' = $ _____ , $B'C' = $ _____

  c) Measure the angles of both triangles.

     $\angle A = $ _____ , $\angle B = $ _____ , $\angle C = $ _____ $\angle A' = $ _____ , $\angle B' = $ _____ , $\angle C' = $ _____

     Are the triangles similar? _____

  d) In your triangles, the scale factor $\dfrac{A'B'}{AB} = \dfrac{A'C'}{AC} = \dfrac{B'C'}{BC} = $ _____ .

     Draw a different pair of triangles with the scale factor 3 and check the angles to see whether the triangles are similar.

B. SAS (side-angle-side)

  a) Measure the sides of the right triangle $\triangle ABC$.

     $AB = $ _____ , $AC = $ _____ , $BC = $ _____

  b) Construct $\triangle A'B'C'$ with right angle A' and

     $A'B' = 3 \times AB$, $A'C' = 3 \times AC$.

     $A'B' = $ _____ , $A'C' = $ _____

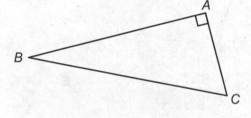

  c) Measure the side $B'C'$. $B'C' = $ _____

  d) Do you have to check the angles of both triangles to say if the triangles are similar? Explain.

  e) **Conjecture:** SAS is a similarity rule:

     If $\angle A = \angle A'$ and $\dfrac{A'B'}{AB} = \dfrac{A'C'}{AC}$, then $\triangle ABC$ is similar to $\triangle A'B'C'$.

     Repeat parts a) to d) with an acute triangle of your choice to check the conjecture.

C. ASA (angle-side-angle)

  a) Draw $\triangle KLM$ with $\angle K = 40°$, $\angle L = 60°$ and side $KL = 3$ cm.

  b) Draw $\triangle K'L'M'$ with $\angle K' = 40°$, $\angle L' = 60°$ and side $K'L' = 12$ cm.

  c) Measure the rest of the sides and angles in both triangles. Are the triangles similar?

  d) What is the scale factor for $\triangle KLM$ and $\triangle K'L'M'$? ____

D. a) Draw another triangle, K*L*M*, with ∠K* = 40° and ∠L* = 60°, but not congruent to △KLM or △K'L'M' from part C.

b) Measure the sides in your triangle and find the ratios $\dfrac{K^*L^*}{KL} = $ ____ $\dfrac{K^*M^*}{KM} = $ ____ $\dfrac{M^*L^*}{ML} = $ ____

What do you notice? _____

c) Without measuring, fill in the blanks: ∠M = ____ and ∠M* = ____ . How do you know?

d) Are △KLM and △K*L*M* similar? ____ If yes, what is the scale factor? ____

e) Conjecture: AA (angle-angle) is a similarity rule:

If ∠A = ∠A' and ∠B = ∠B', then △ABC is similar to △A'B'C'.

Repeat parts b) to d) with different pair of triangles with equal corresponding angles to check the conjecture.

Similarity Rules for Triangles

There are three rules for determining if two triangles are similar:

SSS (side-side-side)   **SAS** (side-angle-side)   **AA** (angle-angle)

If two triangles have ...

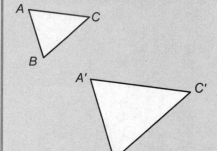

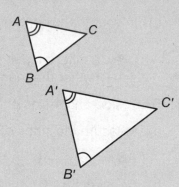

$\dfrac{A'B'}{AB} = \dfrac{A'C'}{AC} = \dfrac{B'C'}{BC}$ $\dfrac{A'B'}{AB} = \dfrac{A'C'}{AC}, \angle A = \angle A'$ $\angle A = \angle A', \angle B = \angle B'$

• three pairs of proportional corresponding sides

• two pairs of proportional corresponding sides and a pair of equal corresponding angles between these sides

• two pairs of equal corresponding angles

...then the triangles are similar.

---

1. Which rule will you use to prove that the triangles are similar?

a)

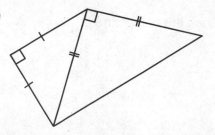

b)

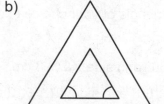

c)

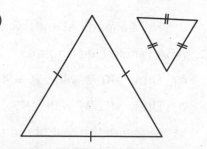

Similarity rule: _____   Similarity rule: _____   Similarity rule: _____

2. Does ASS (angle-side-side) work as a similarity rule? Check the following pair of triangles.

   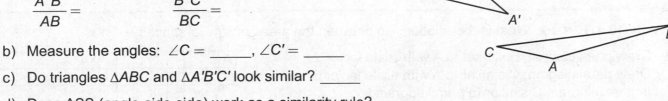

   a) Measure the sides and find the ratios:

   $$\frac{A'B'}{AB} = \qquad \frac{B'C'}{BC} =$$

   b) Measure the angles: $\angle C =$ _____ , $\angle C' =$ _____

   c) Do triangles $\triangle ABC$ and $\triangle A'B'C'$ look similar? _____

   d) Does ASS (angle-side-side) work as a similarity rule? _____

3. Does AS (angle-side) work as a similarity rule? Explain using the example in Question 2.

4. Draw two triangles with $\dfrac{A'B'}{AB} = \dfrac{A'C'}{AC}$ to show that SS (side-side) cannot be a similarity rule.

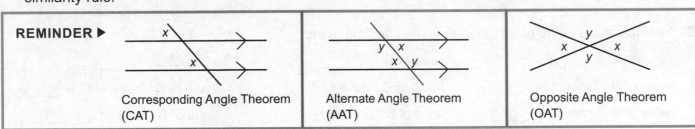

REMINDER ▶		
Corresponding Angle Theorem (CAT)	Alternate Angle Theorem (AAT)	Opposite Angle Theorem (OAT)

5. The lines *BD* and *CE* are parallel.

   a) Mark the angles you know are equal.

   b) Which angles are equal in $\triangle ABD$ and $\triangle ACE$?

   _____

   c) What can you say about $\triangle ABD$ and $\triangle ACE$?

   _____

6. a) Which angle do $\triangle KMN$ and $\triangle KLO$ have in common?

   b) *L* is the midpoint of *KM*, so $KM : KL =$ _____

   O is the midpoint of *KN*, so $KN : KO =$ _____

   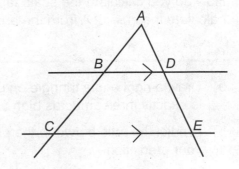

   c) What can you say about $\triangle KMN$ and $\triangle KLO$? Explain.

   d) Which fraction of the length of *KN* is *KO*? How do you know?

   e) Write a pair of corresponding angles for $\triangle KMN$ and $\triangle KLO$. What can you say about these angles? Explain.

   f) What does the relationship between the corresponding angles tell you about the lines *MN* and *LO*? What special quadrilateral is *LMNO*?

7. Explain why SSSS or AAAA do not work as similarity rules for quadrilaterals. Use an example in your answer.

G8-36 Properties of Similar Shapes

INVESTIGATION 1 ▶ What is the relationship between the areas of similar shapes?

A. Draw parallelogram B similar to A with scale factor 2.
Draw parallelogram C similar to A with scale factor 6.
Is parallelogram C similar to parallelogram B? _____
What is the scale factor between B and C? _____

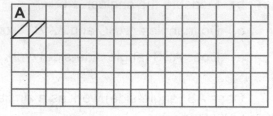

B. Find the base and the height of each parallelogram.

A base = __1__ height = __1__   B base = _____ height = _____   C base = _____ height = _____

How do you calculate the base of B from the base of A and the scale factor?

_____

C. Find the areas of the parallelograms. Then find the ratios.

Area of A = _____   Area of B = _____   Area of C = _____

base of B : base of A = _____   base of C : base of A = _____   base of B : base of C = _____

area of B : area of A = _____   area of C : area of A = _____   area of B : area of C = _____

D. How do you calculate the scale factor from the ratio of the bases? How do you
calculate the area of A from the area of B and the scale factor?

---

1. a) Draw a right angle triangle on grid paper. Then draw a similar triangle that
is exactly three times as high as the first.

b) Predict the ratio between the areas of the triangles, then find the areas to check
your prediction.

c) Explain the ratio you obtained using the formula for the area of a triangle.

2. $\triangle PQR$ is similar to $\triangle UVW$, so that $\angle P = \angle U$, $\angle Q = \angle V$, $\angle R = \angle W$.
Find the ratio $PQ : UV$ from the areas of the triangles below. Explain how you know.

a) Area of $\triangle PQR = 125$ cm². Area of $\triangle UVW = 5$ cm².
b) Area of $\triangle PQR = 1$ cm². Area of $\triangle UVW = 100$ cm².
c) Area of $\triangle PQR = 50$ cm². Area of $\triangle UVW = 25$ cm².

3. $\triangle KLM$ is an isosceles triangle with two angles of 30° and two sides of 2 cm.
$\triangle PQR$ is an isosceles triangle with $\angle R = 120°$.

a) Sketch both triangles. What can you tell about them? Explain.

b) The area of $\triangle PQR$ is 81 times more than the area of $\triangle KLM$. What is the length of
the sides PR and QR? Explain how you know.

INVESTIGATION 2 ▶ What is the relationship between the perimeters of similar shapes?

A. Measure the sides of the triangles.

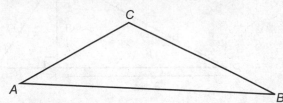 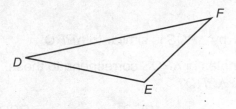

B. Find the ratios between the sides. Are the triangles similar? How do you know?

C. What is the scale factor of the sides of the triangle?

D. Find the perimeter of the triangles.

Perimeter of △ABC _____   Perimeter of △DEF _____

E. How do you calculate the perimeter of △DEF from the perimeter of △ABC and the scale factor? Explain.

F. Draw your own pair of similar shapes with scale factor 5. What is the ratio between their perimeters? Predict the general rule for the ratio between the perimeters of similar shapes.

---

4. ABCD is a trapezoid, with AB ‖ CD, AB = BC, and ∠BCD = 2∠ADC.

   a) Mark the equal sides. Use the given information and what you know about parallel lines to mark the equal angles.

   b) Explain why △ABC is similar to △DAC.

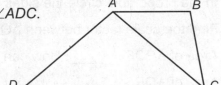

5. △ABC is a right triangle with height BD.

   a) Look at △ABC. ∠BAC + ∠BCA = _____°

   Look at △ABD. ∠BAC + ∠DBA = _____°

   Then ∠DBA = ∠_____.

   What can you tell about △ABC and △ABD? _____

   b) Which angles are equal in △ABC and △BCD? _____

   What can you tell about △ABC and △BCD? _____

   c) Is there another pair of similar triangles in the diagram? Explain.

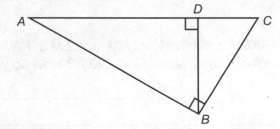

6. A 16 mm picture is projected onto a screen using a light source that is 10 cm behind the picture. The screen is 18 m from the light source. What is the size of the image of the picture on the screen?

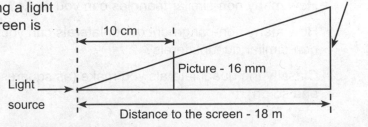

7. Find the area of △PQR using two methods.

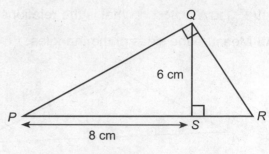

Method 1

a) Explain why △PQS is similar to △PRQ.

b) Which angles in △PQS correspond to these angles in △PRQ?

∠PQR = _____, ∠PRQ = _____, ∠RPQ = _____

c) Finish writing the proportion between the sides of △PRQ and △PQS: $\dfrac{QR}{QS} = \dfrac{PQ}{PS} =$ _____.

In the proportion, circle the sides whose length you know.

d) Which side could you find using the Pythagorean Theorem? _____ Find it. _____ = _____ cm.

e) Find the scale factor between △PRQ and △PQS: $\dfrac{PQ}{PS} =$ _____.

f) What is the area of △PQS? _____

g) The area of △PRQ is _____ times the area of △PQS. Area of △PRQ = _____

Method 2

h) Explain why △PQS is similar to △QRS. Write the pairs of corresponding angles.

i) Finish writing the proportion between the sides of △QRS and △PQS: $\dfrac{QR}{PQ} = \dfrac{RS}{QS} =$ _____

In the proportion, circle the sides whose length you know.

Find the scale factor between △QRS and △PRS. Scale factor = _____

j) Area of △PQS = _____. How can you find the area of △QRS from △PQS using the scale factor?

Area of △QRS = _____

k) Area of △PRQ = _____ + _____ = _____.

8. △KLM is similar to △LNM, and LM ⊥ KN. What is the measure of ∠KLN? How do you know?

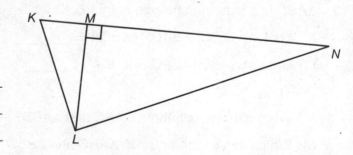

_____

_____

_____

9. On grid paper draw 9 dots in the positions shown. Join sets of dots to make as many triangles or quadrilaterals as you can.

a) How many non-congruent triangles can you make by joining the dots? How many non-similar triangles can you make?

b) How many non-congruent quadrilaterals can you make? How many non-similar quadrilaterals?

c) Classify the quadrilaterals you make (as squares, rectangles, trapezoids, and so on).

PA8-16 Substituting Integers for Variables

1. Add or subtract.

   a) $(-2) + 3 =$ _____   b) $-5 - 3 =$ _____   c) $-5 + 2 =$ _____   d) $4 - 9 =$ _____

   e) $-4) + (+6) =$ _____   f) $(-5) - (-13) =$ _____ g) $(-15) - (+2) =$ _____ h) $+14 + (-29) =$ _____

   i) $(+42) + (-16) =$ _____ j) $5 - (-14) =$ _____   k) $(-1) - (+32) =$ _____ l) $(+61) + (-22) =$ _____

2. Multiply or divide.

   a) $(-2) \times 3 =$ _____   b) $(-4) \times (+3) =$ _____ c) $-6 \times (-2) =$ _____ d) $7 \times (-9) =$ _____

   e) $(-48) \div (+6) =$ _____ f) $(-15) \div (-3) =$ _____ g) $-18 \div (+3) =$ _____ h) $+28 \div (-14) =$ _____

   i) $(-2) \times (-9) =$ _____ j) $-56 \div (-7) =$ _____   k) $(-11) \times 3 =$ _____ l) $(+63) \div (-9) =$ _____

3. Evaluate each expression.

   a) $2x$, $x = -3$ b) $u + 5$, $u = -8$ c) $3r$, $r = -6$ d) $s + 6$, $s = -2$
   $2x = 2(-3)$
   $\quad = 2 \times (-3) = -6$

   e) $2n + 3$, $n = -5$ f) $4t + 26$, $t = -5$ g) $6 + 2n$, $n = -4$
   $2n + 3 = 2(-5) + 3$
   $\quad\quad = -10 + 3 = -7$

   h) $3x + 2$, $x = -7$ i) $z - 2$, $z = -12$ j) $5z - 1$, $z = -10$

   k) $4x + 3$, $x = -3$ l) $3m - 5$, $m = -7$ m) $2 + 3t$, $t = -7$

   n) $-3 + 3x$, $x = -4$ o) $3m + (-5)$, $m = -8$ p) $(-12) - 3t$, $t = -2$

4. Which parts from Question 3 have the same answer? _____ and _____
   Why is this the case?

5. During the day, the temperature on the surface of Mars rises at a rate of 9°C every hour.

   a) How much will the temperature rise in 2 hours? _____ In 3 hours?_____ In n hours? _____

   b) The temperature on the surface of Mars at 9:00 a.m. is -60°C.

   Write an expression to show what the temperature will be n hours after 9:00 a.m.

   _____

   c) Use your expression from b) to find the temperature at 12:00 p.m. _____

   d) What was the temperature at 6:00 a.m.? Hint: What value will you substitute for n

   in the expression from b)? _____

6. Katie saves $5 every week. So far, she has saved a total of $63.

   a) Write an expression for Katie's savings using w for the number of weeks from today.

   b) Use your expression to find out how much money Katie had 5 weeks ago.

7. a) Calculate.

i) $-2 \times 3 =$ ____　　$(-2) \times 3 =$ ____　　$0 - 3 - 3 =$ ____　　$-2(3) =$ ____

ii) $-2 \times 4 =$ ____　　$(-2) \times 4 =$ ____　　$0 - 4 - 4 =$ ____　　$-2(4) =$ ____

iii) $-2 \times 5 =$ ____　　$(-2) \times 5 =$ ____　　$0 - 5 - 5 =$ ____　　$-2(5) =$ ____

iv) $-2 \times 10 =$ ____　　$(-2) \times 10 =$ ____　　$0 - 10 - 10 =$ ____　　$-2(10) =$ ____

b) Circle all the expressions that mean the same thing:

$(-2) \times a$　　　　$-(2 \times a)$　　　　$-2a$　　　　$0 - a - a$　　　　$2a$　　　　$(-2)a$

8. Evaluate each expression.

a) $(-2)x, \quad x = 3$　　　　**b)** $u \times (-5), \quad u = 7$　　　　**c)** $(-3) \times r, \quad r = 4$　　　　**d)** $(-7) \times s, \quad s = -2$

$-2(3) = (-2) \times 3$

$\quad\quad\quad = -2 \times 3 = -6$

e) $(-2)n + 3, \quad n = -5$　　　　**f)** $4 + (-2)t, \quad t = 5$　　　　**g)** $6 + (-4)n, \quad n = 2$

$(-2)(-5) + 3 = (-2) \times (-5) + 3$

$\quad\quad\quad = 10 + 3 = 13$

h) $(-3)x + 2, \quad x = -7$　　　　**i)** $(-6)z - 12, \quad z = -2$　　　　**j)** $-1 + (-5)b, \quad b = -10$

k) $(-4)(x + 3), \quad x = 2$　　　　**l)** $(-3)(m - 5), \quad m = 7$　　　　**m)** $(-2)(3 - t), \quad t = 7$

$(-4)(2 + 3) = (-4) \times (5)$

$\quad\quad\quad = -4 \times 5 = -20$

n) $(-3)(2 + x), \quad x = -5$　　　　**o)** $(3 + m) \times (-5), \quad m = -8$　　　　**BONUS ▶** $(-3)((-12) - t), \quad t = -2$

p) $\dfrac{x}{2}, \quad x = -6$　　　　**q)** $\dfrac{w}{5}, \quad w = -10$　　　　**r)** $\dfrac{q}{-4}, \quad q = +4$

$\dfrac{(-6)}{2} = (-6) \div 2 = -3$

s) $\dfrac{a}{2} + (-4), \quad a = -10$　　　　**t)** $\dfrac{u}{5} - (-3), \quad u = -40$　　　　**u)** $\dfrac{q}{-4} + (-2), \quad q = -16$

9. True or false? If you think the statement is true, explain why. If you think the statement as false, find a counter-example.

a) 3 is less than 5, so $3a$ has to be less than $5a$.

b) For any positive number, $3a$ is less than $5a$.

c) For any negative number, $3a$ is more than $5a$.

d) $3a$ cannot be equal to $5a$ for any value of a.

PA8-17 Solving Equations — Guess and Check

1. a) Calculate $(-3)n = (-3) \times n$ and $(-3)n - 5 = (-3) \times n - 5$ for each value of n given in the chart.

n	-5	-4	-3	-2	-1	0	1	2	3	4	5
$(-3)n$	15	12									
$(-3)n - 5$	10										

b) Use the chart to solve for n.

i) $(-3)n - 5 = 7$

$n =$ _____

ii) $(-3)n - 5 = -20$

$n =$ _____

iii) $(-3)n - 5 = 1$

$n =$ _____

iv) $(-3)n - 5 = -11$

$n =$ _____

2. a) Calculate $x \div (-3) = \dfrac{x}{-3}$ and then $\dfrac{x}{-3} + (-4)$ for each value of x given in the chart.

x	-15	-12	-9	-6	-3	0	3	6	9	12	15	18
$\dfrac{x}{-3}$	5	4	3									
$\dfrac{x}{-3} + (-4)$	1											

b) Use the chart to solve for x.

i) $\dfrac{x}{-3} + (-4) = -9$

$x =$ _____

ii) $\dfrac{x}{-3} + (-4) = 0$

$x =$ _____

iii) $\dfrac{x}{-3} + (-4) = -5$

$x =$ _____

iv) $\dfrac{x}{-3} + (-4) = 1$

$x =$ _____

3. Substitute $n = -8$ and $n = -9$ into the left side of the equation. Is n closer to -8 or -9? Where does n need to be relative to -8 and -9 to make the equation true? What is your next guess?

a) $1 - 4n = 29$

$1 - 4(-8) =$ _1 − (−32) = 33_ is ___more than___ 29.

$1 - 4(-9) =$ _1 − (−36) = 37_ is _further from 29_ than 33.

n is closer to _−8_ than _−9_, so my next guess is _−7_.

b) $1 + 3n = -29$

$1 + 3(-8) =$ _____ is _____ -29.

$1 + 3(-9) =$ _____ is _____

n is closer to _____ than _____, so my next guess is _____.

c) $-5n - 6 = 39$ **d)** $7 - 2n = 13$ **e)** $6n - 10 = -100$

4. Solve for n by guessing small values for n, checking, and revising.

a) $-3(n - 2) = 12$

$n =$ _____

b) $(-5)n - 2 = -12$

$n =$ _____

c) $2n + 7 = 1$

$n =$ _____

d) $\dfrac{n}{2} + (-2) = -5$

$n =$ _____

PA8-18 Solving Equations

1. Write the correct operation and number to get back where you started.

   a) $n + (-3)$ _−(−3)_ $= n$

   b) $n \times (-3)$ _____ $= n$

   c) $(-5)m$ _____ $= m$

   d) $x - (+5)$ _____ $= x$

   e) $x + (-7)$ _____ $= x$

   f) $x \div (-9)$ _____ $= x$

   g) $\dfrac{z}{-5}$ _____ $= z$

   h) $-7y$ _____ $= y$

   i) $r \times 8$ _____ $= r$

2. Circle the expressions that always equal m, for any number m. Check your answers for $m = -5$.

   $6m - 6$ $\qquad$ $-6m \div (-6)$ $\qquad$ $m \div 6 \times 6$ $\qquad$ $6 \div m \times 6$ $\qquad$ $6 + m + (-6)$ $\qquad$ $6 - m + 6$

3. Solve for x by doing the same thing to both sides of the equation. Check your answer.

   a) $(-3)x \qquad = 12$
   $(-3)x \div (-3) = 12 \div (-3)$
   $x = -4$
   Check by replacing x with your answer: $(-3)(-4) = 12$ ✓

   b) $x - 4 = 11$

   c) $-4x = 20$

   d) $3 + x = -9$

   e) $-2x = -6$

   f) $5x = -15$

   g) $-10 + x = 90$

   h) $x + (-4) = -12$

   i) $\dfrac{x}{-3} = 7$

   j) $\dfrac{x}{5} = -7$

4. Solve for the variable. Your answer will be a fraction or decimal. Check your answer by substituting it back into the equation.

   a) $3s = 29$

   b) $2t = 11$

   c) $7y = 8$

   d) $5x = 21$

   e) $6a = 9$

5. Start with -3. Multiply by -2. Then add 4.

   Which sequence of operations will get you back to the number you started with (-3)?

   i)* Divide your answer by -2, then subtract 4.

   ii) Subtract 4 from your answer, then divide by -2.

6. Solve for the variable by undoing each operation, working backwards. Then check your answer by substitution.

   a) $(-8)x + 4 = 28$
   $(-8)x + 4 \underline{\;-4} = 28 \underline{\;-4}$
   $(-8)x = \underline{24}$
   $(-8)x \div \underline{\;(-8)} = \underline{24 \div (-8)}$
   $x = \underline{-3}$
   Check: $\underline{(-8)(-3) + 4 = 24 + 4 = 28}$ ✓

   b) $4h - 3 = -39$
   $4h - 3 + 3 = -39 + $ _____
   $4h = $ _____
   $4h \div 4 = $ _____ $\div$ _____
   $h = $ _____
   Check: _____

   c) $(-3)s - 4 = 29$

   d) $2t + 3 = -11$

   e) $\dfrac{x}{3} + (-5) = 7$

   f) $\dfrac{x}{-2} - 4 = 7$

   g) $3s - 5 = 27$

   h) $3t + 3 = 14$

   i) $(-4) + 5y = 42$

   j) $6z + 14 = 16$

PA8-19 Concepts in Equations

1. The scales are balanced. Find the mass of one triangle in circles. Write your answer as a decimal or as a fraction.

a)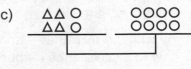

$\Delta = $ _____4.5 circles_____

b)

$\Delta = $ _____

c)

$\Delta = $ _____

2. Here are two ways to solve $(-2)x + 6 = -4$.

Method 1

$(-2)x + 6 = -4$

$(-2)x + 6 - 6 = -4 - 6$ Subtract 6 from both sides

$(-2)x = -10$ Rewrite both sides

$(-2)x \div (-2) = (-10) \div (-2)$ Divide both sides by -2

$x = 5$ Rewrite both sides

Method 2

$(-2)x + 6 = -4$

$(-2)(x + 3) = -4$ Apply the distributive law

$(-2)(x + 3) \div (-2) = -4 \div (-2)$ Divide both sides by -2

$x + 3 = 2$ Rewrite both sides

$x + 3 - 3 = 2 - 3$ Subtract 3 from both sides

$x = -1$ Rewrite both sides

a) Do both methods give the same answer? _____

b) Substitute $x = 5$ into the expression $(-2)x + 6$. Do you get -4? _____

Substitute $x = -1$ into the expression $(-2)x + 6$. Do you get -4? _____

Which method gives the correct answer? _____

c) Substitute $x = 5$ into the left side of each step of Method 2. Where was the mistake made?

d) Correct the mistake in Method 2 and solve the equation using the corrected method.

3. Decide whether each solution is correct by substituting the answer into the original expression.

a) $-3x + 6 = -21$

$(-3)(x - 6) = -21(-3)$

$x - 6 = 7$

$x - 6 + 6 = 7 + 6$

$x = 13$

b) $-3x + 6 = -21$

$(x + 2) = -21$

$x + 2 = 7$

$x + 2 - 2 = 7 - 2$

$x = 5$

c) $-3x + 6 = -21$

$(-3)(x - 2) = -21$

$x - 2 = 7$

$x - 2 + 2 = 7 + 2$

$x = 9$

d) $-3x + 6 = -21$

$-3x + 6 - 6 = -21 - 6$

$-3x = -27$

$(-3)x \div 3 = -27 \div 3$

$x = -9$

4. For each incorrect solution above, describe the mistake. If the solution is correct, write "Correct."

5. To find the average temperature, we add the temperatures and divide the sum by the number of days. Use equations to find the missing temperatures.

City	Day 1	Day 2	Day 3	Average temperature over 3 days
Yellowknife, NWT	$-21°C$	$-34°C$	$x°C$	$-27°C$
Vancouver, BC	$-3°C$	$y°C$	$+5°C$	$+1°C$
Calgary, AB	$z°C$	$-5°C$	$+1°C$	$-9°C$

PA8-20 Formulas

Ariel makes a garden path using square and triangular tiles. He uses 4 triangular tiles for every 1 square tile.

He writes a **formula** — an equation that shows how to calculate the number of triangles from the number of squares:

$$4 \times \text{squares} = \text{triangles}$$

or (for short): $4 \times s = t$

Squares (s)	$4 \times s = t$	Triangles (t)
1	$4 \times 1 = 4$	5
2	$4 \times 2 = 8$	8
3	$4 \times 3 = 12$	12

1. Each chart represents a different design for a path. Complete the charts.

a)

Squares (s)	$5 \times s = t$	Triangles (t)
1	$5 \times \underline{1} = \underline{5}$	5
2	$5 \times \underline{2} = \underline{10}$	
3	$5 \times \underline{3} = \underline{15}$	

b)

Squares (s)	$7 \times s = t$	Triangles (t)
1	$7 \times \underline{1} = \underline{7}$	
2	$7 \times \underline{2} = \underline{}$	
3	$7 \times \underline{3} = \underline{}$	

c)

Squares (s)	$6 \times s = t$	Triangles (t)
2	$6 \times \underline{2} = \underline{}$	
3	$6 \times \underline{} = \underline{}$	
4	$6 \times \underline{} = \underline{}$	

d)

Squares (s)	$9 \times s = t$	Triangles (t)
5	$9 \times \underline{} = \underline{}$	
6	$9 \times \underline{} = \underline{}$	
7	$9 \times \underline{} = \underline{}$	

e)

Squares (s)	$6 \times s = t$	Triangles (t)
1		
3		
5		

f)

Squares (s)	$7 \times s = t$	Triangles (t)
9		
2		
15		

2. Write a formula to show how to calculate the number of triangles (t) from the number of squares (s).

a)

s	t
1	10
2	20
3	30

b)

s	t
1	2
2	4
3	6

c)

s	t
1	8
2	16
3	24

d)

s	t
1	15
2	30
3	45

Sandra makes a border using rectangular and triangular tiles. The number of triangles is always 4 more than the number of rectangles.

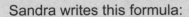

Sandra writes this formula:

rectangles + 4 = triangles

or (for short): $r + 4 = t$

Rectangles (r)	$r + 4 = t$	Triangles (t)
1	$1 + 4 = 5$	5
2	$2 + 4 = 6$	6
3	$3 + 4 = 7$	7

3. Each chart represents a different design for a border. Complete the charts.

a)

Rectangles (r)	$r + 6 = t$	Triangles (t)
1	$1 + 6 = 7$	7
2	$2 + 6 = 8$	8
3	$3 + 6 = 9$	9

b)

Squares (s)	$s + 7 = t$	Triangles (t)
1	$1 + 7 = 8$	8
2	$2 + \_\_\_ = \_\_\_$	
3	$3 + \_\_\_ = \_\_\_$	

c)

Squares (s)	$s + 3 = r$	Rectangles (r)
2	$\underline{2} + 3 = 10$	
3	$\_\_\_ + 3 = \_\_\_$	
4	$\_\_\_ + 3 = \_\_\_$	

d)

Squares (s)	$s + 1 = t$	Triangles (t)
5	$\_\_\_ + 1 = \_\_\_$	
6	$\_\_\_ + 1 = \_\_\_$	
7	$\_\_\_ + 1 = \_\_\_$	

e)

Squares (s)	$s + 2 = k$	Kites (k)
1		
3		
5		

f)

Kites (k)	$k - 1 = t$	Triangles (t)
9	$9 - 1 = \_\_\_$	
2		
15		

4. Write a formula to show how to calculate the number of triangles (t) from the number of squares(s).

a)

s	t
1	10
2	11
3	12

b)

s	t
1	4
2	5
3	6

c)

s	t
1	0
2	1
3	2

d)

s	t
5	3
6	4
7	5

5. Apply the given rule or formula to the numbers in the first column. Write your answer in the second column.

a) **Rule:** Add 4 to each input number.

Input	Output
0	4
1	5
2	6

b) **Rule:** Subtract 4 from each input number.

Input	Output
4	
5	
6	

c) **Rule:** Multiply each input number by 5.

Input	Output
4	
7	
8	

d) **Rule:** Divide each input number by 3.

Input	Output
27	
15	
42	

e) **Rule:** Add 8 to each input number.

Input	Output
18	
19	
20	

f) **Rule:** Multiply each input number by 7.

Input	Output
4	
6	
9	

g) **Formula:**
Input $+ 4 =$ Output

Input	Output
23	
11	
46	

h) **Formula:**
Input $- 3 =$ Output

Input	Output
15	
19	
23	

i) **Formula:**
Input $\times 3 =$ Output

Input	Output
4	
7	
12	

6. For each chart, give a rule or a formula (as in Question 5) that tells how to make the numbers in the second column from the numbers in the first column.

a)

Input	Output
3	18
2	12
1	6

Rule:

b)

Input	Output
16	2
32	4
48	6

Rule:

c)

Input	Output
19	16
15	12
21	18

Rule:

d)

x	y
3	6
4	7
5	8

Formula:

e)

x	y
3	8
5	10
7	12

Formula:

f)

Term Number	Term
1	7
2	14
3	21

Formula:

PA8-21 Formulas for Patterns

1. Fill in the chart and write a formula for the number of blocks in each figure.

a)

Figure 1   **Figure 2**   **Figure 3**

Figure Number	Number of Blocks
1	2
2	4
3	6

Formula: _____ *2 × Figure Number* _____

b)

Figure 1   **Figure 2**   **Figure 3**

Figure Number	Number of Blocks

Formula: _____

c)

     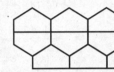

Figure 1   **Figure 2**   **Figure 3**

Figure Number	Number of Blocks

Formula: _____

d)

  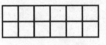

Figure 1   **Figure 2**   **Figure 3**

Figure Number	Number of Blocks

Formula: _____

> In the examples above, you can find the total number of blocks in any figure by multiplying the Figure Number by the <u>same</u> number — the number of blocks in the first figure (**Figure Number × # of blocks in Figure 1**). In such cases, the number of blocks **varies directly** with the Figure Number.

2. Circle the patterns where the number of blocks **varies directly** with the Figure Number.

Figure Number	Number of Blocks
1	4
2	8
3	12

Figure Number	Number of Blocks
1	5
2	8
3	11

Figure Number	Number of Blocks
1	7
2	14
3	21

Figure Number	Number of Blocks
1	3
2	6
3	10

3. Write the formula for the patterns in Question 2 where the number of blocks varies directly with the Figure Number.

4. a) Write a formula for the **number of shaded blocks** in each pattern.

b) Write a formula for the **total number of blocks** in each pattern.

i)

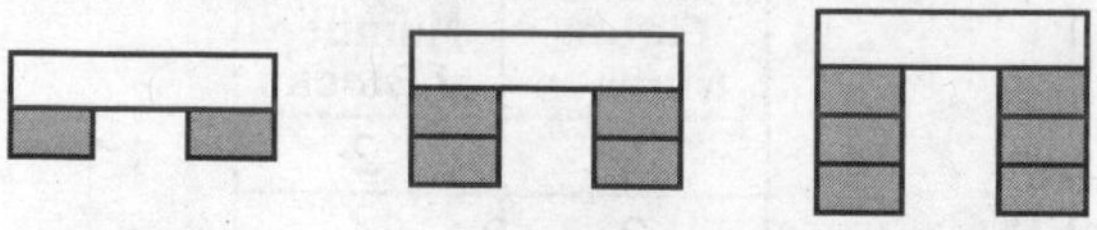

Figure 1   **Figure 2**   **Figure 3**

Formula for the number of shaded blocks:

_____ 2 × Figure Number _____

Formula for the total number of blocks:

_____ 2 × Figure Number + 1 _____

ii)

Figure 1   **Figure 2**   **Figure 3**

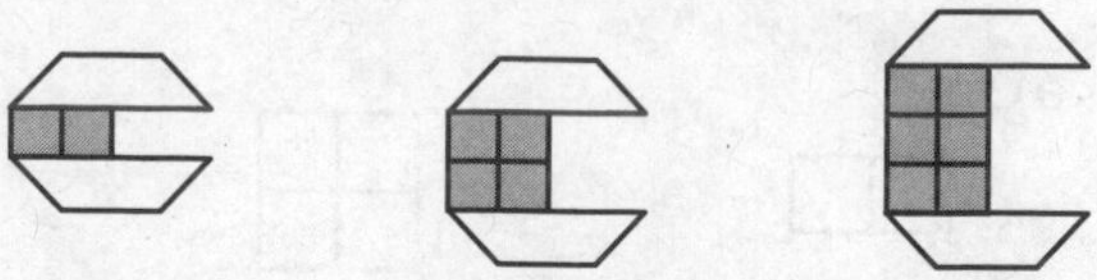

Formula for the number of shaded blocks:

_____

Formula for the total number of blocks:

_____

iii)

Figure 1   **Figure 2**   **Figure 3**

Formula for the number of shaded blocks:

_____

Formula for the total number of blocks:

_____

iv)

Figure 1   **Figure 2**   **Figure 3**

Formula for the number of shaded blocks:

_____

Formula for the total number of blocks:

_____

v)

Figure 1   **Figure 2**   **Figure 3**

Formula for the number of shaded blocks:

_____

Formula for the total number of blocks:

_____

vi)

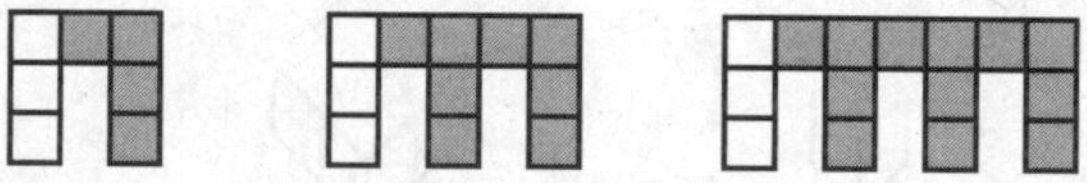

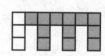
Figure 1   **Figure 2**   **Figure 3**

Formula for the number of shaded blocks:

_____

Formula for the total number of blocks:

_____

c) Compare the formulas for the number of shaded blocks and the <u>total</u> number of blocks.

What varies directly with the figure number: the number of shaded blocks or the <u>total</u> number of blocks?

Which operations are involved in the formulas that show direct variation?

Which operations are involved in the formulas that do not show direct variation?

5. Circle the part of each formula that varies directly with the Figure Number.

a) ⟨2 × Figure Number⟩+ 3   b) 3 × Figure Number − 1   c) 5 × Figure Number

PA8-22 Formulas for Patterns — Advanced

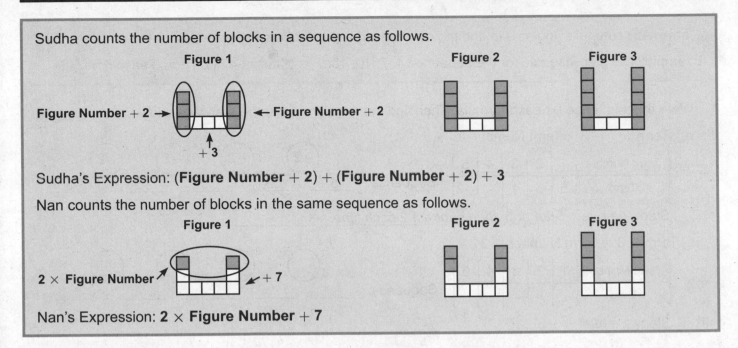

Sudha counts the number of blocks in a sequence as follows.

Sudha's Expression: **(Figure Number + 2) + (Figure Number + 2) + 3**

Nan counts the number of blocks in the same sequence as follows.

Nan's Expression: **2 × Figure Number + 7**

1. Do Suhda's and Nan's expressions give the same number of blocks for each figure? Explain.

2. Show two different ways of calculating the number of blocks, using the Figure Number, in each sequence.

a)

Figure 1   Figure 2   Figure 3

b)

Figure 1   Figure 2   Figure 3

3.

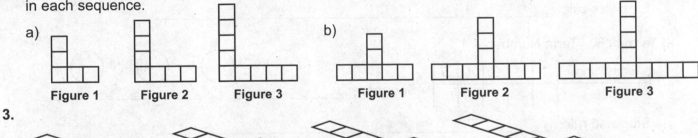

Figure 1   Figure 2   Figure 3   Figure 4

a) How many blocks are added to get the next figure from the previous figure? _____

b) To get Figure 2, we add 2 blocks to Figure 1 _once_.

To get Figure 3, we add 2 blocks to Figure 1 _two_ times. So we add ___4___ blocks.

To get Figure 4, we add 2 blocks to Figure 1 _____ times. So we add _____ blocks.

To get Figure 5, we add 2 blocks to Figure 1 _____ times. So we add _____ blocks.

To get Figure n, we add 2 blocks to Figure 1 _____ times. This is 2 × (_____) blocks.

c) How many blocks are in Figure 1? _____ How many blocks are in Figure n? _____ + _____

d) Use a different method to find the number of blocks in each figure. Let n represent the Figure Number. Did your formula give the same number of blocks in Figure n as your answer in part c)?

e) Use your formula to predict how many blocks are in the 30th term.

f) Use your formula to say which term has 50 blocks.

PA8-23 Stepwise Rules

A **stepwise rule** tells you how to find the next term in a pattern from the previous terms.

Example: The stepwise rule for the sequence 4, 7, 10, 13,… is "Start at 4, then add 3 each time."

1. Write the sequence for each formula. Then find the gaps and write the stepwise rule.

   a) Term = 7 − 2 × Term Number

Term Number	1	2	3	4	5
Term	5	3	1	−1	−3

   Sequence: __5__ __3__ __1__ __−1__ __−3__

   Stepwise rule: _Start at 5, then subtract 2 each time._

   b) Term = 3 × Term Number − 3

Term Number	1	2	3	4	5
Term					

   Sequence: _____ _____ _____ _____ _____

   Stepwise rule: _____

   c) Term = 46 − 4 × Term Number

Term Number	1	2	3	4	5
Term					

   Sequence: _____ _____ _____ _____ _____

   Stepwise rule: _____

   d) Term = 5 × Term Number − 1

Term Number	1	2	3	4	5
Term					

   Sequence: _____ _____ _____ _____ _____

   Stepwise rule: _____

   e) Term = 6 × Term Number − 8

Term Number	1	2	3	4	5
Term					

   Sequence: _____ _____ _____ _____ _____

   Stepwise rule: _____

2. How could you use the stepwise rule to find…

   a) the gap in the sequence?
   b) the first term in the sequence?
   c) the 15th term in the sequence?

3. How could you use the formula to find…

   a) the gap in the sequence?
   b) the first term in the sequence?
   c) the 15th term in the sequence?

4. Would you use the stepwise rule or the formula to find which term in a sequence equals 125? Explain.

5. a) Write the sequence for each formula. Then find the gaps and write the stepwise rule.

   i) Term = 2 × Term Number   ii) Term = 3 × Term Number   iii) Term = 6 × Term Number

   b) Do these sequences vary directly with the term number? How do you see that from the formula? How can you see that from the stepwise rule?

PA8-24 Finding Rules and Formulas

1. Fill in the chart using the rule. Then find the gap between the terms.

a) Rule: Multiply Input by 4 and add 3

Input	Output
1	7
2	
3	

Gap: _____

b) Rule: Multiply Input by 8 and subtract 1

Input	Output
1	
2	
3	

Gap: _____

c) Rule: Multiply Input by 6 and subtract 2

Input	Output
1	7
2	
3	

Gap: _____

d) Rule: Multiply Input by −10 and add 2

Input	Output
1	
2	
3	

Gap: _____

Compare the gap in each pattern above to the rule for the pattern. What do you notice?

_____

2. a) For each pattern below, make a T-table like the one at right. Fill in the total number of blocks (shaded and unshaded) and the gaps.

Can you predict what the gap will be for each pattern before you fill in the chart?

Figure Number	Number of Blocks
1	
2	
3	

Figure 1

Figure 2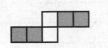

Figure 3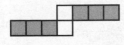

Figure 1

Figure 2

Figure 3

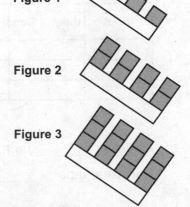

b) Write a formula for each pattern that tells how to find the number of blocks from the figure number.

In the T-table shown here, the term is calculated from the term number by two operations.

To find the operations and write the rule:

Term Number	Term
1	5
2	8
3	11

Step 1: Find the gap between the numbers in the **Term** column.

Term Number (n)	$n \times$ Gap	Term
1		5
2		8
3		11

Gaps: (3) (3)

Step 2: Multiply the **Term Number** by the gap.

Term Number (n)	$n \times$ Gap	Term
1	3	5
2	6	8
3	9	11

Gaps: (3) (3)

Step 3: What must you add to each number in the second column to get the term in the third column?

Term Number (n)	$n \times$ Gap	Term
1	3	5
2	6	8
3	9	11

Gaps: (3) (3)

Add 2

Step 4: Write a rule or a formula for the T-table.

Rule: Multiply the Term Number by 3 and add 2

Formula: Term Number $\times$ 3 + 2

3. Use the steps above to find the rule and formula that tell you how to calculate the output from the input.

a)

Input	Input $\times$ Gap	Output
1		12
2		15
3		18

Add ______

Rule: Multiply by ______ then add ______.

Formula: Input $\times$ ______ + ______

b)

Input	Input $\times$ Gap	Output
1		6
2		8
3		10

Add ______

Rule: Multiply by ______ then add ______.

Formula: Input $\times$ ______ + ______

c)

Input	Input $\times$ Gap	Output
1		4
2		9
3		14

Rule:

Multiply by ______ then subtract ______.

Formula: Input $\times$ ______ − ______

d)

Input	Input $\times$ Gap	Output
1		10
2		25
3		40

Rule:

Multiply by ______ then subtract ______.

Formula: Input $\times$ ______ − ______

4. Which column in the tables in Question 3 varies directly with the Input column? ______

5. Use the gap in the sequence to start writing the formula. Then complete the chart to finish writing the formula.

a)

Term Number (n)	$n \times$ Gap	Term
1	5	3
2	10	8
3	15	13
4	20	18

Formula: _____5n − 2_____

b)

Term Number (n)	$n \times$ Gap	Term
1		2
2		3
3		4
4		5

Formula: _____

c)

Term Number (n)	$n \times$ Gap	Term
1		1
2		5
3		9
4		13

Formula: _____

d)

Term Number (n)	$n \times$ Gap	Term
1		9
2		15
3		21
4		27

Formula: _____

e)

Term Number (n)	$n \times$ Gap	Term
1		3
2		11
3		19
4		27

Formula: _____

f)

Term Number (n)	$n \times$ Gap	Term
1		9
2		19
3		29
4		39

Formula: _____

g) 1, 3, 5, 7, 9

h) 9, 18, 27, 36, 45

i) 7, 15, 23, 31

j) 9, 12, 15, 18, 21

k) 22, 34, 46, 58, 70

l) 56, 58, 60, 62

6. a) Write a formula for the number of toothpicks in each figure.

b) Use your formula to determine the number of toothpicks in the 50ᵗʰ figure.

c) Which figure will have 80 toothpicks?

Figure 1

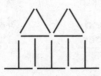

Figure 2

Figure 3

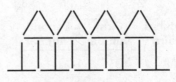

Figure 4

PA8-25 Graphs

A point on a graph or on a coordinate plane can be represented as an **ordered pair** — a pair of numbers where order matters.

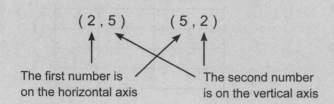

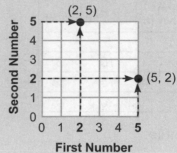

1. For each set of points, write a list of ordered pairs and complete the T-table.

a)

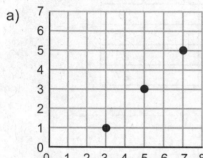

Ordered Pairs	First Number	Second Number
(3 , 1)	3	1
(,)		
(,)		

b)

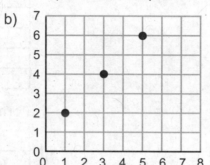

Ordered Pairs	First Number	Second Number
(,)		
(,)		
(,)		

c)

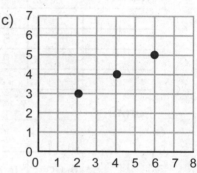

Ordered Pairs	First Number	Second Number
(,)		
(,)		
(,)		

2. Mark 3 grid points on each line segment. Then write a list of ordered pairs and complete the T-table.

a)

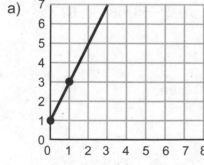

Ordered Pairs	First Number	Second Number
(0 , 1)	0	1
(1 , 3)	1	3
(,)		

b)

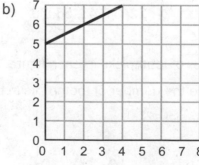

Ordered Pairs	First Number	Second Number
(,)		
(,)		
(,)		

c)

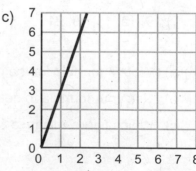

Ordered Pairs	First Number	Second Number
(,)		
(,)		
(,)		

3. a) Make a T-table for each set of points on the coordinate grid.

Line A	
Input	Output
1	2
2	

Line B	
Input	Output

Line C	
Input	Output

b) Write a formula for each T-table.

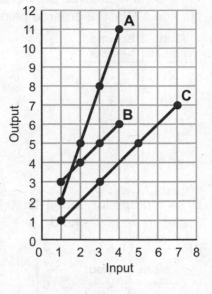

To graph the sequence **2 4 6 8 10**:

Step 1: Make a list of ordered pairs.
(1, **2**) (2, **4**) (3, **6**) (4, **8**) (5, **10**)

Step 2: Plot the ordered pairs on a graph.

4. a) Draw a line through the points on the grid.

b) Mark 3 more grid points that lie on the line you drew. Then make a T-table for your set of points.

c) Write a formula for your T-table.

d) A point on your line has coordinates (*x*, 15). Mark the point. *x* = _____.

e) Why is there not a 0 marked on the horizontal axis?

Term Number	Term

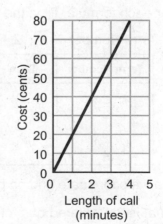

5. The graph shows the cost of making a telephone call to India.

a) Fill in the T-table.

b) Write a formula for the T-table.

c) How much would you pay to talk for 10 minutes?

d) If you paid $1, how long would you be able to talk for?

Length of call (min.)	Cost (¢)
1	
2	
3	
4	

BONUS ▶ If your call is 30 seconds long, how much will you pay?

6. Write a list of ordered pairs based on the T-table provided. Plot the ordered pairs.

First Number	Second Number	
2	1	(,)
3	3	(,)
4	5	(,)
5	7	(,)

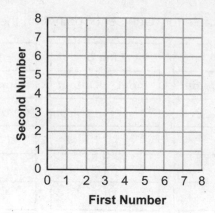

7. Draw a graph for each T-table (as in Question 6). Make sure you look carefully at the scales in parts c) and d).

a)

Input	Output
2	4
4	5
6	6
8	7

b)

Input	Output
1	6
2	5
3	4
4	3

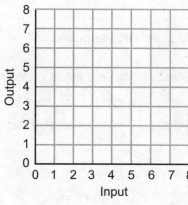

c)

Input	Output
2	4
4	8
6	12
8	16

d)

Input	Output
1	6
3	8
5	10
7	12

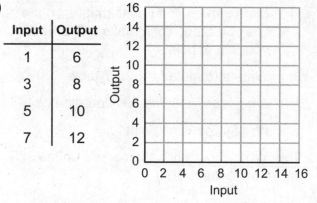

8. a) For each formula, fill in the table, then make a list of ordered pairs: (Term Number, Term).

i) Term Number × 3 + 2

Term Number	Term	Ordered Pair
1	5	(_1_ , _5_)
2		(,)
3		(,)
4		(,)

ii) Term Number × 4 − 3

Term Number	Term	Ordered Pair
1		(,)
2		(,)
3		(,)
4		(,)

b) Draw a coordinate grid on grid paper. Plot the ordered pairs on the grid.

c) What is the ordered pair for Term Number 40?

PA8-26 Sequences and Ordered Pairs

You can think of a sequence as a set of ordered pairs with the form (Term Number, Term).

Example: In the sequence **3,   5,   7,   9,   11**, …
                 11 has term number 5, because 11 is the 5th term.
                 The ordered pairs are (1, **3**), (2, **5**), (3, **7**), (4, **9**),   (5, **11**), …

1. Complete the T-table for each sequence.

    a) 5 8 11 14 17

Term Number	Term	Ordered Pair
1	5	(1 , 5)
2	8	
3		
4		
5		

    b) 4 6 8 10 12

Term Number	Term	Ordered Pair
1		
2		
3		
4		
5		

    c) 4 8 12 16 20

Term Number	Term	Ordered Pair
1		
2		
3		
4		
5		

2. Change each sequence to a set of ordered pairs.

    a) 1 7 13 19 25

        (1, 1), (2, 7), (3, 13), (4, 19), (5, 25)

    b) 3 5 7 9 11

        (1,   ), (2,   ), (3,   ), (4,   ), (5,   )

    c) 41 38 35 32 29

    d) 10 20 40 80 160

3. a) Change each set of ordered pairs to a sequence of numbers.

        A (1, 0), (2, 6), (3, 12), (4, 18), (5, 24)   B (1, 64), (2, 32), (3, 16), (4, 8), (5, 4)

        C (1, 64), (2, 32), (3, 16), (4, 32), (5, 64)   D (1, 4), (2, 9) (3, 4), (4, 9), (5, 4) (6, 9), (7, 4), (8, 9)

        E (1, 55), (2, 46), (3, 37), (4, 28), (5, 19)   F (1, 3), (2, 6), (3, 11), (4, 18), (5, 27)

    b) Which sequence from part a) matches each description?

        i)   decreases then increases _____   ii) increases by the same amount _____

        iii) repeats _____   iv) decreases by different amounts _____

        v) increases by different amounts _____ vi) decreases by the same amount _____

    c) Plot each set of ordered pairs on a separate coordinate grid and join the points in order.

    d) Describe the graphs. How are the graphs of increasing and decreasing
        sequences different? How can you tell from the graph that a sequence repeats?

PA8-27 Graphing Sequences

1. a) Graph each sequence of numbers by first making a list of ordered pairs.

   i) 0, 1, 3, 6, 10, 15

   (1, *0*) (2, *1*) (3, *3*)
   (4,   ) (5,   ) (6,   )

   ii) 1, 3, 5, 7, 9, 11

   (1,   ) (2,   ) (3,   )
   (4,   ) (5,   ) (6,   )

   iii) 0, 3, 6, 9, 12, 15

   (1,   ) (2,   ) (3,   )
   (4,   ) (5,   ) (6,   )

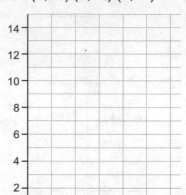
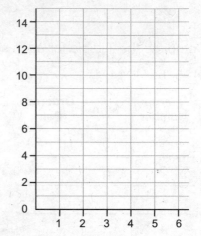

   iv) 1, 5, 9, 12, 14, 15

   (1,   ) (2,   ) (3,   )
   (4,   ) (5,   ) (6,   )

   v) 4, 2, 0, −2, −4, −6

   (1,   ) (2,   ) (3,   )
   (4,   ) (5,   ) (6,   )

   vi) 14, 10, 8, 4, 3, 0

   (1,   ) (2,   ) (3,   )
   (4,   ) (5,   ) (6,   )

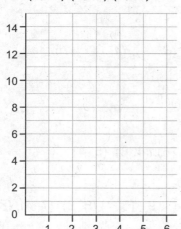
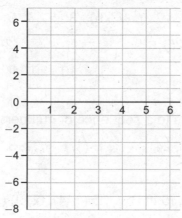
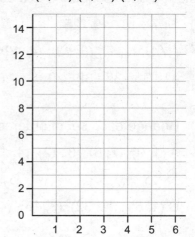

   b) Join the points on each graph by a line. Is the line straight?

   i) _____ ii) _____ iii) _____ iv) _____ v) _____ vi) _____

   > A sequence is called **linear** if the points on its graph can be joined by a straight line.

2. Which of the sequences in Question 1 are linear? _____

3. Graph each sequence on grid paper by first making a list of ordered pairs.
   Then decide whether the sequence is linear or not.

   a) 3, 2, 1, 0, −1   b) 1, −2, 3, −4, 5, −6   c) −8, −5, −2, 1, 4

Patterns and Algebra 8-27

INVESTIGATION 1 ▶ How can you tell from the gaps whether or not a sequence is linear?

A. Which sequences from Question 1 are linear? Find their gaps.

_____ ii) _____ 1 (+2) 3 ◯ 5 ◯ 7 ◯ 9 ◯ 11 _____

_____ ◯ ◯ ◯ ◯ ◯ _____

_____ ◯ ◯ ◯ ◯ ◯ _____

B. Which sequences from Question 1 are not linear? Find their gaps.

_____ ◯ ◯ ◯ ◯ ◯ _____

_____ ◯ ◯ ◯ ◯ ◯ _____

_____ ◯ ◯ ◯ ◯ ◯ _____

C. How can you tell by looking at the gaps of a sequence whether or not the sequence is linear?

---

4. a) Decide which of these decreasing sequences is linear by finding the gaps between terms.

A 12, 10, 7, 5, 2   **B** 14, 11, 8, 5, 2

_____ is linear because _____

b) Check your answer by graphing both sequences on grid paper and joining the points.

INVESTIGATION 2 ▶ How can you tell from the formula whether or not a sequence is linear?

A. For each formula, write the first 4 terms of the sequence. Then find the gaps.

i) Term Number × 2 + 1
◯ ◯ ◯
_3_ _5_ ___ ___

ii) Term Number + 5
◯ ◯ ◯
___ ___ ___ ___

iii) Term Number × Term Number
◯ ◯ ◯
___ ___ ___ ___

iv) Term Number × 3 − 2
◯ ◯ ◯
___ ___ ___ ___

v) Term Number ÷ 4
◯ ◯ ◯
_0.25_ ___ ___ ___

vi) Term Number × (Term Number − 1)
◯ ◯ ◯
___ ___ ___ ___

B. Looking at the gaps, predict which sequences are linear.

C. Choose one sequence that you think is linear and another that you think is not linear. Check your predictions by graphing the sequences on grid paper and joining the points.

D. How are the formulas for non-linear sequences different from the formulas for linear sequences?

Patterns and Algebra 8-27

PA8-28 Graphing Formulas

1. Evaluate each expression for $n = 1, 2, 3, 4$, and 5. Write your answers in the T-table.

a) $2n + 3$

n	$2n + 3$
1	
2	
3	
4	
5	

b) $3n - 2$

n	$3n - 2$
1	
2	
3	
4	
5	

c) $2n - 1$

n	$2n - 1$
1	
2	
3	
4	
5	

2. a) Complete each T-table. Then plot the ordered pairs on the graph and join the points with a line.

i)

n	$2n + 3$	$(n, 2n + 3)$
1	5	$(1, 5)$
2		
3		
4		
5		

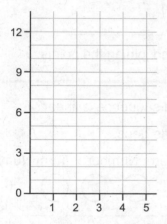

ii)

n	$2n - 2$	$(n, 2n - 2)$
1		
2		
3		
4		
5		

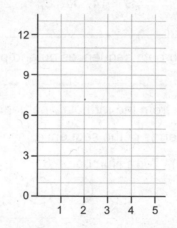

iii)

n	$2n$	$(n, 2n)$
1		
2		
3		
4		
5		

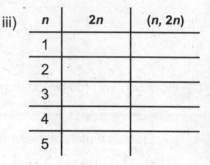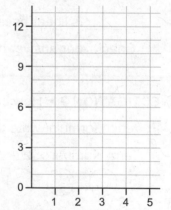

b) Compare the algebraic expressions used to create the graphs. How are they similar? How are they different?

c) Copy all three graphs to the same grid using different colours. Do the lines ever intersect, even if extended? Use the formulas for the graphs to explain why or why not.

3. Make a graph for each formula by substituting the numbers from 1 to 5, making ordered pairs as in Question 2, and plotting the ordered pairs on grid paper.

a) $3n + 2$ b) $4n - 2$ c) $4n - 3$ d) $5n - 1$ e) $10n$

PA8-29 Investigating Patterns

1. Use the graph to find the missing values in the table.

a)
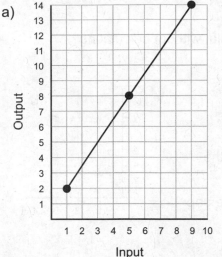

Input	Output
1	2
3	
5	8
	11
9	14

b)
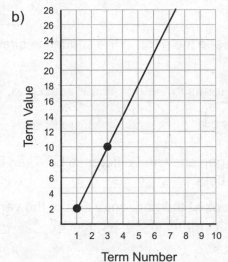

Term Number	Term Value
1	2
2	
3	10
	14
5	
	26

2. Extend the line to find the value of the 11th term.

a)
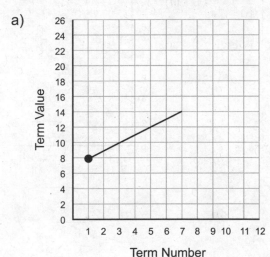

Value of the 11th term _____

b)
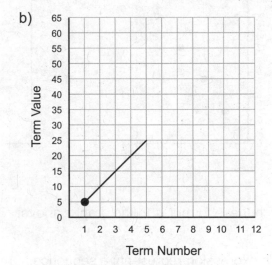

Value of the 11th term _____

3. a) For each sequence, make a table of values for the term numbers and the term values. Draw a graph for your table and extend the graph to find the value of the 7th term.

   i) 2, 6, 10, 14   ii) 1, 4, 7, 10   iii) 2, 9, 16, 23

b) Find a formula for each sequence and check your answer by substitution.

c) Is there a term that has value 46? If yes, which term? If no, explain why not.

4. Draw a graph to show how many toothpicks would be needed for the 8th figure. Then check your answer by finding a formula for the number of toothpicks.

a) ▱ ▱▱ ▱▱▱   b) |∨| |∨||∨| |∨||∨||∨|

5. Find the gaps in the sequence represented by the formula.

 a) $75 - 3n$ b) $5 + 4n$ c) $2n + 4$ d) $5 - n$ e) $5n + 4$

     -3 _____   _____   _____   _____

How can you see the gaps in the sequence directly from the formula, without calculating?

6. a) Write the terms in the non-linear sequence. Then find the gaps.

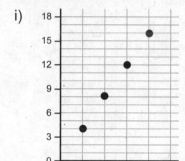

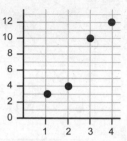

 _____   _____   _____   _____

b) Does the gap show the difference between the term values or the term numbers? _____

c) Will you look at the horizontal axis or the vertical axis to see the gap between the terms of the sequence? _____

7. a) Without writing the sequence for the graph, find the gaps in the sequence.

  i) 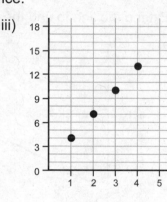   ii) 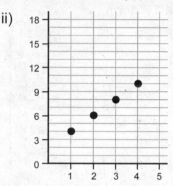   iii)

    _____   _____   _____

b) Match these formulas to the graphs above: $3n + 1$ _____ $4n$ _____ $2n + 2$ _____

8. a) Each expression represents a sequence.

Evaluate the expression at $n = 1$ to find the first term of the sequence.

  i) $3n + 3$ _____   ii) $3n + 1$ _____   iii) $3n - 2$ _____

b) Each graph represents a sequence.

Find the first term of the sequence by finding the second coordinate when the first coordinate is 1. Then match each graph to one of the formulas in part a).

  A 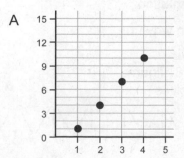   B 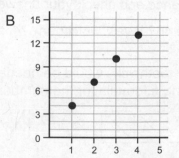   C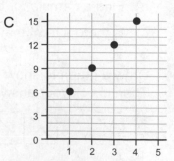

9. Match each graph to a formula.

A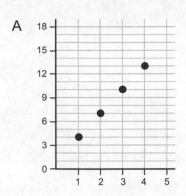

B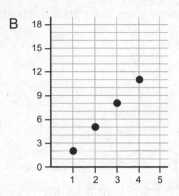

C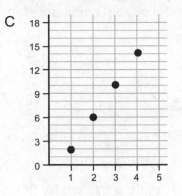

$3n - 1$ matches _____ $4n - 2$ matches _____ $3n + 1$ matches _____

10. Finish writing 5 different expressions with numbers of your choice.

$3n +$ _____ $2n +$ _____ $4n +$ _____ $3n +$ _____ $2n +$ _____

Draw the 5 graphs on grid paper, out of order. Have a partner match the expressions to the graphs.

11. A car is travelling at a constant speed of 60 km/h.

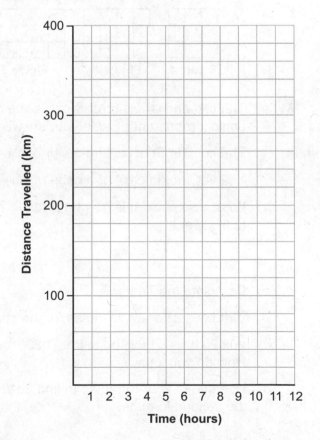

a) Write an expression for the distance the car travelled after h hours.

Distance = _____

b) Fill in the table of values for the distance the car travelled after h hours.

h hours	Distance travelled (km)
1	
2	
3	

c) Write the ordered pairs from the table of values:

(,) (,) (,)

Plot the points on the graph.

d) Join the points on the graph with a straight line.
If the car travelled 4.5 hours, how far would it go?

_____

e) How many hours would it take the car to travel 360 km?
Extend the line to find out. _____

f) Check your answer in part e) using your formula from part a).

PA8-30 Problems and Puzzles

1. If the pattern continues, how many times does the number 49 appear in the triangle?

```
              1
          4       4
        7     7     7
     10    10    10    10
   13    13    13    13    13
```

2. For each pattern below:

a) Write a sequence giving the number of blocks in each figure.

b) Write a formula for the number of blocks. Use *n* for the Figure Number.

c) Say which figure (if any) will have 100 blocks. If there is no such figure, explain how you know.

i)

Figure 1   **Figure 2**   **Figure 3**

ii)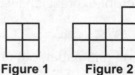

Figure 1   **Figure 2**   **Figure 3**

iii)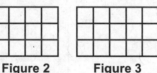

Figure 1   **Figure 2**   **Figure 3**

iv)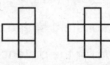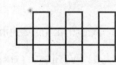

Figure 1   **Figure 2**   **Figure 3**

3. a) The title and labels for this graph are missing. Which of these events could it represent? Circle your answer. Explain your reasoning.

The cost (in $) of renting a pair of skates for *n* hours

The volume (in cm³) of a cube of side length *n* cm

b) What else could this graph represent? Add your own title and labels to the graph.

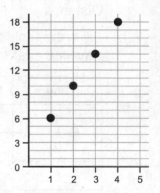

4. a) Complete the T-table.

b) Write two different formulas for the number in the nth row of the T-table.

c) Will $2010^2 - 2009^2$ be in the 2009th row or the 2010th row? How do you know?

d) Use one of your formulas to find $2010^2 - 2009^2$. Check using the second formula.

1	$2^2 - 1^2 =$
2	$3^2 - 2^2 =$
3	$4^2 - 3^2 =$
4	$5^2 - 4^2 =$
5	$6^2 - 5^2 =$
6	$7^2 - 6^2 =$

5. a) Write an expression for the perimeter of each figure.

b) Which figure would have perimeter 76?

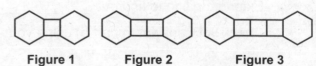

Figure 1   **Figure 2**   **Figure 3**

PA8-31 Investigating Equations — Advanced

Look at these equations:

$2 \times 3 = 3 + 3$ $2 \times 0 = 0 + 0$ $2 \times (-5) = (-5) + (-5)$ $2 \times 26 = 26 + 26$

The equations are all different, but they have the same form. They all look like this:

$2 \times a = a + a$ for some number a

The letter a is a **variable** — it represents a number.

1. Replace the number that changes in each group of equations with the variable m.

   a) $5 \times 3 \div 3 = 5$

       $7 \times 3 \div 3 = 7$

       $12 \times 3 \div 3 = 12$

       $\underline{m \times 3 \div 3 = m}$

   b) $7 + 3 - 3 = 7$

       $18 + 3 - 3 = 18$

       $25 + 3 - 3 = 25$

       _____

   c) $7 + 3 - 3 = 7$

       $7 + 4 - 4 = 7$

       $7 + (-12) - (-12) = 7$

       _____

   d) $16 \div 2 \times 2 = 16$

       $(-12) \div 2 \times 2 = -12$

       $7 \div 2 \times 2 = 7$

       _____

   e) $9 - 5 + 5 = 9$

       $15 - 5 + 5 = 15$

       $-21 - 5 + 5 = -21$

       _____

   f) $9 - 5 + 5 = 9$

       $9 - 0 + 0 = 0$

       $9 - (-7) + (-7) = 9$

       _____

2. Tara notices that these equations have the same right side:

   $7 \times 3 \div 3 = 7$ $7 \times 5 \div 5 = 7$ $7 \times 200 \div 200 = 7$

   a) Tara thinks that $7 \times a \div a = 7$ will be true for any number a. Is she correct?
   Hint: Are there any numbers that you are not allowed to divide by?

   b) Choose a number a that you think will make $7 \times a \div a = 7$ true. $a = $ _____
   Check your answer.

3. Calculate each expression for $a = 12$ and $b = 3$.

   a) $a - b = \underline{\;\;12\;\;} - \underline{\;\;3\;\;}$

       $= \underline{\;\;9\;\;}$

   b) $a + b = \underline{\;\;12\;\;} + \underline{\;\;3\;\;}$

       $= \underline{\;\;\;\;\;}$

   c) $a \times b = \underline{\;\;\;\;\;} \times \underline{\;\;\;\;\;}$

       $= \underline{\;\;\;\;\;}$

   d) $a \div b = \underline{\;\;\;\;\;} \div \underline{\;\;\;\;\;}$

       $= \underline{\;\;\;\;\;}$

   e) $b \times a = \underline{\;\;\;\;\;} \times \underline{\;\;\;\;\;}$

       $= \underline{\;\;\;\;\;}$

   f) $b \div a = \underline{\;\;\;\;\;} \div \underline{\;\;\;\;\;}$

       $= \underline{\;\;\;\;\;}$

4. Circle two expressions from Question 3 that have the same answer.
   Check whether they will also have the same answer when…

   a) $a = 4$ and $b = -7$ b) $a = -3$ and $b = 5$ c) $a = $ _____ and $b = $ _____ (your choice)

5. Write an equation to show that the two expressions you circled in Question 3 always

   have the same answer. _____ = _____

To **verify** that an equation is true, calculate both sides and make sure they both equal the same number.

6. Verify that each equation is true for $a = 3$ and $b = -5$.

a) $a \times (b + 2) = a \times b + a \times 2$

$3 \times (-5 + 2) \quad 3 \times (-5) + 3 \times 2$

$= 3 \times (-3) \quad = -15 + 6$

$= -9 \quad\quad = -9$

equal

b) $a \times (b + 3) \quad\quad = \quad\quad a \times b + a \times 3$

$\underline{\quad} \times (\underline{\quad} + \underline{\quad}) \quad \underline{\quad} \times \underline{\quad} + \underline{\quad} \times \underline{\quad}$

$= \underline{\quad} \times \underline{\quad} \quad\quad\quad = \underline{\quad} + \underline{\quad}$

$= \underline{\quad} \quad\quad\quad\quad\quad = \underline{\quad}$

c) $a \times (b + 4) = a \times b + a \times 4$ d) $a \times (b + 5) = a \times b + a \times 5$ e) $a \times (b - 6) = a \times b + a \times (-6)$

7. All the equations in Question 6 have this form: $a \times (b + c) = a \times b + a \times c$.
This is an equation in 3 variables.

In Question 6 c), you used $a = \underline{\quad 3 \quad}$, $b = \underline{\quad -5 \quad}$, and $c = \underline{\quad 4 \quad}$.

In Question 6 d), you used $a = \underline{\quad\quad}$, $b = \underline{\quad\quad}$, and $c = \underline{\quad\quad}$.

In Question 6 e), you used $a = \underline{\quad\quad}$, $b = \underline{\quad\quad}$, and $c = \underline{\quad\quad}$.

8. Use $a \times (b + c) = a \times b + a \times c$ to find the values of a, b, and c in each equation.

a) $5 \times (-2 + 7) = 5 \times (-2) + 5 \times 7$ $a = \underline{\quad\quad}$ $b = \underline{\quad\quad}$ $c = \underline{\quad\quad}$

b) $3 \times (2 - 5) = 3 \times 2 + 3 \times (-5)$ $a = \underline{\quad\quad}$ $b = \underline{\quad\quad}$ $c = \underline{\quad\quad}$

c) $-4 \times (12 + 83) = (-4) \times 12 - 4 \times 83$ $a = \underline{\quad\quad}$ $b = \underline{\quad\quad}$ $c = \underline{\quad\quad}$

9. Use $a \times (b + c) = a \times b + a \times c$ to finish writing each equation.

a) $3 \times (5 + 1) = 3 \times \underline{\quad\quad} + 3 \times \underline{\quad\quad}$ b) $4 \times (2 - 6) = \underline{\quad\quad} \times 2 + \underline{\quad\quad} \times (-6)$

c) $-7 \times (0 + 3) = \underline{\quad} \times \underline{\quad} + \underline{\quad} \times \underline{\quad}$ d) $0 \times (3 + 4) = \underline{\quad\quad\quad\quad\quad\quad\quad\quad}$

10. Calculate $(a + b) \times c$ and $a \times c + b \times c$ for the values of a, b, and c given.

a) $a = -3, b = 5, c = 4$ b) $a = 2, b = -3, c = 1$ c) $a = 5, b = 2, c = -10$

What do you notice about your answers? Write an equation using the variables a, b, and c.

11. Use the equation from Question 10 to fill in the blanks.

a) In the expression $(5 + 3) \times 6$

$a = \underline{\quad 5 \quad}$ $b = \underline{\quad 3 \quad}$ $c = \underline{\quad 6 \quad}$

So $(5 + 3) \times 6 = \underline{\quad} \times 6 + \underline{\quad} \times 6$

b) In the expression $(8 + 5) \times (-3)$

$a = \underline{\quad\quad}$ $b = \underline{\quad\quad}$ $c = \underline{\quad\quad}$

So $(8 + 5) \times 3 = 8 \times \underline{\quad} + 5 \times \underline{\quad}$

c) In the expression $(7 - 2) \times 9$

$a = \underline{\quad\quad}$ $b = \underline{\quad\quad}$ $c = \underline{\quad\quad}$

So $(7 - 2) \times 9 = \underline{\quad} \times \underline{\quad} + \underline{\quad} \times \underline{\quad}$

d) In the expression $(-3 + 2) \times 0$

$a = \underline{\quad\quad}$ $b = \underline{\quad\quad}$ $c = \underline{\quad\quad}$

So $(-3 + 2) \times 0 = \underline{\quad\quad\quad\quad\quad}$

PA8-32 Advanced Algebra

In an equation, a term may be moved to the other side of the equal sign, but only if the sign (+ or −) of the term is changed.

Examples: If $7 = 5 + 2$ If $10 - 2 = 8$ If $a + b = c$ If $a + b = -c + d$
Then $7 - 2 = 5$ Then $10 = 8 + 2$ Then $c - b = a$ Then $a + b + c = d$

1. **Variable terms** include a variable (Examples: $3x$, $-19x$). Move all variable terms to the same side of the equal sign.

a) $4x = 2x + 8$

$4x \underline{\ -2x\ } = 8$

b) $5x = 3x + 6$

$5x \underline{\hphantom{xxxx}} = 6$

c) $2x = 12 - 4x$

$2x \underline{\hphantom{xxxx}} = 12$

d) $-2x = 4x - 8$

$-2x \underline{\hphantom{xxxx}} = -8$

e) $14 - 3x = 4x$

$14 = 4x \underline{\hphantom{xxxx}}$

f) $7 - 2x = 5x$

$7 = 5x \underline{\hphantom{xxxx}}$

2. Solve each equation by first moving all variable terms to the same side of the equal sign.

a) $2x = -3x + 15$
$2x + 3x = 15$
$5x = 15$
$x = 15 \div 5$
$x = 3$

b) $5x = 2x + 9$

c) $8x = 3x + 20$

d) $x = -3x - 16$

e) $3x + 2x = 4x + 13$

3. Move all variable terms to one side of the equal sign and all numbers to the other side.

a) $-2x + 5 = -4x + 2$
$-2x + 4x = 2 - 5$

b) $4x - 2 = 2x + 8$

c) $-3x - 4 = 2x - 14$

d) $5x - 3 = 2x + 9$

4. Solve each equation by first grouping like terms.

a) $3x + 2x = 10 + 15$
$5x = 25$
$5x \div 5 = 25 \div 5$
$x = 5$

b) $6x - 4x = 10 - 2$

c) $4x - 3x + 2x = 13 - 4$

5. Solve each equation. (Group like terms first if necessary.)

a) $5x + 3 = -3x + 27$
$5x + 3x = 27 - 3$
$8x = 24$
$8x \div 8 = 24 \div 8$
$x = 3$

b) $4x + 2 = 2x + 6$

c) $-7x - 2 = -3x + 10$

d) $5 + 3x = 2x + 1$

e) $6x - 4 = 2x + 7 - 3$

f) $11x - 2 = 7 + 2x$

g) $2x + 3x - 4 = 3x + 10$

6. A box contains some red and yellow beads. Let x represent the number of red beads in the box. Write the number of yellow beads in terms of x.

a) 4 more yellow beads than red beads

red: _____ x _____

yellow: _____ $x + 4$ _____

b) 3 fewer yellow beads than red beads

red: _____

yellow: _____

c) 5 more red beads than yellow beads

d) 4 times as many yellow beads as red beads

e) 2 fewer red beads than yellow beads

f) 4 times as many red beads as yellow beads

7. A box contains 20 red and yellow beads. Find the number of red and yellow beads.

a) There are 4 more red beads than yellow beads.

red: _____ x _____ yellow: _____ $x - 4$ _____

Equation: $x + x - 4 = 20$

$2x - 4 = 20$

$2x = 20 + 4$

$2x = 24$

$2x \div 2 = 24 \div 2$

$x = 12$

b) There are 3 more yellow beads than red beads.

c) There are 3 times as many yellow beads as red beads.

d) There are 2 more red beads than yellow beads.

e) There are twice as many red beads as yellow beads.

8. Write expressions for the number of red, green, and yellow beads in a box. Hint: Underline the colour that appears in both sentences. Let x represent that colour.

a) There are 3 more yellow beads than <u>green</u> beads.
There are 4 times as many red beads as <u>green</u> beads.

red: _____

green: _____ x _____

yellow: _____

b) There are 4 fewer yellow beads than red beads.
There are 5 times as many green beads as yellow beads.

c) There are 2 fewer red beads than green beads.
There are 3 more yellow beads than green beads.

9. There are 5 more red beads than green beads in a box. There are 3 times as many yellow beads as green beads. The number of red and green beads is equal to the number of yellow beads. How many beads are in the box?

10. Pam and Ari went surfing together. Pam paid $7 to rent her wind surfer, plus $3 for each hour she surfed. Ari paid $10 for his wind surfer, plus $2 for each hour she surfed. Pam and Ari paid the same amount. How many hours did they wind surf together?

11. The boxes have the same perimeter. Find the perimeter of each box.

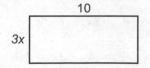

NS8-104 Introduction to Powers

Multiplication is a short form for repeated addition. Example: $5 \times 3 = 3 + 3 + 3 + 3 + 3$

Add five 3s

A **power** is a short form for repeated multiplication. Example: $3^5 = 3 \times 3 \times 3 \times 3 \times 3$

Multiply five 3s

The **exponent** in a power tells you how many times to write the **base** in the product.

base $\longrightarrow 3^5 \longleftarrow$ exponent

1. Write the exponent and base for the power.

   a) 2^3

      base: __2__ exponent: __3__

   b) 3^2

      base: ____ exponent: ____

   c) 7^4

      base: ____ exponent: ____

2. Write the power as a product.

   a) $9^2 = 9 \times 9$

   b) $7^3 =$

   c) $8^4 =$

3. Write the product as a power.

   a) $3 \times 3 \times 3 =$

   b) $4 \times 4 \times 4 \times 4 =$

   c) $9 \times 9 =$

   d) $8 \times 8 \times 8 \times 8 =$

4. Evaluate the power.

   a) $2^3 = 2 \times 2 \times 2$

      $= \underline{\hspace{1cm}}$

   b) $3^4 = 3 \times 3 \times 3 \times 3$

      $= \underline{\hspace{1cm}}$

   c) $4^2 = 4 \times 4$

      $= \underline{\hspace{1cm}}$

   d) $5^2 = 5 \times 5$

      $= \underline{\hspace{1cm}}$

   e) $2^4 = 2 \times 2 \times 2 \times 2$

      $= \underline{\hspace{1cm}}$

   f) $5^3 = 5 \times 5 \times 5$

      $= \underline{\hspace{1cm}}$

5. Circle two powers from Question 4 that have the same answer.

INVESTIGATION ▶

In a product, changing the order of the numbers does not affect the answer.
(Example: $2 \times 4 = 4 \times 2$)

In a power, does changing the order of the numbers affect the answer?
(Example: $2^4 = 4^2$ but does $2^3 = 3^2$?)

A. Calculate the powers.

   i) $2^3 = 2 \times 2 \times 2 = \underline{\hspace{1.5cm}}$ and $3^2 = 3 \times 3 = \underline{\hspace{1.5cm}}$

   ii) $3^5 = 3 \times 3 \times 3 \times 3 \times 3 = \underline{\hspace{1.5cm}}$ and $5^3 = 5 \times 5 \times 5 = \underline{\hspace{1.5cm}}$

   iii) $10^2 = 10 \times 10 = \underline{\hspace{1.5cm}}$ and $2^{10} = 2 \times 2 \times 2 \times 2 \times 2 \times 2 \times 2 \times 2 \times 2 \times 2 = \underline{\hspace{1.5cm}}$

B. Does changing the order of the numbers change the answer in a power? _____

6. Evaluate the power.

a) $3^1 =$ _____   b) $5^1 =$ _____   c) $8^1 =$ _____   d) $13^1 =$ _____   e) $2057^1 =$ _____

> $3^1 = 3$ is the **first power** of 3.
>
> $3^2 = 3 \times 3$ is the **second power** of 3.
>
> $3^3 = 3 \times 3 \times 3$ is the **third power** of 3.

7. Write the power as a product. Example: The fourth power of 2 is $2 \times 2 \times 2 \times 2$.

a) the fourth power of 3   b) the fifth power of 3   c) the sixth power of 3

d) the fourth power of 5   e) the fifth power of 4   f) the seventh power of 8

8. Write the power as a product and evaluate.

a) the second power of 8   b) the third power of 3   c) the fifth power of 2

9. Write the product as a power of 1.

a) $1 \times 1 =$ _____   b) $1 \times 1 \times 1 =$ _____   c) $1 \times 1 \times 1 \times 1 =$ _____   d) $1 \times 1 \times 1 \times 1 \times 1 =$ _____

10. Evaluate the power of 1.

a) $1^1 =$ _____   b) $1^2 =$ _____   c) $1^3 =$ _____   d) $1^4 =$ _____   e) $1^{523} =$ _____

11. The table shows the buttons you should press on a calculator to calculate a power.

a) How many times would you press the $\boxed{=}$ button to calculate the power?

i) 2^7 _____ times   ii) 5^3 _____ times

iii) 8^5 _____ times   iv) 3^{15} _____ times

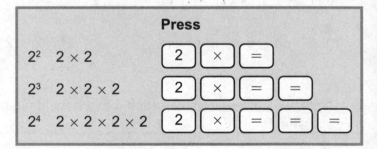

b) Write the power as a product and then use a calculator to find the answer.

i) $6^3 =$ ii) $4^5 =$ iii) $7^4 =$

12. Evaluate the powers, then multiply, divide, add, or subtract. Show your work.

a) 5×2^2 b) 3×2^3 c) $4^2 \div 2$ d) 2×5^2 e) $2^2 \times 3^2$

   $= 5 \times 4$

   $= 20$

f) $3^2 \times 2^3$ g) $10^2 \div 5^2$ h) $2^2 + 3^2$ i) $7^2 + 6^2$ j) $8^2 - 2^2$

NS8-105 Investigating Powers

1. a) Evaluate the power of 2.

   $2^1 =$ _____ $2^2 =$ _____ $2^3 =$ _____ $2^4 =$ _____ $2^5 =$ _____

   b) Find the gaps in the sequence from part a) to continue the sequence. What is 2^8?

   ◯   ◯   ◯   ◯   ◯   ◯   ◯

   _____   _____   _____   _____   _____   _____   _____

   c) How can you obtain 2^9 from 2^8? _____

   d) If 2^{11} is 2 048, what is 2^{12}? _____

2. a) Use your answers to Question 1 to complete the chart.

n	1	2	3	4	5	6	7	8	9	10
2^n	2	4	8							

   b) Evaluate the product and write the answer as another power of 2.

   Then add the exponents.

   i) $2^2 \times 2^3 = 4 \times 8$
   $= 32$
   $= 2^5$

   ii) $2^3 \times 2^4 =$

   iii) $2^1 \times 2^5 =$

   $2 + 3 =$ ____ $3 + 4 =$ ____ $1 + 5 =$ ____

   iv) $2^2 \times 2^5 =$

   v) $2^6 \times 2^4 =$

   vi) $2^5 \times 2^4$

   ____ + ____ = ____   ____ + ____ = ____   ____ + ____ = ____

   What do you notice about your answers? _____

   > $3^4 \times 3^5 = \overbrace{3 \times 3 \times 3 \times 3}^{3^4} \times \overbrace{3 \times 3 \times 3 \times 3 \times 3}^{3^5}$
   >
   > $= 3^{4+5}$ ◀—There are $4 + 5 = 9$ threes in the product altogether.
   >
   > $= 3^9$

3. Write the product as a power.

   a) $3^2 \times 3^7 =$ __3^9__   b) $4^5 \times 4^3 =$ ____   c) $3^1 \times 3^5 =$ ____   d) $6 \times 6^8 =$ ____   e) $5^3 \times 5^7 =$ ____

   f) $8^6 \times 8^3 =$ ____   g) $7^5 \times 7^2 =$ ____   h) $4^5 \times 4^5 =$ ____   BONUS ▶ $5^2 \times 5^3 \times 5^6 \times 5^4 \times 5^7 =$ ____

4. Write the power of 9 as a power of 3. Remember: $9 = 3 \times 3$.

a) $9^2 = 9 \times 9$

     $= (3 \times 3) \times (3 \times 3)$

     $= 3^4$

b) 9^3

c) 9^4

d) 9^5

e) 9^6

f) 9^7

g) 9^8

BONUS ▶ $9^{125} = 3^{\boxed{}}$

5. Without evaluating the powers, order them from smallest to greatest. Explain your answer.

3^{12} 3^5 3^7 3^4 3^{20} 3^{17}

6. Write the power as a power of 2.

a) $4^7 = (2 \times 2) \times (2 \times 2) \times (2 \times 2) \times (2 \times 2) \times (2 \times 2) \times (2 \times 2) \times (2 \times 2) = \underline{\hphantom{000000}}$

b) $8^5 = (2 \times 2 \times 2) \times (2 \times 2 \times 2) \times (2 \times 2 \times 2) \times (2 \times 2 \times 2) \times (2 \times 2 \times 2) = \underline{\hphantom{000000}}$

c) $16^3 =$

d) $32^4 =$

7. Order the numbers from Question 6 from smallest to largest. $\underline{\hphantom{0000}} < \underline{\hphantom{0}4^7\hphantom{0}} < \underline{\hphantom{0000}} < \underline{\hphantom{0000}}$

8. To find the number that makes the equation true, try the numbers in order, starting at 1, until it works.

a) $2^x = 16$

    $2^1 = \underline{\hphantom{0}2\hphantom{0}}$

    $2^2 = \underline{\hphantom{0}4\hphantom{0}}$

    $2^3 = \underline{\hphantom{0}8\hphantom{0}}$

    $2^4 = \underline{\hphantom{0}16\hphantom{0}}$

    $2^5 = \underline{\hphantom{000}}$

    $x = \underline{\hphantom{0}4\hphantom{0}}$

b) $3^x = 81$

    $3^1 = \underline{\hphantom{000}}$

    $3^2 = \underline{\hphantom{000}}$

    $3^3 = \underline{\hphantom{000}}$

    $3^4 = \underline{\hphantom{000}}$

    $3^5 = \underline{\hphantom{000}}$

    $x = \underline{\hphantom{000}}$

c) $x^4 = 81$

    $1^4 = \underline{\hphantom{000}}$

    $2^4 = \underline{\hphantom{000}}$

    $3^4 = \underline{\hphantom{000}}$

    $4^4 = \underline{\hphantom{000}}$

    $5^4 = \underline{\hphantom{000}}$

    $x = \underline{\hphantom{000}}$

d) $x^3 = 125$

    $1^3 = \underline{\hphantom{000}}$

    $2^3 = \underline{\hphantom{000}}$

    $3^3 = \underline{\hphantom{000}}$

    $4^3 = \underline{\hphantom{000}}$

    $5^3 = \underline{\hphantom{000}}$

    $x = \underline{\hphantom{000}}$

e) $x^5 = 32$

f) $2^x = 8$

g) $4^x = 16$

h) $5^x = 625$

i) $x^2 = 64$

j) $x^3 = 64$

k) $x^2 = 49$

l) $6^x = 36$

9. Which prime number less than 10 (2, 3, 5, or 7) divides evenly into the given number? How did you check?

a) 256   b) 3125   c) 343   d) 243

10. Write the number as a power of a prime number. Start by dividing to see which prime number divides evenly into the number given.

a) $8 = 2^3$ b) $27 =$ c) $49 =$ d) $64 =$

e) $256 =$ f) $3125 =$ g) $343 =$ h) $243 =$

11. a) Write 64 three ways: as a power of 2, a power of 4, and a power of 8.

    b) Write 729 as a power in three different ways.

NS8-106 Powers and Expanded Form

1. Use the pattern in parts a) through c) to predict the number of zeros in the expression.

   a) $10^2 = 100$

   b) $10^3 = 1\ 000$

   c) $10^4 = 10\ 000$

   d) $10^5 = $ _____

   e) $10^7 = $ _____

   f) $10^8 = $ _____

2. Write the number as a power of 10.

   a) $10\ 000 = \underline{\quad 10^4 \quad}$

   b) $1\ 000\ 000 = $ _____

   c) $10\ 000\ 000 = $ _____

3. Write the number as a power of 10. Show your work.

   a) $1\ 000 \times 10\ 000$

   $= \underline{\quad 10\ 000\ 000 \quad} = \underline{\quad 10^7 \quad}$

   b) $10\ 000 \times 1\ 000\ 000$

   $= $ _____ $= $ _____

   c) $10\ 000\ 000 \div 1\ 000$

   $= $ _____ $= $ _____

   d) $10 \times 1\ 000 \times 10\ 000$

   $= $ _____ $= $ _____

4. Write the number in expanded form in two ways.

   a) 78 752

   $= \underline{\quad 7 \times 10\ 000 + 8 \times 1\ 000 + 7 \times 100 + 5 \times 10 + 2 \quad}$

   $= \underline{\quad 7 \times 10^4 + 8 \times 10^3 + 7 \times 10^2 + 5 \times 10 + 2 \quad}$

   b) 36 982

   $= $ _____

   $= $ _____

   c) 4 025 901

   $= $ _____

   $= $ _____

5. Write the number in standard form.

   a) $7 \times 10^4 + 3 \times 10^3 + 5 \times 10^2$

   $= \underline{\quad 73\ 500 \quad}$

   b) $4 \times 10^5 + 3 \times 10^4 + 4 \times 10^3 + 5 \times 10^2 + 1 \times 10 + 9$

   $= $ _____

   c) $3 \times 10^3 + 5 \times 10$

   $= $ _____

   d) $9 \times 10^5 + 5 \times 10^3 + 3 \times 10 + 7$

   $= $ _____

   e) $9 \times 10^5 + 3 \times 10^2 + 7$

   $= $ _____

   f) $7 \times 10^8 + 9 \times 10^7$

   $= $ _____

6. Write $>$ or $<$ in the square to show which number is greater.

   a) $5 \times 10^4 + 2 \times 10^3 + 7$ ☐ $5 \times 10^4 + 2 \times 10^2 + 7$

   b) $9 \times 10^5 + 3 \times 10^3 + 2 \times 10^2$ ☐ $9 \times 10^5 + 7 \times 10^3 + 2 \times 10^2$

NS-107 Powers of Negative Numbers

We can write powers of negative numbers too.

Example: $(-2)^3 = (-2) \times (-2) \times (-2)$

$$= \quad 4 \quad \times \quad (-2)$$
$$= \quad -8$$

Remember:

$+(+) = +$

$+(-) = -$

$-(+) = -$

$-(-) = +$

1. a) Evaluate the first seven powers of (-2) and the first seven powers of 2.

$(-2)^1 = \underline{\quad -2 \quad}) \times (-2)$ and $2^1 = \underline{\quad 2 \quad}) \times 2$

$(-2)^2 = \underline{\quad 4 \quad}) \times (-2)$ and $2^2 = \underline{\quad 4 \quad}) \times 2$

$(-2)^3 = \underline{\qquad}) \times (-2)$ and $2^3 = \underline{\qquad}) \times 2$

$(-2)^4 = \underline{\qquad}) \times (-2)$ and $2^4 = \underline{\qquad}) \times 2$

$(-2)^5 = \underline{\qquad}) \times (-2)$ and $2^5 = \underline{\qquad}) \times 2$

$(-2)^6 = \underline{\qquad}) \times (-2)$ and $2^6 = \underline{\qquad}) \times 2$

$(-2)^7 = \underline{\qquad}$ and $2^7 = \underline{\qquad}$

b) For which values of the exponent n (1, 2, 3, 4, 5, 6, or 7) is $(-2)^n$ positive?

_____, _____, and _____

c) Predict the next value of n for which $(-2)^n$ will be positive. _____

d) How does $(-2)^n$ compare to 2^n when n is even?_____

How does $(-2)^n$ compare to 2^n when n is odd? _____

e) If 2^{13} is 8 192, what is $(-2)^{13}$? _____

If 2^{14} is 16 384, what is $(-2)^{14}$? _____

2. a) Evaluate each term in the pattern.

$(-1)^1 = \underline{\qquad}$ $(-1)^2 = \underline{\qquad}$ $(-1)^3 = \underline{\qquad}$ $(-1)^4 = \underline{\qquad}$ $(-1)^5 = \underline{\qquad}$ $(-1)^6 = \underline{\qquad}$

b) Predict $(-1)^{973}$. Explain your prediction. _____

_____

3. Order the powers from least to greatest. Use your answers to Question 1.

$(-2)^1$ $\qquad$ $(-2)^2$ $\qquad$ $(-2)^3$ $\qquad$ $(-2)^4$ $\qquad$ $(-2)^5$ $\qquad$ $(-2)^6$ $\qquad$ $(-2)^7$

_____, _____, _____, _____, _____, _____, _____

4. a) Predict the order of these powers from least to greatest.

$(-3)^1$ $\qquad$ $(-3)^2$ $\qquad$ $(-3)^3$ $\qquad$ $(-3)^4$ $\qquad$ $(-3)^5$ $\qquad$ $(-3)^6$ $\qquad$ $(-3)^7$

_____, _____, _____, _____, _____, _____, _____

b) Check your prediction in part a) by calculating the powers.

NS-108 Exponents, Integers, and Order of Operations

When adding, subtracting, multiplying, and dividing integers, we use brackets to avoid writing two operation signs next to each other. Example: We write $3 \times (-2)$ instead of 3×-2.

We also use brackets to show which operations are done first. The correct order of operations is:

1. Do operations in brackets.
2. Calculate exponents and evaluate powers.
3. Do multiplication and division, from left to right.
4. Do addition and subtraction, from left to right.

1. Do any operations in brackets first. Then calculate the powers, and evaluate the expression.

a) $(7 - 5)^3$
b) $(3 + (-5))^4$
c) $(3 + (-3))^4$
d) $3^4 + (-3)^4$
e) $(2 + (-2))^5$
f) $2^5 + (-2)^5$
g) $(-5 + 3)^3$
h) $-5 + 3^3$

2. Calculate the exponent before calculating the power.

a) $3^{6 - (1 + 3)}$
$= 3^{6 - 4}$
$= 3^2$
$= 9$

b) $7^{(7 - 5) \div 2}$
c) $(-2)^{(4 + 2) \div 2}$
d) $(-2)^{4 + 2 \div 2}$

3. Calculate using the correct order of operations.

a) $4 \times (-2) \times 3$
b) $4 \div (-2) \times 3$
c) $5 + (-3) \times 9$
d) $5 \times (-3 + 9)$
e) $1 \times 7 - (-6) \div 2$
f) $(-1)^5 - 3$
g) $(-8) \div (3 - 7)$
h) $7 - (3 - 5)$
i) $(4 - 12) \div (-2)$
j) $(12 - 3) \times (-4) \div 3$
k) $(-2) \times (-3) - (4 + 7)$
l) $(3 - 5)^2$
m) $(24 + 2 \times (-6)) \div 4$
n) $(-3)^2 + 4 \times (-5)$
o) $3^2 - 5^2$

4. Add brackets where necessary to the equation to make it true.

a) $3 - 5 \times 2 = -4$
b) $2 - 5 \times 3 + 4 = -5$
c) $5 + (-2) \times (-3) = -9$
d) $2 - 5 \times 3 + 4 = -21$
e) $2 - 5 \times 3 + 4 = -33$
f) $3 - 5^2 = 4$
g) $2^3 \div 4 - 8 = -2$
h) $(-2)^3 + 2 \times 4 = 0$
i) $(-2)^3 + 2 \times 4 = -24$
j) $(-2)^{6 + 3 - 1} = -8$
k) $2 - 5^2 = 9$
l) $-4 + 3 - 2^5 = -3$

5. Translate the description into an expression and evaluate the expression.

Example: Add 7 and 5.
Then divide by 3.
Then add 2.

Answer: $(7 + 5) \div 3 + 2 = 12 \div 3 + 2$
$= 4 + 2$
$= 6$

a) Multiply -2 and -3.
Subtract 7.
Add 4.

b) Subtract 9 from -6.
Then add 7.
Raise the result to the second power.

c) Divide 6 by -3.
Then add -10.
Then subtract -12.

d) Add 2 and -8.
Divide by 3.
Raise the result to the fourth power.

6. Write the expression in words.

a) $(6 + (-8)) \times 3$
b) $(5 - 3) \times 3 + (-2)$
c) $4 \times (3 + (-2) \times (-5))$
d) $((7 - 9) \div 2)^3$

NS-109 Concepts in Powers

1. a) Evaluate the product by regrouping and using the fact that $2 \times 5 = 10$.

   $2 \times 2 \times 5 = \underline{\quad 20 \quad}$

   $2 \times 2 \times 2 \times 5 \times 5 = \underline{\qquad\qquad}$

   $2 \times 2 \times 2 \times 2 \times 5 \times 5 \times 5 = \underline{\qquad\qquad}$

   $2 \times 2 \times 2 \times 2 \times 2 \times 5 \times 5 \times 5 \times 5 = \underline{\qquad\qquad}$

   $2 \times 2 \times 2 \times 2 \times 2 \times 2 \times 5 \times 5 \times 5 \times 5 \times 5 = \underline{\qquad\qquad}$

   b) Write each product from part a) as a product of two powers.

   $\underline{\qquad\quad 2^2 \times 5^1 \qquad\quad}$

   $\underline{\qquad\qquad\qquad\qquad\qquad}$

   $\underline{\qquad\qquad\qquad\qquad\qquad}$

   $\underline{\qquad\qquad\qquad\qquad\qquad}$

   $\underline{\qquad\qquad\qquad\qquad\qquad}$

   c) What is $2^8 \times 5^7$? $\underline{\qquad\qquad}$ How do you know? $\underline{\qquad\qquad\qquad}$

   $\underline{\qquad\qquad\qquad\qquad\qquad\qquad\qquad\qquad\qquad\qquad\qquad\qquad}$

2. a) Write the first eight powers of 2.

   b) What is the pattern in the ones digit of your answers?

   c) What is the ones digit of the following powers?   i) 2^{10} ii) 2^{15}

3. Write the first six powers of 5. What is the ones digit of 5^{20}? How do you know?

4. a) Use a calculator to fill in the chart.

3^n	3^1	3^2	3^3	3^4	3^5	3^6	3^7	3^8	3^9	3^{10}	3^{11}	3^{12}
=	3	9	27									
ones digit	3	9	7									

   b) Describe the pattern in the ones digits of the powers of 3.

   c) Write the first three powers of 3 that have ones digit 9. Then write an expression for the nth exponent in the sequence. How much less than a multiple of 4 is every exponent in the sequence?

   d) Which of these powers of 3 have ones digit 9? Start by finding any exponents that are a multiple of 4.

   i) 3^{13} 3^{14} 3^{15} 3^{16} ii) 3^{17} 3^{18} 3^{19} 3^{20} iii) 3^{95} 3^{96} 3^{97} 3^{98} 3^{99} 3^{100}

   e) What is the ones digit of 3^{1000}? How do you know?

   BONUS ▶ Predict the ones digit of $2^{17} + 3^{17} + 4^{17} + 5^{17}$, then check your answer on a calculator.

5. In the square at right, each row, column, and both diagonals, multiply to the same number. Find the missing terms.

6. a) Evaluate these numbers that all use three 3s.

   i) $3^3 + 3$ ii) $3^3 \div 3$ iii) $(3 + 3) \div 3$

   iv) 33^3 v) 3^{3+3} vi) $3^{3 \div 3}$

   b) Use three 3s to make…

   i) 81   ii) 24   iii) 18   iv) 27   v) 0

NS-110 Negative Fractions and Decimals

1. Fill in the blank and mark the number on the number line.

   a) 1.4 is $\frac{4}{10}$ of the way from 1 to 2.

   b) 4.8 is _____ of the way from 4 to 5.

   So −1.4 is $\frac{4}{10}$ of the way from −1 to −2.

   So −4.8 is _____ of the way from −4 to −5.

2. a) Mark these positive numbers on a number line. Then order them from smallest to largest.

   A 3   B 1.4   C $2\frac{1}{2}$ D 2.8   E $\frac{4}{3}$ F 1.7   G $3\frac{3}{4}$

   _____, _____, _____, _____, _____, _____, _____

   b) Mark these negative numbers on a number line. Then order them from smallest to largest.

   A −3   B −1.4   C $-2\frac{1}{2}$ D −2.8   E $-\frac{4}{3}$ F −1.7   G $-3\frac{3}{4}$

   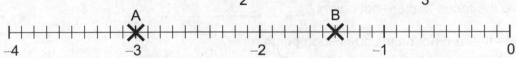

   _____, _____, _____, _____, _____, _____, _____

   c) Compare the lists from parts a) and b). What do you notice?

   REMINDER ▶ The **opposite** of an integer is the integer that adds with it to make 0.

   To get the opposite integer, change the sign from + to − or from − to +.

   Example: 3 + (−3) = 0 so 3 and −3 are opposites.

3. On grid paper, draw a number line from −3 to 3 and mark each of the following numbers.

   A the opposite of 2.8   B the opposite of $-\frac{4}{5}$ C 1 more than $-\frac{7}{5}$ D 2 less than $\frac{5}{4}$

4. Order the numbers from smallest to largest.

   a) 0.134 $\frac{1}{8}$ 0.032

   b) −2.715 $-\frac{14}{5}$ $-2\frac{3}{4}$

   c) 7.56   −9.126 $-9\frac{1}{8}$ $7\frac{1}{2}$ 0.3   −0.2

   d) 3.257   −3.257 $-3\frac{1}{4}$ $3\frac{1}{4}$ $3\frac{1}{3}$ $-3\frac{1}{3}$

ME8-9 Right Prisms

Prisms have faces, edges, vertices, and bases.

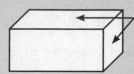

The faces are the flat surfaces.

The dotted lines show hidden edges.

Edges meet at vertices.

Faces meet at edges.

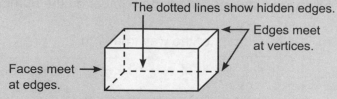

Every prism has two **bases**. The bases of a prism are always congruent polygons. The prism is named for the shape of the base.

pentagonal prism

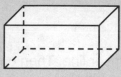

rectangular prism

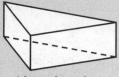

triangular prism

1. a) Shade one base of the prism, then name the prism.

i)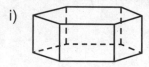

ii)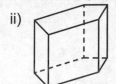

iii)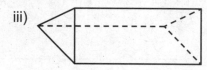

_____   _____   _____

b) What shape are the faces that are not bases? _____

c) How many faces that are not bases does each prism have?

i) _____   ii) _____   iii) _____

2. How many of each type of face would you need to make the prism shown?

a)

 △ = _____

▭ = _____

b)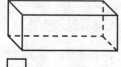

□ = _____

▭ = _____

c)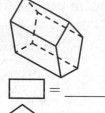

▭ = _____

⬠ = _____

When a prism stands on one base, the other base becomes the top face.

In a **right prism**, the top face is directly above the bottom face.
The side edges are vertical.

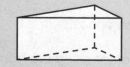

3. a) Sort the 3-D shapes.

A   B   C   D   E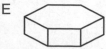

Right prisms: _A,_ _____   Not prisms: _____

b) Choose one 3-D shape that you said was not a prism and explain why it is not a prism.

146

Measurement 8-9

How to sketch a right prism

Step 1: Sketch two congruent bases.

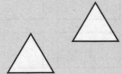

Step 2: Join the corresponding vertices.

Step 3: Use an eraser to make the hidden edges dashed.

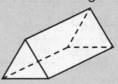

4. Finish sketching the right prism.

a)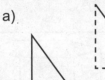

b)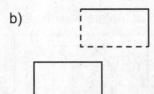

c)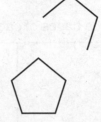

5. Now sketch two different rectangular prisms. Make the hidden edges dashed, and make sure none of your edges overlap!

How to sketch a right prism standing on its base

Step 1: Sketch two congruent polygons, one directly above the other.

Step 2: Join the corresponding vertices.

Step 3: Use an eraser to make the hidden edges dashed.

6. Follow the steps above to sketch three prisms with bases of different shapes.

7. Match each set of dimensions to the sketch that fits best. Then mark the length, height, and width of each prism on the sketch.

 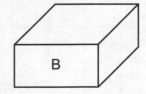 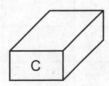

_____ 5 m, 3 m, 7 m

_____ 3 cm, 3 cm, 4 cm

_____ 2 km, 4 km, 4 km

8. a) Write 200 as a multiple of three numbers in three different ways.

200 = _____ × _____ × _____   200 = _____ × _____ × _____   200 = _____ × _____ × _____

b) Use the numbers from part a) to sketch three rectangular prisms with volume 200 cm³.

ME8-10 Nets of Right Prisms

1. The polygons below are faces of a prism. Mark the equal sides on all the faces.
   Name the prism you could make if you assembled the faces.

   a)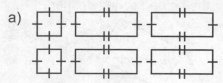

   b)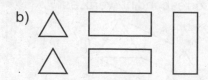

   c)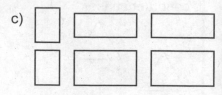

   _____ _____ _____

2. Shade the bases of each shape and then complete the chart.

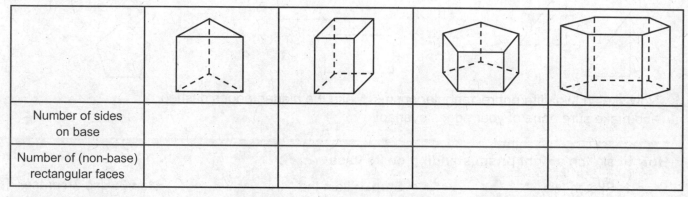

Number of sides on base				
Number of (non-base) rectangular faces				

   What relationship do you see between the number of sides on the base of a prism

   and the number of (non-base) rectangular faces? _____

3. Draw a net for the box on the grid and label each face.

   a)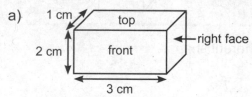
      1 cm
      top
      → right face
      2 cm
      front
      3 cm

   b)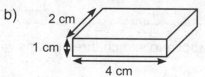
      2 cm
      1 cm
      4 cm

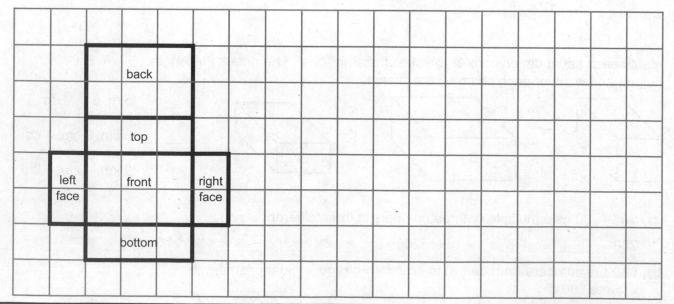

4. How many copies of each face do you need to make the prism? Mark the dimensions on each face.

a)
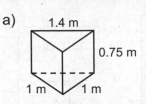

1 m 1.4 m 1 m

0.75 m 1.m

0.75 m 1.4 m

_____2_____ copies   _____2_____ copies   _____1_____ copies

b)
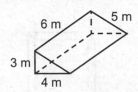
6 m 5 m 3 m 4 m

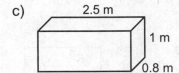

_____ copies   _____ copies   _____ copies   _____ copies

c)

2.5 m 1 m 0.8 m

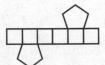
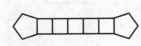

_____ copies   _____ copies   _____ copies

5. Circle the sketch or sketches that could be the net for the prism.

a)
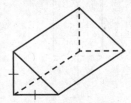

b)
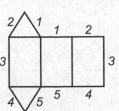
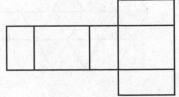

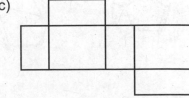

c) Explain what is wrong with the sketches you did not circle.

6. Mark the edges that will be glued together with the same number.

a)

2 1 1 2 3 3 4 5 5 4

b)

c)
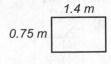

7. Circle the shape that could be the missing face for the net. Then add this face to the net.

a)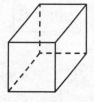

b)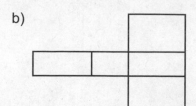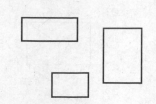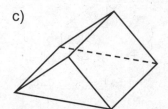

8. Sketch a net for the prism. Name the prism.

a) 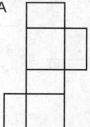   b) 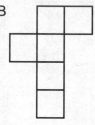   c) 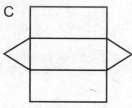   d)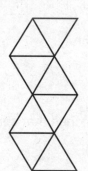

9. Match each net to a 3-D shape.

A 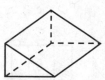   B   C   D   E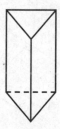

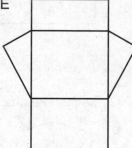

_____   _____   _____   _____   _____

BONUS ▶ Match the 3-D shapes to the nets.

A   B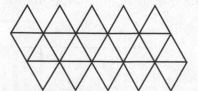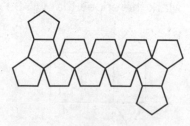

_____   _____

ME8-11 Volume of Rectangular Prisms

Volume is the amount of space taken up by a three-dimensional object.

To measure volume, we can use 1 cm³ blocks. They are also called centimetre cubes.

1 cm³ block

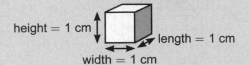

height = 1 cm

length = 1 cm

width = 1 cm

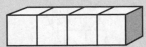

This object, made of centimetre cubes, has a volume of 4 cubes or 4 cubic centimetres (written 4 cm³).

1. Blocks are stacked to make boxes.

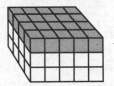

a) How many blocks are in the shaded layer?   _$3 \times 2 = 6$_   _____   _____

b) How many blocks are in each layer?   _6_   _____   _____

c) How many horizontal layers are there?   _2_   _____   _____

d) How many blocks are in the whole box?   _$6 \times 2 = 12$_   _____   _____

2. A box is ℓ blocks long, w blocks wide, and h blocks tall.

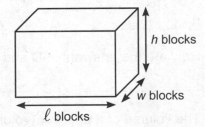

a) How many blocks are in each horizontal layer? _____

b) How many layers are there? _____

c) How many blocks are in the whole box? _____

d) Write a formula for the volume of the box (V) using the words length, width, and height.

$V =$ _____

h blocks

w blocks

ℓ blocks

3. Find the volume of the box.

a)

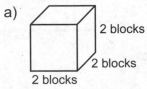

2 blocks

2 blocks

2 blocks

width: _____

length: _____

height: _____

volume = _____

b)

2 m

2 m

3 m

width: _____

length: _____

height: _____

volume = _____

c)

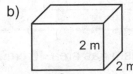

2 cm

2 cm

4 cm

width: _____

length: _____

height: _____

volume = _____

d)

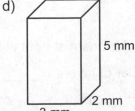

5 mm

2 mm

3 mm

width: _____

length: _____

height: _____

volume = _____

INVESTIGATION ▶ In a rectangular prism made of blocks, how is the area of the base related to the volume?

These prisms are made from 1 cm³ blocks:

i) 　　ii) 　　iii) 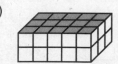　　iv)

A. The base is shaded. What is the area of the base in each prism?

i) _____12 cm²_____　ii) _____　iii) _____　iv) _____

B. What is the volume of one horizontal layer of blocks in each prism?

i) _____12 cm³_____　ii) _____　iii) _____　iv) _____

C. How are the answers in A and B related? Are the numbers the same? The units?

_____

D. How many horizontal layers are in each prism?

i) _____　ii) _____　iii) _____　iv) _____

E. What is the height of each prism?

i) _____　ii) _____　iii) _____　iv) _____

F. How are the answers in D and E related? Are the numbers the same? The units?

_____

G. The volume of a prism = (volume of one horizontal layer) × (number of horizontal layers).

Find the volume of each prism.

i) _____　　ii) _____　　iii) _____　　iv) _____

H. What can you multiply by the area of the base to get the volume of a prism?

V = (area of base) × _____

_____

4. The base of a rectangular prism has area 15 cm². The volume of one horizontal layer is _____ cm³.

The height of the prism is 4 cm. How many 1 cm layers are there? _____

The volume of the prism is _____ cm³ × _____ = _____ cm³.

5. Find the area of the rectangular prism at right in two ways.

Volume of one layer × number of layers = _____ cm³ × _____ = _____ cm³

Area of base × height = _____ cm² × _____ cm = _____ cm³

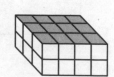

The volume of a rectangular prism = area of base × height.

6. Look at the prism at right.

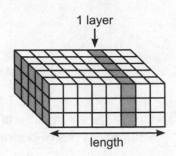

1 layer

length

a) What is the area of the left side? _____ cm²

What is the volume of the leftmost layer? _____ cm³

Compare your answers. Are the numbers the same? Are the units the same? Explain.

b) How many vertical layers are there? _____

What is the length of the prism? _____ cm

Compare your answers. Are the numbers the same? Are the units the same? Explain.

c) The volume of a right rectangular prism made of centimetre cubes is (number of layers in prism) × (number of cubes in each layer).

Explain why this formula gives the same answer as (length of prism) × (area of left face of prism).

7. What do you multiply each area by to find the volume of a rectangular prism — length, width, or height?

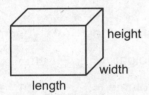

height

width

length

a) area of top × _____

b) area of right side × _____

c) area of bottom × _____

d) area of back × _____

e) area of left side × _____

f) area of front × _____

8. Find the volume of the prism in three different ways.

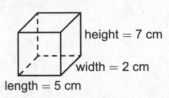

height = 7 cm

width = 2 cm

length = 5 cm

a) area of top × _____ *height* _____

= _____ cm² × _____ cm = _____ cm³

b) area of front × _____

= _____ cm² × _____ cm = _____ cm³

c) area of right side × _____

= _____ cm² × _____ cm = _____ cm³

Did you get the same answer all three ways?

_____

9. Find the volume of each right rectangular prism. Include the units in your answer.

a)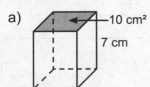
10 cm²
7 cm

b)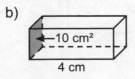
10 cm²
4 cm

c)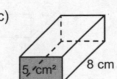
5 cm²
8 cm

d)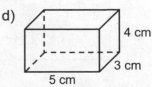
4 cm
3 cm
5 cm

10. Mentally rotate the prisms in Question 9 so that the shaded base is on the bottom.
Sketch the results.

a)

b)

c)

d)

e) Calculate the volume of each prism using this formula:
volume = area of bottom face × height.

Do you get the same answer? Why is this the case?

11. a) Find the volume of the rectangular prism. All lengths are in centimetres.

i)

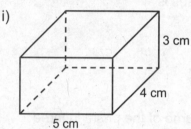
3 cm
4 cm
5 cm

ii)

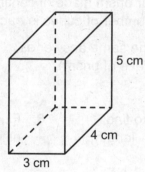
5 cm
4 cm
3 cm

iii)

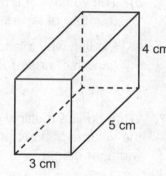
4 cm
5 cm
3 cm

area of top = _____ cm²

height = _____ cm

volume = _____ cm³

area of top = _____ cm²

height = _____ cm

volume = _____ cm³

area of top = _____ cm²

height = _____ cm

volume = _____ cm³

b) What do you notice about the volumes of the three prisms in part a)? Why is
this the case?

12. Without calculating the volumes, decide which two prisms have the same volume.
How did you decide?

A.

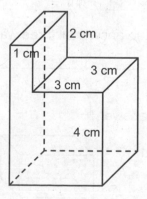
2 cm
1 cm
3 cm
3 cm
4 cm

B.

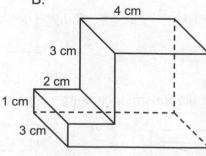
4 cm
3 cm
2 cm
1 cm
3 cm

C.

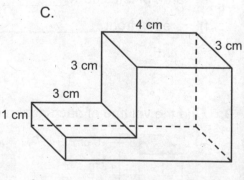
4 cm
3 cm
3 cm
3 cm
1 cm

ME8-12 Volume of Polygonal Prisms

INVESTIGATION 1 ▶ Does the volume of any prism made from centimetre cubes = area of base × height?

i)   ii) 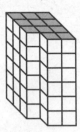   iii)

A. Complete the chart for each prism shown.

Figure	i)	ii)	iii)
Volume of one layer (cm³)	11		
Number of layers	2		
Volume of structure (cm³)	22		
Area of base (cm²)	11		
Height of structure (cm)	2		

B. Is the volume of any prism made from blocks equal to (area of base) × (height)? _____

INVESTIGATION 2 ▶ Does the volume of a triangular prism = area of base × height?

A. What fraction of the rectangle is the triangle? Explain.

a) 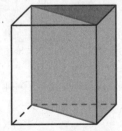   b) 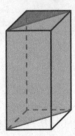   c)

B. What fraction of the rectangular prism is the triangular prism? Explain.

a) 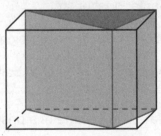   b)   c)

C. How can you use the volume of the rectangular prisms to find the volume of the triangular prisms?

volume of triangular prism = (volume of rectangular prism) ÷ _____

D. The volume of the rectangular prism at right is

(area of rectangle) × (_____ of prism)

= 2 × (area of _____) × (_____ of prism)

So the volume of a triangular prism is

(area of _____) × (_____ of prism)

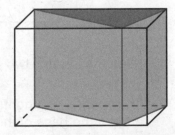

1. Imagine rotating the prism so that the shaded base is on the bottom. Trace an edge that shows the height.

a)

b)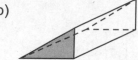

c)

2. The bases of the prism are shaded.

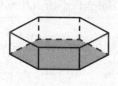

a) Label the height h along one of the edges.

b) Explain why the volume of the prism is $15 \times h + 20 \times h$.

c) Is the expression $15 \times h + 20 \times h$ equal to the expression $(15 + 20) \times h$? Check for $h = 1$, $h = 2$, and $h = 3$.

d) How do your answers to parts b) and c) show that the volume of the prism is equal to **area of base** $\times$ **height**?

3. Decompose the base into triangles and rectangles. Then find the area of the base and the volume of the prism.

a)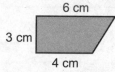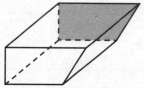

b)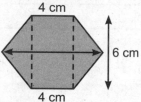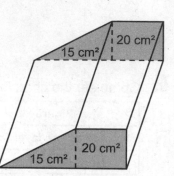

Any polygon can be decomposed into triangles. The volume of a polygonal prism is the sum of the volumes of the triangular prisms.

Example: Volume of pentagonal prism

$=$ area of $\times$ height $+$ area of $\times$ height $+$ area of $\times$ height $=$ area of $\times$ height

So **volume of polygonal prism = area of base $\times$ height**

4. Estimate, then calculate, the volume of a prism with height 10 cm and the base shown.

a)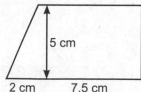

b)

3 cm

8.4 cm

5 cm

c)

12.1 cm

9.3 cm

5. Sketch and label two prisms with different heights that have volume 300 cm³.

6. The volume of a right triangular prism is 600 cm³. Its height is 15 cm. What is the area of the base of this prism? Explain how you found your answer.

ME8-13 Volume of Cylinders

1. Calculate the volume of the prism.

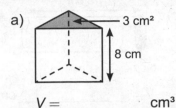 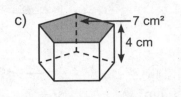 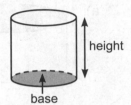 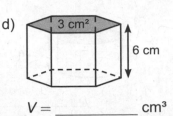

a) — 3 cm² 8 cm

b) 6 cm² 5 cm

c) — 7 cm² 4 cm

d) 3 cm² 6 cm

V = _____ cm³   V = _____ cm³   V = _____ cm³   V = _____ cm³

> A **cylinder** is like a prism, but with circles for bases.

INVESTIGATION ▶ What is the formula for the volume of a cylinder?

A. Predict the formula for the volume of a cylinder in terms of its base and height. Explain your prediction.

B. The volume of a can of food is given on the label. Bilal estimates the inside radius and inside height of four cans, and creates this table.

Can	Inside Radius (*r*)	*r²*	Inside Height (*h*)	*h* × *r²*	Volume of Food (*V*)	$\frac{V}{hr^2}$
pea soup	4.8 cm		11 cm		796 cm³	
pasta sauce	4.1 cm		13 cm		680 cm³	
mixed beans	4 cm		10.8 cm		540 cm³	
tomato paste	2.5 cm		8 cm		156 cm³	

Bilal measured the outside height of the pea soup can to be 11.8 cm. Why did he estimate a smaller number for the inside height? _____

Bilal measured the outside diameter of the pea soup can to be 10 cm. What is the outside radius? _____ Why did he estimate 4.8 cm for the inside radius? _____

C. Complete Bilal's table.

D. Which column has values always close to π ≈ 3.14? _____

E. Use your answer in part D to write a formula for the volume of a can.

π ≈ V ÷ (_____) so the formula is: V = π × _____

F. The base of a cylinder is a circle with radius *r*. The area of the circle is _____.

G. Use your answer in F to rewrite your formula from E for the volume of a cylinder:

V = (area of base circle) × _____

H. How is the formula for the volume of a cylinder like the formula for the volume of a prism? Why does this make sense? Hint: Think about how cylinders are like prisms.

_____

_____

I. Was your prediction in part A correct? _____

2. The volume of a cylinder is equal to (area of base) × height. Find the volume (V) of the cylinder.

a)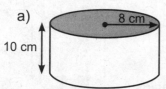

$V =$ _____ cm³

b)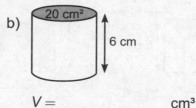

$V =$ _____ cm³

c)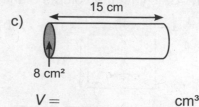

$V =$ _____ cm³

3. Use the radius or diameter to find the area of the base and the volume of the cylinder.

a)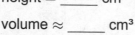

area of base ≈ _____ cm²

height = _____ cm

volume ≈ _____ cm³

b)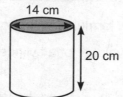

area of base ≈ _____ cm²

height = _____ cm

volume ≈ _____ cm³

4. Tina has a jar 20 cm high. She can fit 30 candies flat on the bottom of the jar. Each candy is 1 cm high. How many candies can she fit into the jar if…

a) the jar is a cylinder?

b) the jar is a right prism?

Are the two answers the same? Why does this happen?

5. Regular polygons with many sides look a lot like circles. Some Canadian pennies are circular, but some are polygonal.

a) Estimate the volume of a penny by pretending all pennies are perfect cylinders.

Step 1: Measure the diameter of a penny. Diameter = _____ mm

Step 2: Calculate the radius of the penny. Radius = _____ mm

Step 3: Measure the height of the penny.

First, measure the height of one coin individually. _____ mm.

Next, measure the height of 10 coins by stacking them.

Then divide your answer by 10.

    Height of 1 coin = Height of 10 coins ÷ 10

                = _____ cm ÷ 10

                = _____ mm

Which answer for the height of one coin is more accurate? Explain.

Step 4: Calculate the volume of the penny using the radius and height you found.

_____

b) Sara fills a graduated cylinder to the 30 mL mark. She then adds 10 pennies. Where should the water level be now?

ME8-14 Capacity

A centimetre cube has **volume** 1 cm³. It can hold 1 mL of water, so its **capacity** is 1 mL.

1. a) 1 L = _____ mL   b) A 1 L jar has volume _____ cm³.

2. A juice carton has a capacity of 1.89 L. What is its volume? _____

3. A rectangular juice carton can hold 2 L of juice. It is 25 cm tall. What is the area of the base of the carton?

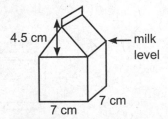

4. A small milk carton holds 250 mL of milk. Use the measurements given on the sketch to find the total height of the carton.

5. a) Find the volume of the can of orange juice.

   b) To make orange juice, you add 3 cans of water for each can of concentrate. How much juice (in L) will you have if you use 2 cans of concentrate?

6. A cake recipe calls for the use of either 2 round pans or 1 rectangular pan:

  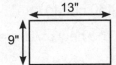

   a) If you use the same recipe, in which type of pan will the cake mix reach a higher level?

   b) You need to bake thicker cakes for longer. In which type of pan will you need to bake the cake for longer?

7. A recipe says to mix $\frac{1}{4}$ cup butter, 5 cups miniature marshmallows, 6 cups crisp rice cereal and pour the mixture in a pan 20 cm by 30 cm by 6 cm. If 1 cup = 240 mL, how high will the mixture be in the pan?

8. Tegan just bought an aquarium. The aquarium is 90 cm long, 45 cm high, and 40 cm wide.

   a) 1 L of water weighs 1 kg. Can Tegan fill her aquarium at a water source and then carry it to where she wants it? Explain.

   b) If Tegan has a 6 L pail, how many trips will she need to make from the water source to the aquarium to fill it with water?

   c) Do an Internet search to find reasons why Tegan might need to know the volume of her aquarium. Some things that might depend on volume include:

   • the number of fish Tegan can put in the aquarium,
   • the amount of medication she needs to provide if her fish get sick,
   • the amount of water she must occasionally replace with fresh tap water.

ME8-15 Changing Units of Area and Volume

1. Use the picture to fill in the blanks.

a)

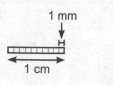

1 cm = _____ mm

b)

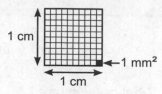

1 cm² = _____ mm²

c)

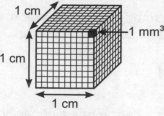

1 cm³ = _____ mm³

d)

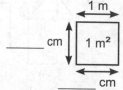

1 m² = _____ × _____ cm²

= _____ cm²

e)

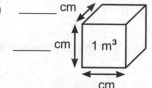

1 m³ = ___ × ___ × ___ cm³

= _____ cm³

f)

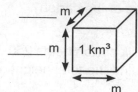

1 km³ = _____ × _____ × _____ m³

= _____ m³

2. Change the following units.

a) 15 000 cm² to m²

The new units are ___*100²*___ times ___*bigger*___.

So I need ___*10 000*___ times ___*fewer*___ units.

So I ___*divide*___ by ___*10 000*___.

15 000 cm² = ___*1.5*___ m²

b) 460 cm³ to mm³

The new units are _____ times _____.

So I need _____ times _____ units.

So I _____ by _____.

460 cm³ = _____ mm³

c) 15 000 m² to km²   d) 460 mm³ to cm³   e) 4 mm² to m²   f) 0.4 m³ to cm³

g) 5.2 m² to cm²   h) 0.01 m³ to cm³   i) 0.01 m² to km²   j) 2400 cm³ to m³

3. Don says a rectangular prism with length 4 m, width 80 cm, and height 50 cm has a volume of 16 000 cm³. What mistake did he make? Explain.

4. a) A circle has circumference 0.16 m. What is its area in cm²?
b) A rectangle has perimeter 0.16 m. Can you tell its area in cm² from this information?
c) If the rectangle in part b) is a square, does that change your answer?

5. 1 cm² tiles cost 10¢ each. About how much would it cost to tile an area of 0.15 m²? Why is this only an approximation?

6. a) A circular pool has diameter 8 m and the water is 120 cm deep. How much water is in the pool? Write your answer in terms of m³ and L. Which unit is a more reasonable unit of measurement?

b) During a drought year in a country with very little water, water costs $7.50/m³. How much does it cost to fill the pool in part a)?

ME8-16 Surface Area of Prisms

Note: Pictures are not drawn to scale.

1. In each prism, shade **all** the edges that have the same length as the edge marked.

a)   b) 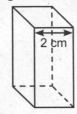   c) 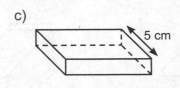   d)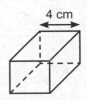

2. Find the missing edge length for the prism.

a) 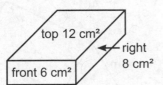   b) 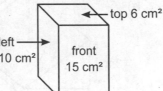   c)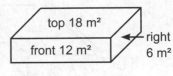

3. Shade the face that has the same area as the shaded face.

a) 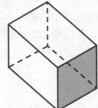   b) 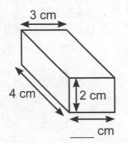   c)

4. The area of each visible face is given. What is the area of each hidden face?

a)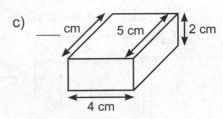

top 12 cm²
front 6 cm²
right 8 cm²

back _____

bottom _____

left _____

b)

top 6 cm²
left 10 cm²
front 15 cm²

back _____

bottom _____

right _____

c)

top 18 m²
front 12 m²
right 6 m²

back _____

bottom _____

left _____

5. Write the area of each visible face directly on the face. Then double each area to find the total area of each pair of congruent faces.

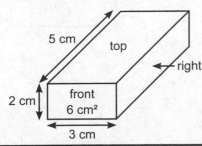

5 cm, top, right, 2 cm, front 6 cm², 3 cm

front   +   back   = _6 cm² × 2_ = _12 cm²_

top   +   bottom   = _____ = _____

_____ + _____ = _____ = _____

The **surface area** of a 3-D shape is the total area of all the faces of the shape.

6. Calculate the surface area of the prism.

a)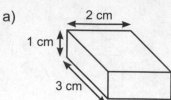

b)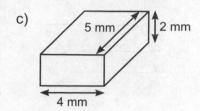

c)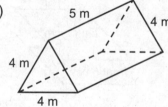

7. Miki calculates the surface area of the prism to be 40 cm². What did she do wrong?

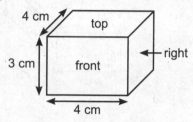

8. a) Alexandra says that she needs to find the area of only two faces of this prism to calculate the surface area. Is she correct? Explain.

b) What is the surface area of the prism?

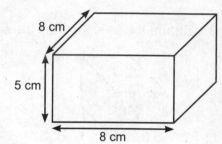

9. Write the name of each face of the prism on the net, then mark the length of each edge on the net.

a)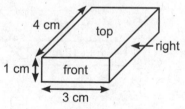

b)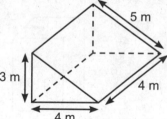

c)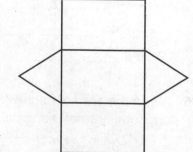

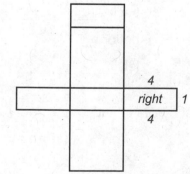

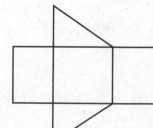

10. Find the surface area of each prism from Question 9. Include the units.

a) _____

b) _____

c) _____

How is the surface area of a prism related to the area of its net? Explain.

162

11. Find the missing length.

a)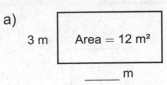

3 m | Area = 12 m²

_____ m

b)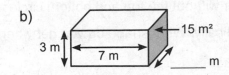

5 m

_____ m | Area = 15 m²

c)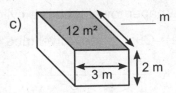

2 m | Area = 14 m²

_____ m

12. Find the missing edge length.

a)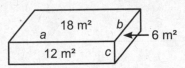

_____ m

20 m²

4 m   6 m

b)

_____ m

3 m   7 m   15 m²

_____ m

c)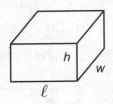

_____ m

12 m²   3 m   2 m

13. Edges a, b, and c have lengths that are whole numbers. The surface area of each face is written directly on the face. What are some possible lengths for edges a, b, and c? (Hint: Why can edge a not be 4 m long?)

18 m² b

a 6 m²

12 m² c

14. Write a formula for the surface area of the prism using the length (ℓ), width (w), and height (h).

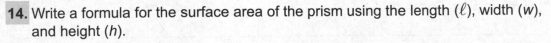

h w ℓ

15. Calculate the surface area of the prism. Be careful with the units!

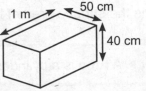

1 m   50 cm   40 cm

16. It costs \$0.40 per square metre to paint a room. How much would it cost to paint the walls of this room (not including the door and windows)?

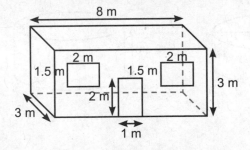

8 m

2 m   2 m

1.5 m   1.5 m   3 m

2 m

3 m   1 m

17. Look at the prism at right. It is not drawn to scale.

a) Draw a better sketch.

b) Find the volume and surface area of this prism.

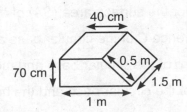

40 cm   0.5 m

70 cm   1.5 m

1 m

18. a) Write a rule that tells you how to calculate the surface area of the figures from the figure number. (Each cube has length, width, and height 1 cm.)

b) Use your rule to predict the surface area of the 20ᵗʰ figure.

Figure 1   Figure 2   Figure 3

ME8-17 Surface Area of Cylinders

REMINDER ▶ A **cylinder** is like a prism, but with circles for bases.

1. A paper towel tube is a cylinder without the top and bottom circles.

   a) Cut a paper towel tube vertically. What shape do you get when you open it up?

   _____

   b) Cut a paper towel tube diagonally. What shape do you get when you open it up?

   _____

   c) If the tube has circumference 15 cm and height 12 cm, what are the base and height of the shapes in parts a) and b)?

   a) _____   b) _____

   d) Do the shapes in parts a) and b) have the same area? _____

   Why does this make sense? _____

   _____

   e) What is the surface area of the tube? _____

REMINDER ▶ A **tube** is a cylinder without the top and bottom circles.

2. Find the surface area of the tube by finding the length and width of a rectangle with the same area.

   a)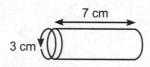

   b)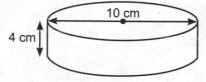

   c)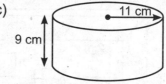

3. Write a formula for the surface area (SA) of a tube in terms of…

   a) the circumference C of the circular base and the height h. $SA = $ _____

   b) the diameter d of the circular base and the height h. $SA = $ _____

   c) the radius r of the circular base and the height h. $SA = $ _____

4. Which of these shapes can be the net for a tube? _____ Explain.

   | A | B | C | D | E | F |

5. A can of food is a cylinder. It has both top and bottom circles.

a) Find the surface area of the can.

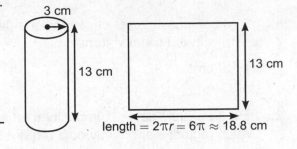

Area of rectangle   = _____

Area of top circle   = _____

+ Area of bottom circle   = _____

Surface area of can   = _____

length $= 2\pi r = 6\pi \approx 18.8$ cm

b) Which net matches the can in part a)? What is wrong with the other net?

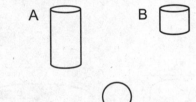

18.8 cm

6 cm   13 cm

or

6 cm

18.8 cm   13 cm

6. a) Which cylinder matches each net?

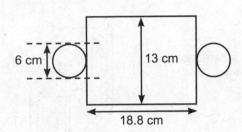

A   B   C   D   E

_____   _____   _____

b) Sketch nets for the two cylinders that were not matched.

c) How does the surface area of a cylinder compare to the area of its net? Explain.

7. Find the surface area of each can by first finding the area of a rectangle and the area of the top and bottom circles.

a)

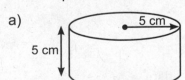

5 cm

5 cm

b)

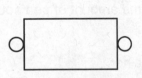

9 cm

2 cm

c)

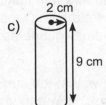

2 cm

9 cm

8. A cylindrical can has a circular base of radius r and height h. Write a formula for its surface area. Do not forget to include the top and bottom.

ME8-18 Surface Area and Volume

1. Write one possible set of dimensions (length, width, and height) for a rectangular prism with the given volume.

   a) 12 cm³   b) 8 cm³   c) 18 m³

2. Find 3 possible sets of dimensions for a rectangular prism with volume 24 cm³. Which rectangular prism would require the least amount of material to construct?

3. This is the top view (and mat plan) of a rectangular prism made of 1 cm³ blocks: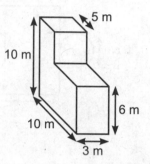

   a) What is its surface area in cm²?
   b) What is its volume in cm³?

4. Find the volume and surface area of the shape. Explain your strategy.

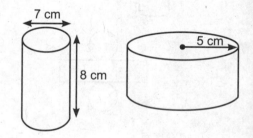

5. a) A prism has a square base that measures 10 cm by 10 cm. A cylinder has a base with the same area as the base of the prism.

   b) If both the prism and the cylinder are 20 cm high, which container will require less material to make?

   c) Do both containers have the same volume? Explain.

6. The two containers shown hold the same amount of pea soup.

   a) How tall is the second container?

   b) Find the surface area of each container.

   c) It costs 8¢ for each cm² of metal to make a can. How much will it cost to make each can? Which can is cheaper?

7. Each square is 3 cm by 3 cm.

   a) Find the area of the large circle.

   b) Find the area of the 9 small circles.

   c) Ten cylinders with height 5 cm and bases equal to the circles shown are made. Does the large cylinder hold more than, less than, or the same volume as the 9 smaller cylinders together?

8. Crystal knows that the surface areas of the front, top, and right faces of a prism add to 20 cm². How can she find the **total** surface area of the prism? Explain.

9. Determine the capacity, volume, and surface area of the box.

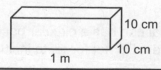

10. a) Calculate the volume and surface area of both cylinders.

A

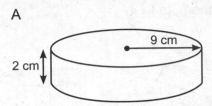

2 cm   9 cm

B

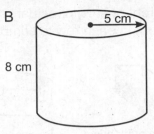

5 cm

8 cm

Volume = _____

Surface Area = _____

Volume = _____

Surface Area = _____

b) Which cylinder has the larger volume? _____

c) Which cylinder has the larger surface area? _____

11. a) Calculate the surface area and volume of this rectangular prism.

b) Find a cube with a larger volume and a smaller surface area.

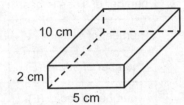

10 cm

2 cm

5 cm

12. Satya has the two containers shown.

a) Predict which container will hold more.

b) Calculate the volume of each container. Which one will hold more?

c) Satya fills the cylinder with water. How can he check which container will hold more without first finding the volume of each?

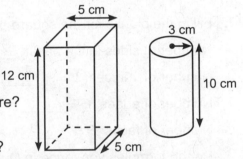

5 cm

3 cm

12 cm

10 cm

5 cm

13. a) Fold a standard (22 cm by 28 cm) sheet of paper into a tube in two ways.

A

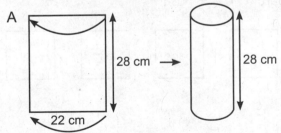

28 cm → 28 cm

22 cm

B

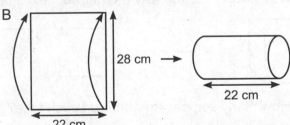

28 cm →

22 cm

22 cm

b) Add a top and bottom to the tubes to make a can. Calculate the volume and surface area of each can.

c) Which can has the larger volume and surface area?

d) Which can has a lower cost of material per unit volume?

14. A cylinder has a radius and height that are whole numbers (measured in cm), and a volume of $36 \times \pi$ cm². What is the smallest surface area it can have?

G8-37 Euler's Formula

1. Use the drawings of different prisms, or actual prisms if you have them, to fill in the chart. Look for a pattern in each row to complete the last column.

A
Triangular prism

B
Rectangular prism

C
Pentagonal prism

D
Hexagonal prism

E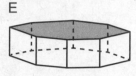
Octagonal prism

Prism	A	B	C	D	E	*n*-gonal prism
shape of base	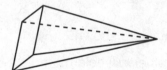					polygon with *n* sides
number of sides in base	3					*n*
number of vertices (V)						
number of edges (E)						
number of faces (F)						

2. Fill in the blanks for the square pyramid at right.

   Number of sides in the base: _____

   Number of vertices: V = _____

   Number of edges: E = _____

   Number of faces: F = _____

   Do the formulas you found in Question 1 for prisms apply to the square pyramid? _____

3. In a cube, F × (number of vertices on each face) = V × (number of faces that meet at each vertex). To see why this is true, take a cube apart:

    → | top | | bottom | | front | | back | | left | | right |

   a) How many vertices are there on each face? _____

   b) Number of faces: F = _____

   c) How many vertices are there in total on all faces?

      F × (number of vertices on each face) = _____ × _____ = _____

   d) How many vertices are on a cube before you take it apart? V = _____

   e) List the faces that meet at each vertex.

    _____ *top, front* _____
   _____ *and right faces* _____

    _____
   _____

    _____
   _____

f) How many faces meet at each vertex of a cube? _____

So $V \times$ (number of faces that meet at each vertex) = _____ $\times$ _____ = _____

g) In part c), when you calculated the number of vertices on all the square faces, how many times did you count each vertex in the cube? _____ Explain.

INVESTIGATION ▶ In a cube, is
$F \times$ (number of edges on each face) = $E \times$ (number of faces that meet at each edge)?

A. How many edges are on each face of a cube? _____

So $F \times$ (number of edges on each face) = _____ $\times$ _____ = _____

B. Which faces meet at each edge?

<u>front</u>
<u>left</u>

_____
_____

_____
_____

_____
_____

How many faces meet at each edge? _____

C. How many edges does a cube have? $E =$ _____

So $E \times$ (number of faces that meet at each edge) = _____ $\times$ _____ = _____

D. In a cube, is
$F \times$ (number of edges on each face) = $E \times$ (number of faces meeting in each edge)? _____

A 3-D shape is called a **Platonic solid** if all its faces are congruent regular polygons and there is the same number of faces meeting at each vertex.

4.
A
Rectangular prism

B
Cube

C
Triangular prism

D
Pentagonal prism

E
Square pyramid

F
Triangular pyramid with faces that are equilateral triangles

a) Which of the shapes have the same number of faces meeting at each vertex?

_____

b) Which of the shapes have all faces congruent? _____

c) Which of the shapes are Platonic solids? _____

BONUS ▶

a) Which prism is a Platonic solid? _____

b) Which pyramid is a Platonic solid? _____

Explain why any other pyramid is not a Platonic solid.

c) Consider a shape made from two triangular pyramids with equilateral faces. Is it a Platonic solid? Explain.

There are 5 Platonic solids. Their names come from ancient Greek. In Greek, "edron" means "face." The names of some Platonic solids tell you how many faces they have.

tetrahedron	cube	octahedron	dodecahedron	icosahedron
tetra = four		octo = eight	dodeca = twelve	icosi = twenty
4 faces	6 faces	8 faces	12 faces	20 faces

5. a) Sort the Platonic solids by the shape of their faces.

   triangular faces: _____

   square faces: _____

   pentagonal faces: _____

   b) Sort the Platonic solids by the number of faces that meet at each vertex.

   3 faces: _____

   4 faces: _____

   5 faces: _____

In any Platonic solid:
$F \times$ (number of vertices on each face) $= V \times$ (number of faces that meet at each vertex)
$F \times$ (number of edges on each face) $= E \times$ (number of faces that meet at each edge)

6. Use the charts to find the number of vertices (V) and the number of edges (E) in the Platonic solids.

	F	vertices on each face	faces at each vertex	Equation for V	V
tetrahedron	4			____ × ____ = ____ × ____	
cube	6	4	3	_6_ × _4_ = _3_ × _V_	8
octahedron	8			____ × ____ = ____ × ____	
dodecahedron	12			____ × ____ = ____ × ____	
icosahedron	20			____ × ____ = ____ × ____	

	F	edges on each face	faces at each edge	Equation for E	E
tetrahedron	4			____ × ____ = ____ × ____	
cube	6	4	2	_6_ × _4_ = _3_ × _V_	12
octahedron	8			____ × ____ = ____ × ____	
dodecahedron	12			____ × ____ = ____ × ____	
icosahedron	20			____ × ____ = ____ × ____	

7. a) Fill in the table for each shape. Use the tables from Question 6.

Shape					
number of vertices (V)					
number of faces (F)					
number of edges (E)					
V + F					

b) Look for relationships between the rows. What do you notice? _____

_____

> A famous 18th century mathematician named Leonhard Euler discovered that for many 3-D shapes $V + F = E + 2$. This is called **Euler's formula**.

8. Complete the chart. Then check Euler's formula for each prism.

Prism	Number of…				Does Euler's formula hold?
	sides in base	faces	edges	vertices	
rectangular prism	4	6	12	8	Yes: $6 + 8 = 12 + 2$
pentagonal prism					
hexagonal prism					
n-gonal prism	n				

9. A soccer ball is made of 12 pentagons and 20 hexagons. Euler's formula holds for it.

a) How many faces does a soccer ball have? $F =$ _____

b) If we count the edges once in each face, we get $12 \times$ _____ $+ 20 \times 6 =$ _____ edges.

Is that the number of edges of the soccer ball? _____

c) How many faces meet at each edge of a soccer ball? _____

How many times did we count each edge in b)? _____ (Hint: See Investigation part B.)

How many edges does a soccer ball have? $E =$ _____

d) Substitute the numbers for E and F (from above) into Euler's formula, $F + V = E + 2$,

to get an equation. _____

e) Solve the equation from d) for V. What is the number of vertices on the soccer ball? _____

f) Is a soccer ball a Platonic solid? Why or why not?

G8-38 Tessellations and Transformations

squares

equilateral triangles

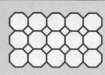

octagons and squares

1. Finish the tessellation using the shapes given.

   a) hexagons and rhombuses

   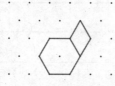

   b) trapezoids

   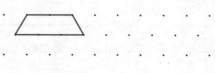

2. Show two different tessellations using the same shape.

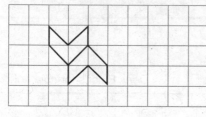

   Translate the shape 2 units left or right repeatedly.

   Reflect each shape in the row through a horizontal line and translate it 1 unit up and 1 unit right.

   Translate both rows together 2 units up or down repeatedly.

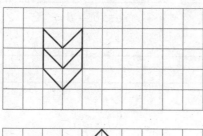

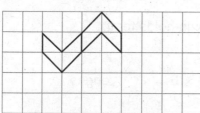

3. a) Which transformation (translation, reflection, or rotation) could you use to move shape 1 onto…

   i) shape 2?   ii) shape 3?   iii) shape 4?

   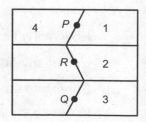

   b) Philip says: "I can move shape 3 onto shape 4 using a 180° rotation and then a translation." Is he correct? Explain.

   c) Explain how you could move shape 3 onto shape 4 using a single rotation. What is the centre of rotation?

   d) Does shape 1 tessellate? Describe the tessellation or explain why it does not tessellate.

4. Show how to make a large L shape out of 4 small L shapes like the one shown. Then use 4 large Ls to make an even larger L. Explain how this strategy will allow you to tessellate a grid.

5. a) Find a pair of shapes that is connected by…

   i)   a reflection in the *y*-axis. _____

   ii) 180° rotation about the point (0, 6). _____

   iii) reflection in a horizontal line through (0, 6). _____

   iv) 180° rotation about the point (3, 3). _____

   v) translation 6 units right and 6 units up. _____

   vi) translation 6 units left and 6 units up. _____

   vii) reflection through a vertical line and translation. _____

   viii) 180° rotation and translation. _____

b) Identify the line of reflection and describe the translation in part vii).

c) Identify the centre of rotation and describe the translation in part viii).

6. a) Which transformations take…

   i)   shape A to shape B?   ii) shape B to shape C?

b) Describe a pair of transformations that will take shape A to shape C, then describe a single transformation that will do it. Draw and label the mirror lines or centres of rotation.

7. Identify a pair of shapes (from A, B, C, D, or E) in the tessellation that is connected by each transformation or combination of transformations.

a) reflection in a vertical line (Draw the mirror line.) _____

b) reflection in a slant line (Draw the mirror line.) _____

c) a 120° rotation around a common vertex _____

   (Mark the centre of rotation.) _____

d) a translation (Draw the translation arrow.) _____

Hint: Use your answers in parts a) to d) in the next parts. There might be more than one answer!

e) a reflection and a translation _____

f) a reflection and a rotation _____

g) a translation and a rotation _____

BONUS ▶ Describe how you could create this tessellation starting from shape A.

G8-39 Angles in Polygons and Tessellations

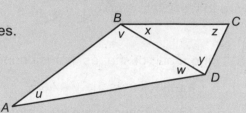

1. A pentagon can be divided into three triangles. Find the sum of the angles in each pentagon. Then check your answer by measuring the angles.

a)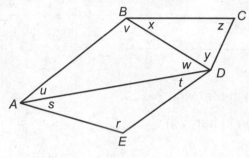

$\angle A + \angle B + \angle C + \angle D + \angle E$

$= (s + u) + (v + x) + z + (y + w + t) + r$

$=$ _____

b)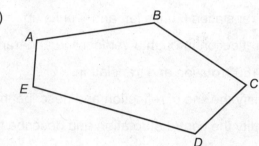

$\angle A + \angle B + \angle C + \angle D + \angle E$

$=$ _____

$=$ _____

2. Use a protractor to measure the interior angles that are smaller than 180° in this pentagon. Use the sum of the angles in a pentagon (from Question 1) to find the fifth angle.

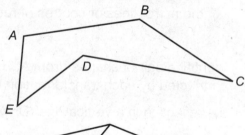

3. What is the sum of the angles around a point? Use a picture to explain your answer.

4. Sidra divides this pentagon into 5 triangles and adds all the interior angles. How much greater is her total than the sum of the angles in the pentagon alone? How do you know?

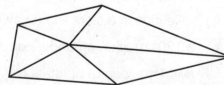

5. a) An equilateral triangle has all its angles equal.

   What is the measure of each angle? _____

   b) Six equilateral triangles can fit around a common vertex without gaps or overlaps.

   Why is this possible? _____

   c) How many squares can fit around a common vertex with no gaps or overlaps? How do you know?

   d) Show how you can tessellate using equilateral triangles.

   e) Show how you can tessellate using squares.

6. Divide each polygon into triangles that all meet at one of the vertices of the polygon.
Then fill in the table below and find the sum of the interior angles of the polygons.

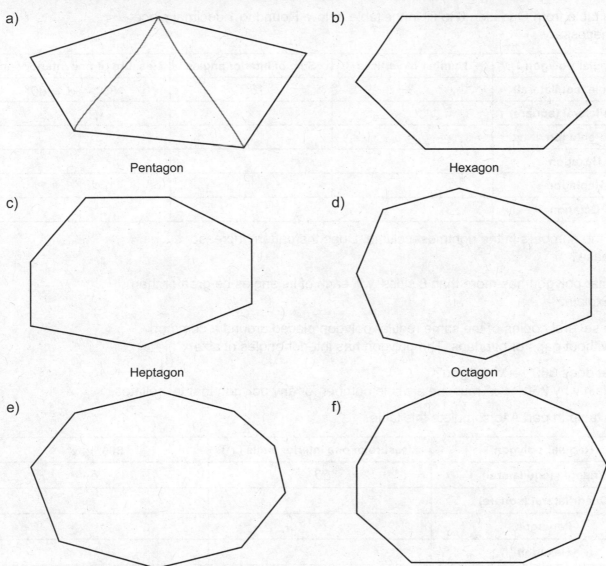

a) Pentagon

b) Hexagon

c) Heptagon

d) Octagon

e) Nonagon

f) Decagon

Polygon	Number of sides	Number of triangles created by diagonals	Expression for the sum of interior angles	Sum of interior angles
Quadrilateral	4	2	180° × 2	360°
Pentagon	5	3	180° ×	
Hexagon				
Heptagon				
Octagon				
Nonagon				
Decagon				
n-sided polygon	*n*			

INVESTIGATION ▶ A **regular polygon** has all sides and all angles equal. Which regular polygons tessellate?

A. Use the table from Question 6 to fill in the table below. Round to 1 decimal place where necessary.

Regular polygon	Number of vertices	Sum of interior angles	Measure of one interior angle
Triangle (equilateral)	3	180°	180° ÷ 3 = 60°
Quadrilateral (square)			
Pentagon			
Hexagon			
Heptagon			
Octagon			

B. Look at the numbers in the rightmost column. Does the pattern increase or decrease?

If a regular polygon has more than 8 sides, will each of its angles be greater than 135°? Explain.

C. Imagine several copies of the same regular polygon placed around a common vertex without gaps or overlaps. The polygon has interior angles of size $x°$.

a) What does $360° \div x°$ tell you?
b) Explain why $360° \div x°$ must be a whole number for any polygon that tessellates.

D. Use the table in part A to complete this table.

Regular polygon	Measure of one interior angle ($x°$)	$360° \div x°$
Triangle (equilateral)	60°	6
Quadrilateral (square)		
Pentagon		
Hexagon		
Heptagon		
Octagon		

E. Use the table in part D to determine which of the regular polygons listed tessellate. Explain your answer.

F. Use your answer in part B to explain why no regular polygon with more than 8 sides can tessellate. (Can you place more than two copies without overlapping? How do you know? If you place two copies without overlapping, will there be a gap? How do you know?)

---

7. This tessellating polygon has all sides equal.

a) How many sides does this polygon have?

b) Why is this polygon not a counter-example to the results of your investigation?

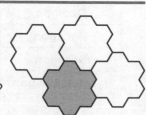

G8-40 Tessellating Polygons

1. Rectangles are not regular polygons but they tessellate. Use what you know about the size of their angles to explain why they can tessellate.

2. a) Describe how you can tessellate with any parallelogram using translations.

   b) Draw a scalene triangle. Will you use a rotation, a reflection, or a translation to obtain a second triangle, congruent to the first, so that the two triangles together produce a parallelogram?

   c) Does your triangle tessellate? Explain.

3. a) Finish tessellating the grid using each triangle. Identify the transformations you used.

   i)    ii)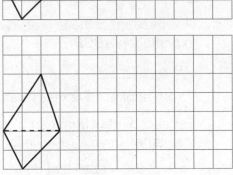

   b) Add six more quadrilaterals to tessellate the grid. Describe the transformations you used.

   c) On grid paper, draw a quadrilateral with a horizontal diagonal. Explain how the strategy from part b) will help you tessellate the grid with your quadrilateral.

4. Quadrilaterals 2 and 3 were obtained from quadrilateral 1 using a 180° rotation around the midpoints of the common edges.

   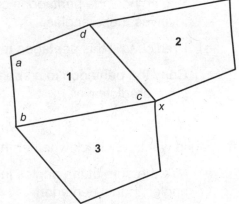

   a) Label the interior angles in quadrilaterals 2 and 3.

   b) What is the size of angle *x*? How do you know?

   c) Mark the equal line segments on this diagram.

   d) Draw a fourth copy of the same quadrilateral to close the gap around the common vertex. Which transformation would take this quadrilateral to quadrilateral 1? quadrilateral 2? quadrilateral 3?

   e) Why can you always place 4 copies of the same quadrilateral around a point?

5. Mirek wants to create a tessellation using regular octagons and another polygon.

   a) Mirek places two octagons so that they share a side. Can he place a third octagon so that it shares a vertex with the first two without creating an overlap? Why or why not?

   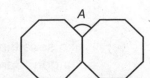

   b) What is the degree measure of ∠A in the picture? How do you know?

   c) What polygon could Mirek use to fill in the gap between the octagons?

6. Olesya uses the octagon shown, together with another polygon, to create a tessellation. All the angles of the octagon are equal.

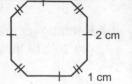
2 cm
1 cm

a) What are the angles of the octagon? _____

b) Olesya places two octagons so that they share a longer side.

What is the degree measure of ∠A in the picture? _____

c) What polygon could Olesya use to fill in the gap between the octagons? _____

What are the lengths of this polygon's sides? _____

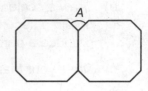
A

d) Kong places Olesya's octagons so that they share a shorter side. Describe the polygon he needs to fill in the gap between the octagons for the new tessellation.

7. Check whether pentagon *ABCDE* tessellates.

a) Use the sum of the angles in a pentagon to find the measures of these angles in pentagon *ABCDE*.

∠B = _____   ∠D = _____

b) Which angles have measures that divide into 360°? _____

c) For each vertex from part b), sketch how the pentagons will be placed around that vertex in your tessellation.

d) Look at the angles that do not divide into 360°.

Which combinations of angles add together to 360°? _____

Sketch how the pentagons could be placed around the common vertex that involves these angles.

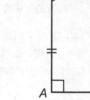

e) Predict: Will this pentagon tessellate? _____

Copy the pentagon to a sheet of paper and cut out several copies to check your prediction.

8. Keiko wants to check whether this pentagon tessellates.

a) Use the sum of the angles in a pentagon to find the measures of the missing angles in this pentagon.

∠a = _____

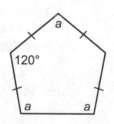
120°

b) Keiko places three copies of the pentagon around a common vertex.

Find the measures of the angles *x*, *y*, and *z*.

∠x = _____   ∠y = _____   ∠z = _____

c) Keiko sees that the measure of *x* is more than any of the angles of the pentagon. Can she place two copies of the pentagon to fill in angle *x*? If yes, sketch how she can do it. If no, explain why not.

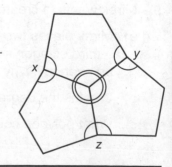

9. Use angle measures to predict whether the pentagon tessellates.

Copy the polygon to a sheet of paper, cut out several copies of it, and check your prediction.

a)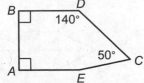

b)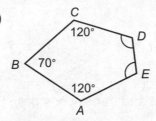

c)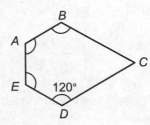

10. a) Use the sum of the angles in a hexagon to find the measure of each angle in the hexagon.

i)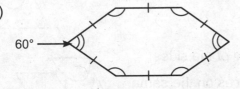

ii)

b) Use the measure of the angles from part a) to predict whether each hexagon tessellates (alone).

c) Copy each hexagon to a sheet of paper and cut out several copies to check your predictions in part b).

d) Describe the transformations used to make each tessellation that works.

11. a) Pair the shapes that will tessellate together.

_____ and _____, _____ and _____, _____ and _____

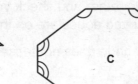

b) Use angle measurements to justify your answers in part a).

c) Which shapes will tessellate alone? _____

12. Nellie wants to create a tessellating shape. She starts with a rectangle because rectangles tessellate. She cuts out a part of the rectangle, cuts the part in two, and tapes the two pieces to the other side.

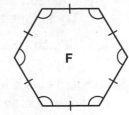

a) Is the area of Nellie's new shape the same as the area of the rectangle? _____

b) Nellie thinks that in her shape, $\angle a + \angle b = \angle c$. Is she correct? _____

c) Nellie thinks that because $\angle a + \angle b = \angle c$, the other angles are right angles, and the area is the same, her shape will tessellate. Is she correct? Explain.

G8-41 Creating Tessellating Shapes

1. **a)** Create a shape that will tessellate: Cut out a grid paper rectangle. Cut the rectangle into two pieces (any way you want). Tape the two opposite ends together. Example:

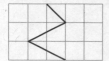    

b) Create a tessellation using your shape and translations only. Sketch your tessellation.

c) Create a different tessellation by reflecting your shape in the straight sides and translating it. Sketch your tessellation.

2. **a)** Create another shape that will tessellate:

Cut out a paper parallelogram. Mark the midpoint of one of the sides.

Draw a curved line from the midpoint to one of the vertices on the same side. Cut along the line you drew.

Rotate the piece you cut off 180° and tape it back to the second half of the side.

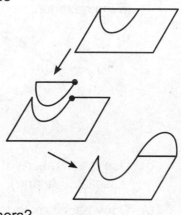

b) Create a tessellation using your shape. Sketch your tessellation. Which transformations are used to move one shape in the tessellation to the others?

3. Lina creates a tessellating shape using the method of Question 1 applied to a hexagon. She cuts a hexagon in two as shown and tapes the pieces together.

a) On the original hexagon, trace the two sides that Lina taped together.

b) Predict whether Lina's new shape will tessellate. Cut out six hexagons and cut them the way Lina did. Tape the pieces together and check your prediction. Try to tape the pieces together so that no curved edges are on the outside.

c) Sketch your tessellation or explain why the shape does not tessellate.

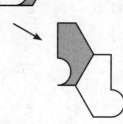

4. Ahmad cuts a hexagon the same way Lina did in Question 3, but he tapes the pieces together in a different way.

a) On the original hexagon, trace the two sides that Ahmad taped together.

b) Predict whether Ahmad's new shape will tessellate. Use at least seven hexagons to check your prediction.

c) Sketch your tessellation or explain why the shape does not tessellate.

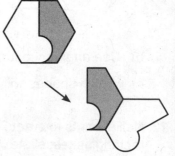

5. Predict which of the shapes below will tessellate. Check your predictions.

A 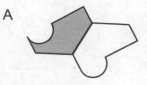   B 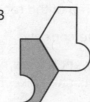   C

G8-42 3-D Drawings, Top and Front Views

Follow these steps to draw a cube on isometric dot paper.

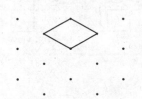  

Step 1: Draw the top square with 4 vertices at 4 different dots.

Step 2: Draw vertical lines from 3 vertices to the dots below.

Step 3: Join the new vertices.

1. Draw the structure made from connecting cubes on isometric dot paper.

a)

b)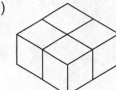

c)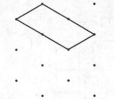

d)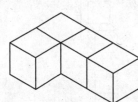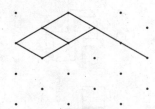

e)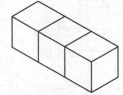

f)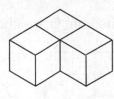

2. Build the structure with blocks or connecting cubes.

a)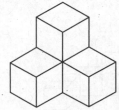

b)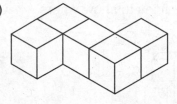

c)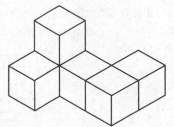

d)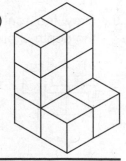

When you look at a structure from one side only, you see a side view. There are six possible side views of a 3-D structure:

front view   left side view   top view

back view   right side view   bottom view

front view

3. Draw the front view of the structure.

a)

b)

c)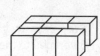

d)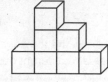

4. Shade the front face of the layer that is closer to you. Shade the same square on the front view. Then add thick lines to show where the depth changes.

a)

b)

c)

d)

Now draw the thick lines on the front face without shading.

e)

f)

g)

h)

5. Draw the front view of the structure. Include thick lines to show where the depth changes.

a)

b)

c)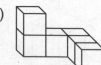

                                          Geometry 8-42

When you look at a structure from the top, you see the **top view**. The front edge is at the bottom.

top view

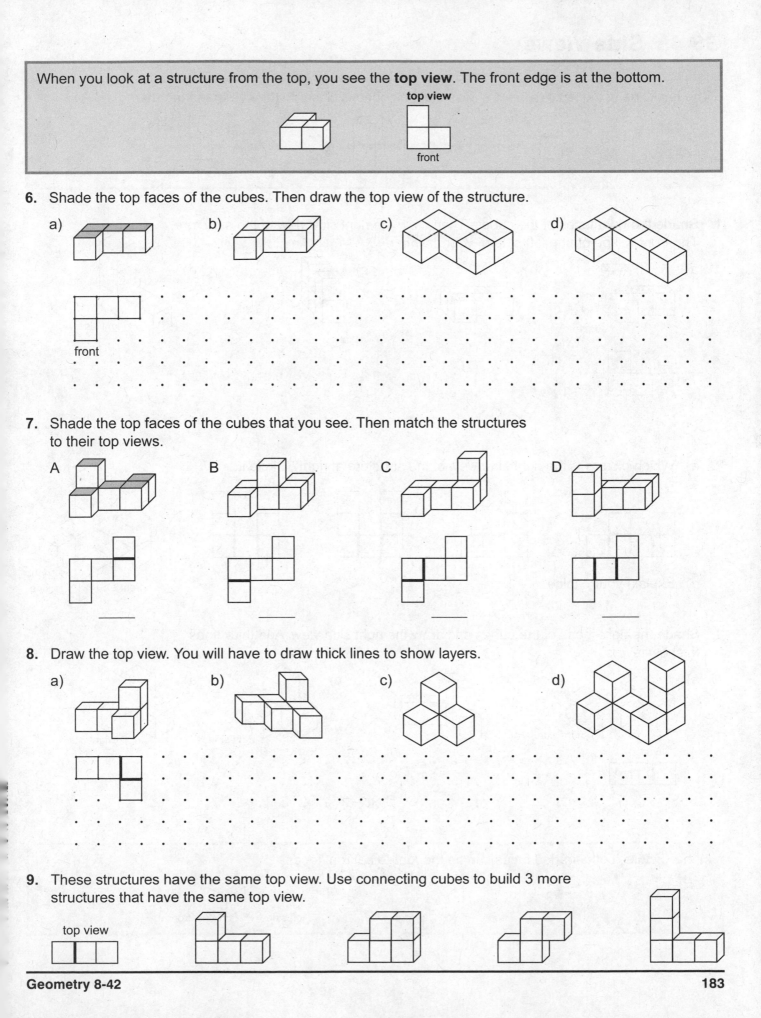

6. Shade the top faces of the cubes. Then draw the top view of the structure.

a)

b)

c)

d)

front

7. Shade the top faces of the cubes that you see. Then match the structures to their top views.

A

B

C

D

8. Draw the top view. You will have to draw thick lines to show layers.

a)

b)

c)

d)

9. These structures have the same top view. Use connecting cubes to build 3 more structures that have the same top view.

top view

G8-43 Side Views

The thick line in the left side view shows that one cube is closer to the eye than the others.

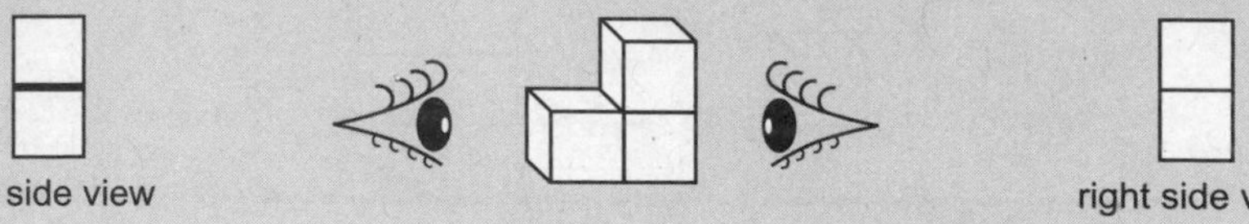

left side view   right side view

1. Shade the right faces of the cubes. Then draw the right side view of the structure.
    The front will be on the left side of your drawing.

    a) 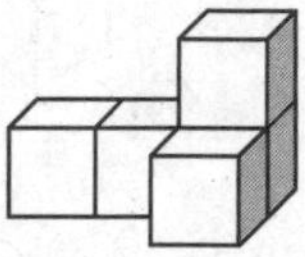   b) 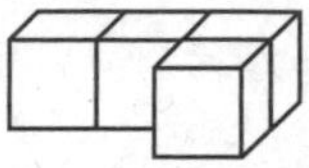   c) 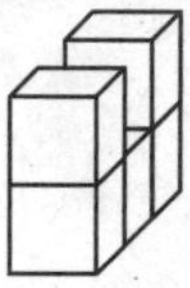   d)

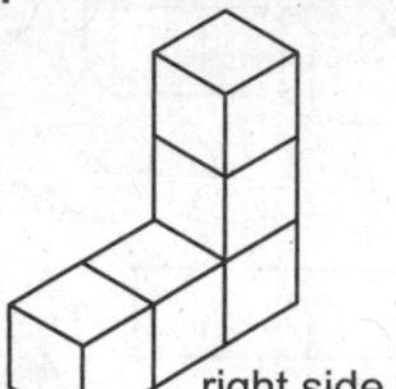

                                                                        right side

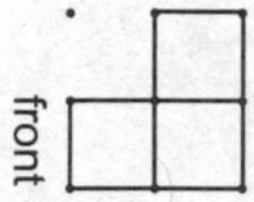

    front

2. a) Which picture is the right side view of the structure at right? Circle it.

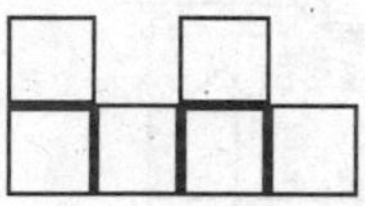

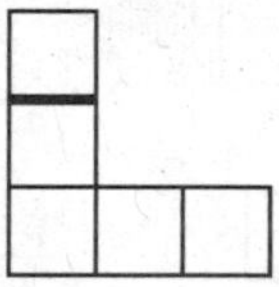

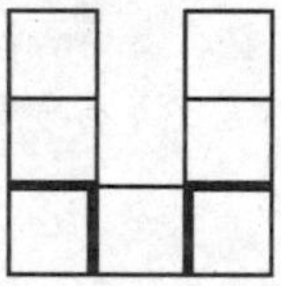

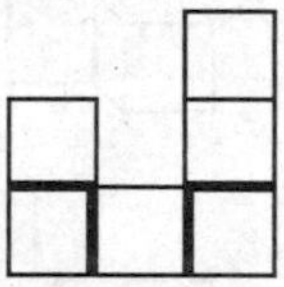

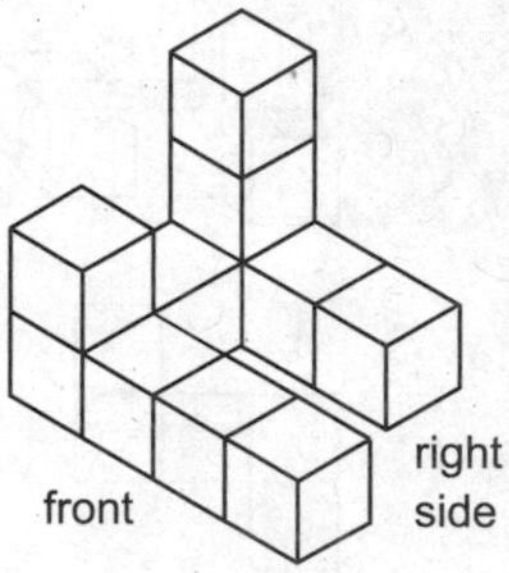

    b) Explain your choice.

                                                                        right
                                                            front   side

3. Shade the right faces of the cubes and draw the right side view. Add thick lines
    to show layers.

    a) 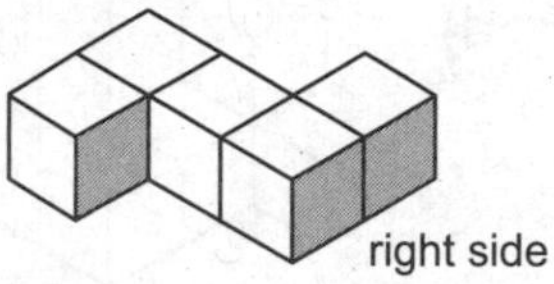   b) 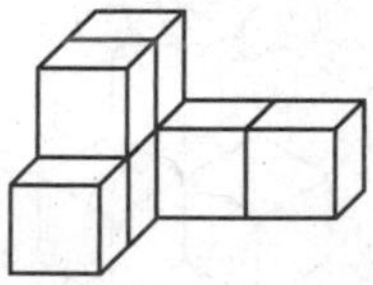   c) 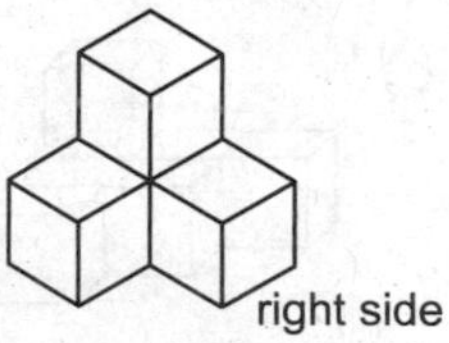   d)

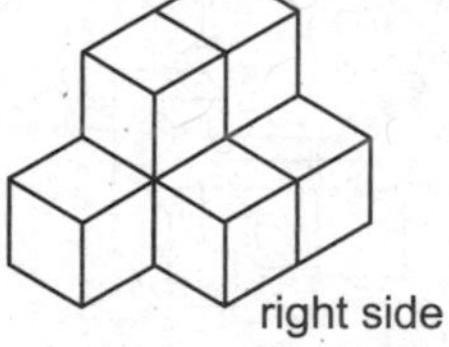

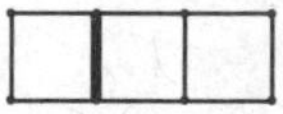

        right side   right side   right side

In this picture, both shaded faces can be thought to be front faces.

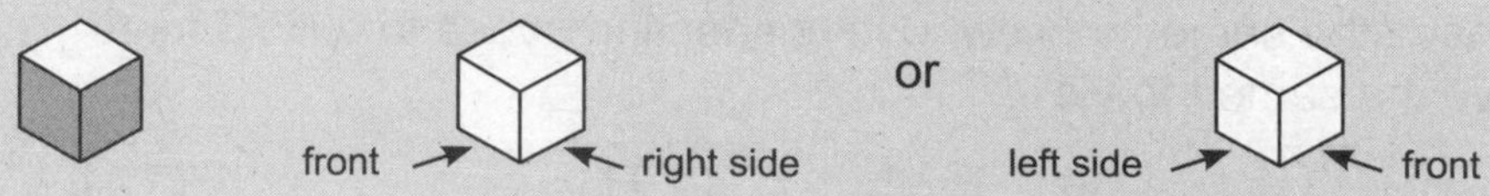

                                                    or

            front →   ← right side   left side →   ← front

4. a) Shade the front faces.

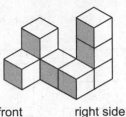

front   right side

Draw the front view.

b) Shade the left faces.

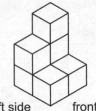

left side   front

Draw the left side view.

c) Shade the front faces.

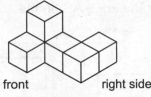

front   right side

Draw the front view.

5. Which of these pictures shows the left side view, front view, and top view of this structure?

_____   _____   _____

6. Draw the front, top, and right side views for the structure.

a)

top view

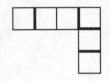

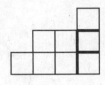

front

right side

front view

right side view

b)

top view

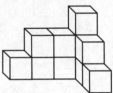

front   right side

front view   right side view

c)

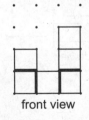

left side   front

d)

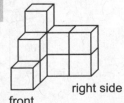

front

right side

e)

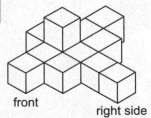

front

right side

7. Use 8 connecting cubes to build 2 different structures. Draw the front, top, and both side views of your structures.

G8-44 Side Views of Structures Built from Prisms

1. Mark the edge AB on the side views.

a)
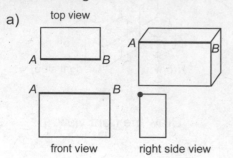

top view

A ▭ B

A ▭ B

front view

right side view

b)
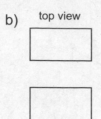

top view

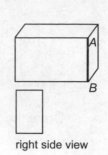

front view

right side view

c)
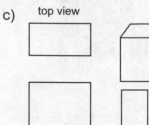

top view

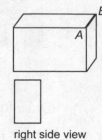

front view

right side view

2. Mark the dimensions on the side views of the prism.

a)
top view

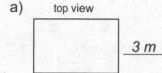

_5 m_   _3 m_

5 m   2 m   3 m

_5 m_   _2 m_

_3 m_   _2 m_

front view

right side view

b)
top view

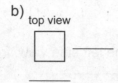

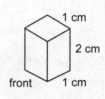

1 cm

2 cm

front   1 cm

front view

right side view

c)
top view

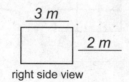

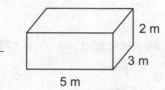

2 m

1 m

2 m

front view

right side view

d)
top view

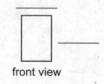

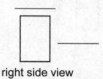

7 mm

2 cm   25 mm

front

front view

right side view

3. Sketch the side views of the prism. Mark the dimensions on the sketch.

a) top view

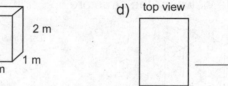   

3 cm

25 mm

5 cm

b)
top view

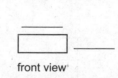   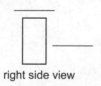

10 m

25 m

left side   8 m

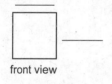   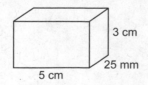   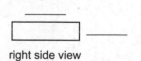   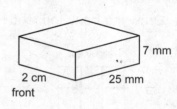   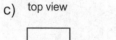

front view   right side view   left side view   front view

4. Sketch and label the top, front, and side views of the structure.

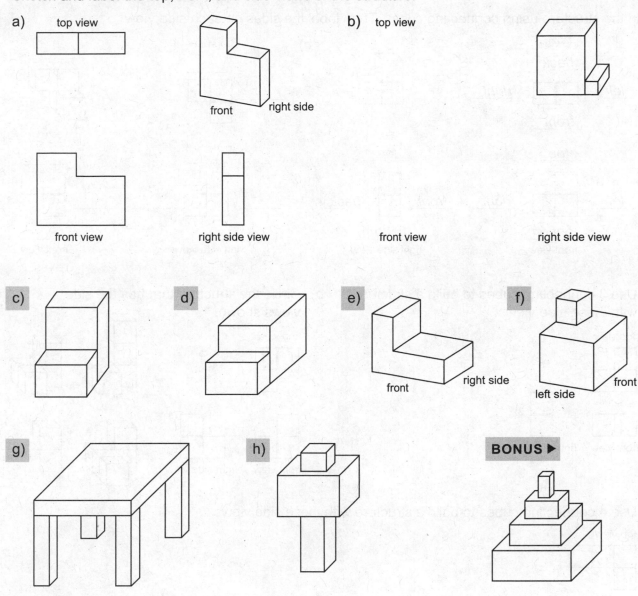

a)   top view

front   right side

front view   right side view

b)   top view

front view   right side view

c)

d)

e)   front   right side

f)   left side   front

g)

h)

BONUS ▶

BONUS ▶ Sketch the bottom view of the structure in g).

5. Sketch and label the top, front, and side views of the object.

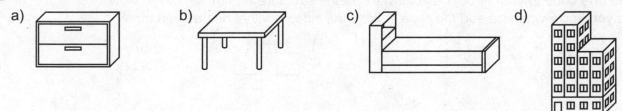

a)   b)   c)   d)

G8-45 Building Structures from Side Views

1. Build the structure using connecting cubes. Then label the sides on each side view.

a)
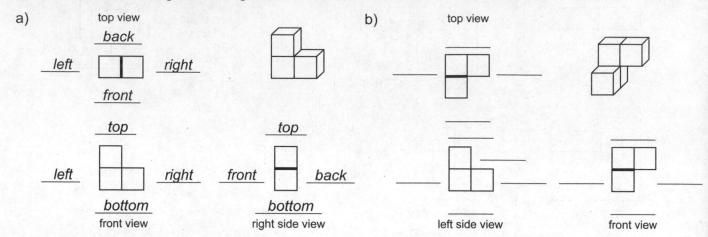

top view

back

left   right

front

top   top

left   right   front   back

bottom   bottom

front view   right side view

b)

top view

left side view   front view

2. a) Use 3 connecting cubes to build a structure with these side views.

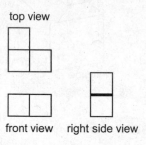

top view

front view   right side view

b) Circle the structure that has the side views shown.

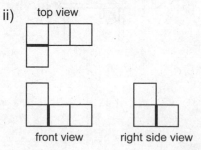

top view

front view   right side view

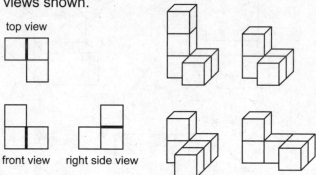

3. a) Use 4 connecting cubes to build a structure with these side views.

top view

front view   right side view

b) Add one cube to your structure from a) to get the structure with these views. How did you know where to add the cube? Circle the side view that helped you most.

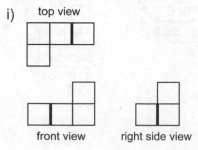

i)   top view

front view   right side view

ii)   top view

front view   right side view

c) Add two cubes to your structure in a) to get the structure with these views.

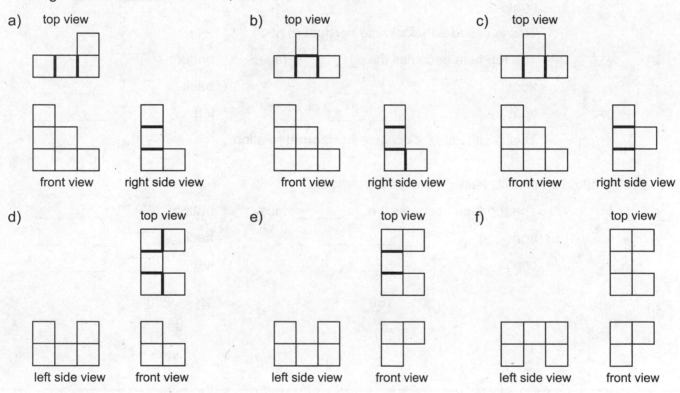

i) top view   front view   right side view

ii) top view   front view   right side view

iii) top view   front view   right side view

4. Use 7 connecting cubes to create a structure with these side views. Start by building the largest face without thick lines, then add more cubes.

a) top view   front view   right side view

b) top view   front view   right side view

c) top view   front view   right side view

d) top view   left side view   front view

e) top view   left side view   front view

f) top view   left side view   front view

5. Turn your structure from Question 4 f) so that it has the side views of another part in Question 4.

Which part is that? _____

6. Draw the left side view and the right side view (without the thick lines) of each structure you built in Question 4. What do you notice about the left side view and the right side view of the same structure? Explain why this happens.

7. Build a structure from 10 connecting cubes. Draw and label its side views. Have a partner make the structure with the side views that you have drawn.

G8-46 Rotating Structures

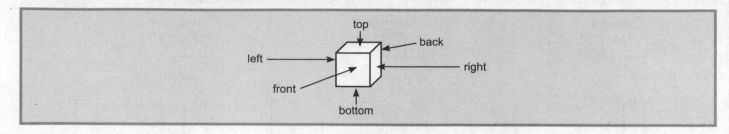

1. A die is rotated 90° as shown. How do the faces change?

a)

The top face becomes the ___*right*___ face.   bottom ⟶ ___*left*___

front ⟶ ___*front*___   back ⟶ _____

right ⟶ _____   left ⟶ _____

This is called 90° clockwise **vertical** rotation.

b)

The top face becomes the _____ face.   bottom ⟶ _____

front ⟶ _____   back ⟶ _____

right ⟶ _____   left ⟶ _____

This is called 90° clockwise **horizontal** rotation.

2. A die is rotated as shown. How do the faces change?

a) 90°

The top face becomes the _____ face.   bottom ⟶ _____

front ⟶ _____   back ⟶ _____

right ⟶ _____   left ⟶ _____

b) 180°

c) 180°

d) 270°

INVESTIGATION 1 ▶ How does the top view change in a horizontal rotation?

A. Build this structure from connecting cubes. Draw its top view in the first column of the table below.

B. Rotate the structure horizontally by the angles given. Draw the top views in the table.

before rotation	after 90° counter clockwise rotation	after 180° counter clockwise rotation	after 270° counter clockwise rotation

C. How did the top view change?

INVESTIGATION 2 ▶ How do side views change in a horizontal rotation?

top view

A. Build the structure given by these views from connecting cubes.

B. Draw the missing side views before rotation in the table below.

C. Rotate the structure horizontally by the angles given. Draw the back, front, and both side views after rotation.

front view   right side view

	left side view	front view	right side view	back view
before rotation				
after 90° clockwise rotation				
after 180° clockwise rotation				
after 270° clockwise rotation				
after 90° counter clockwise rotation				

D. What do you notice about the right side view and the left side view in each row? What do you notice about the back view and the front view in each row? Explain.

E. Compare the side views in one row to the side views in the next row. Describe the changes between the views when you rotate the structure.

F. Predict the side views when you rotate the structure 180° and 270° counter-clockwise horizontally. Which rows of the table will these views match? Explain your thinking.

PDM8-15 Mean, Median, Mode, and Range

The **leaf** of a number is its rightmost digit. The **stem** is all its digits except the rightmost digit. Note: The stem of a one-digit number is 0 since there are no digits except the rightmost one.

stem   leaf

A **stem and leaf plot** puts all the data in a set in order.

To build a stem and leaf plot for the data set 538, 529, 526, 542, 543, 534, follow these steps:

Step 1: Write the stems in order, from smallest to largest.	Step 2: Write each leaf in the same row as its stem.	Step 3: Put the leaves in each row in order, from smallest to largest.

stem	leaf
52	
53	
54	

stem	leaf
52	9 6
53	8 4
54	2 3

stem	leaf
52	6 9
53	8 4
54	2 3

1. For each plot, put the leaves in the correct order. Then list the data from smallest to largest.

   a)
stem	leaf
32	5 1
34	8 5 1
35	6 2

   →

stem	leaf
32	1 5
34	
35	

   _321_ _325_ ____ ____ ____ ____ ____ ____

   b)
stem	leaf
0	7
1	9 3
2	5 8 0

   →

stem	leaf

   ____ ____ ____ ____ ____ ____

2. Use the data set to make a stem and leaf plot.

   a) 8 7 13 18 10

   b) 99 97 103 99 101

   c) 77 91 105 97 112 114 96 78

What you can learn from a stem and leaf plot

The **smallest number** is 981 and the **largest number** is 1006.

stem	leaf
98	1 4 9
99	8 8 8
100	2 3 3 6

The **range** is

the largest   _   the smallest
 number   number

1006   –   981 = 25

The number that occurs most often is called the **mode**. There are two modes here: 998 and 1003 both occur twice.

stem	leaf
98	1 4 9
99	**8 8** 8
100	2 **3 3** 6

---

3. Make a stem and leaf plot and find the range and the mode of the set.

   a) 24 27 29 21 29
      30 31 26 23 29

   b) 0 25 0 10 12 12 0
      5 2 1 13 29 21 3

   c) 7432 7456 7418 7435
      7421 7416 7430 7444

4. The set 2, 3, 3, 4, 5, 5 has two modes: 3 and 5. What data value could you add to the set so that…

   a) the number of modes decreases? ____

   b) the number of modes increases? ____

   c) the largest number increases? ____

   d) the range increases? ____

To find the **median** of a data set, put the data in order. Count from either end until you reach the middle.

2   3   ⑥   7   11   2   3   ⑦ ⑨ 11   15

The median is 6.   The median is halfway between 7 and 9. The median is 8.

5. Find the median.

a) 9 20 22 _____   b) 38 40 42 _____   c) 10 15 20 25 30 _____

6. Make a stem and leaf plot to put the data in order. Then find the median, the mode, and the range.

a) 15 18 40 32 25   b) 29 21 27 16 22 17 15   c) 40 25 10 15 20

d) 35 34 31 36 35 34 47   e) 235   219   248   216   230   225
    37 42 28 31 30 45 39   241   207   222   227   231   219

How to find the **mean** of a set of numbers	
Step 1: Add the data values.	**Step 2:** Divide the result by the number of data values.
Set: 4 2 2 4 5 Sum of data values $= 4 + 2 + 2 + 4 + 5$ $= 17$	**Mean** = **Sum** of data values $\div$ **Number** of data values $= 17 \div 5 = 3\frac{2}{5} = 3.4$

7. Find the mean. Note: The last three answers will not be whole numbers.

a) 0 3 4 6 7

sum of data values: __20__

number of data values: __5__

mean: __20 ÷ 5 = 4__

b) 1 3 5 6 7 8

sum of data values: _____

number of data values: _____

mean: _____

c) 2 5 6 7

sum of data values: _____

number of data values: _____

mean: _____

d) 2 6 7 9 11

e) 7 8 10 11

f) 5 8 9 11 12

g) 0 1 2 3 4 5

h) 24 25 27 29 21

i) 0 25 10 12

8. a) John has 3 apples, Cynthia has 5 apples, and Noa has 10 apples. How many apples should Noa give John and Cynthia if the three people want to share the apples equally?

b) Find the mean of the data set 3, 5, 10. How is your answer related to part a)?

c) Bilal has 6 apples. Does he have to give any apples to Noa, John, or Cynthia for the apples to be shared equally among the four people? Do any of the others have to give apples to Bilal? Explain.

PDM8-16 Understanding Mean, Median, Mode, and Range

INVESTIGATION 1 ▶ How does adding 1 to each data value affect the mean?

A. Find the mean of each data set.

    i) 0 2 4 5 9   ii) 1 3 5 6 10   iii) 2 4 6 7 11

    How are these sets related? _____

    How are their means related? _____

B. Find the mean of the data set. Then create another data set by adding 1 to each data value and find the new mean.

    data set: 4 7 7 8 9 13   new data set: _____ _____ _____ _____ _____ _____

    mean: _____   new mean: _____

C. Create a data set with 5 data values and mean 6. _____ _____ _____ _____ _____

    Create a new data set by adding 1 to each data value. _____ _____ _____ _____ _____

    Predict the new mean. Explain your prediction.

    Check your prediction by calculating the new mean.

D. Find the mean of this data set: 23 16 21 22 30 20

    Create a new data set by adding 5 to each data value. _____ _____ _____ _____ _____

    Predict the new mean. Explain your prediction.

    Check your prediction by calculating the new mean.

INVESTIGATION 2 ▶ Does repeating each data value the same number of times change the mean?

A. Find the mean.

    a) 4 5 5 10   (_____ + _____ + _____ + _____) ÷ 4   = _____

    b) 4 5 5 10 4 5 5 10   (_____ + _____ + _____ + _____) × 2 ÷ 8 = _____

    c) 4 5 5 10 4 5 5 10 4 5 5 10 (_____ + _____ + _____ + _____) × 3 ÷ 12 = _____

    d) 2 5 4 1   (_____ + _____ + _____ + _____) ÷ _____   = _____

    e) 2 5 4 1 2 5 4 1 2 5 4 1 (_____ + _____ + _____ + _____) × _____ ÷ _____ = _____

B. Construct a data set with 5 data values and mean 4. _____ _____ _____ _____

    Repeat each data value to construct a new data set with 10 values.

    _____ _____ _____ _____ _____ _____ _____ _____ _____ _____

    Predict the mean of your new data set. Explain your prediction.

    Check your prediction by calculating the new mean.

C. Does repeating each data value the same number of times change the mean? Explain.

INVESTIGATION 3 ▶ Does repeating each data value the same number of times affect the mode and the median?

Do the mode and the median change? How? Make up your own data to check.

---

1. Sally surveyed 50 families on her street to find the number of cars they have. She displays her results in both a frequency table and a circle graph.

# of cars	frequency
0	10
1	25
2	15

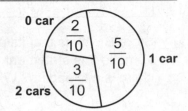

To find the mean (the average number of cars per family),

Sally uses the frequency table:

$(0 + 0 + 0 + 0 + 0 + 0 + 0 + 0 + 0 + 0 +$

$1 + 1 + 1 + 1 + 1 + 1 + 1 + 1 + 1 + 1 +$

$1 + 1 + 1 + 1 + 1 + 1 + 1 + 1 + 1 + 1 +$

$1 + 1 + 1 + 1 + 1 + 2 + 2 + 2 + 2 + 2 +$

$2 + 2 + 2 + 2 + 2 + 2 + 2 + 2 + 2 + 2) \div 50$

Tina uses the circle graph:

$(0 + 0 + 1 + 1 + 1 + 1 + 1 + 2 + 2 + 2) \div 10$

a) Do Sally and Tina get the same answer? Explain why this happened.

b) Whose method do you like better? Why?

c) If Sally accidentally divides her sum by 20 instead of by 50, what answer will she get for the mean? How can she tell immediately that she made a mistake?

d) If Tina accidentally divides her sum by 20 instead of by 10, what answer will she get for the mean? How can she tell immediately that she made a mistake?

2. The circle graph shows the percentage of families in a city having each number of cars.

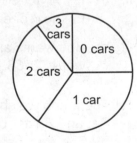

a) Use the circle graph to find the mean, median, and mode. Use a protractor. Hint: Pretend the city has only 100 people.

b) Explain why you do not need to know the population of the city to determine the mean, median, or mode.

3. Create a data set, not all numbers equal, where the mean, mode, and median are all the same.

4. When a soccer player moved from Team A to Team B, the mean age of **both** teams increased. Give an example of data to show how this could happen.

5. You have a set of 6 whole numbers (some of them can be 0). Find the lowest possible sum of all the numbers in the set if...

a) the median is 500.   b) the mean is 500.   c) the mode is 500.

d) Show sets having these sums and compare the sets.

PDM8-17 Using the Mean, Median, Mode, and Range

1. This table shows the price for the same pair of shoes at seven different stores.

Store	A	B	C	D	E	F	G
Price ($)	83	85	84	86	86	82	81

   Store B claims that its prices are lower than average. Which average could they use to make this statement true: the mean, the mode, or the median? Do you think the claim is misleading? Why?

2. You work at a clothing store, and your manager says that every week you need an average daily sales of at least $500. What kind of average do you think your manager is talking about — a mean, a mode, or a median? Why?

3. A grade 8 student needs to average at least 85% to get into a high school that has a special arts program. Which average do you think this is referring to — the mean, the median, or the mode? Why?

4. A shoe store asks a famous athlete to sign the running shoes she designed. The store can have only one size of the running shoe at the signing. To decide which size to order, which average shoe size sold at the store should the store owner determine — the mean, the median, or the mode? Why?

5. The mean of a set of data is 10. The data values are 2, 19, 7, 4, 15, and one other number. Let x represent the missing number. Write the expression for the mean, and solve the equation.

6. a) If you got 80, 93, and 91 on the first 3 history tests, what do you need to get on the next one to average 90 on the first 4 history tests?

   b) Bob wants an average of 85 on all 6 history tests. His marks on the first 5 tests were 72, 86, 92, 73, and 76. Can he do it? Explain.

7. The mean weight of three dogs, Tippy, Pat and Baxter, is 25 kg. Tippy weighs 31 kg. Pat and Baxter both weigh the same amount. What is Pat's weight?

8. A family drives at 110 km/h for 6 hours and then 60 km/h for 4 hours.

   a) How far did the family drive in the first 6 hours? _____

   b) How far did the family drive in the last 4 hours? _____

   c) How far did the family drive altogether? _____

   d) What was the mean speed for the whole trip?

   Mean speed = $\dfrac{\text{distance travelled}}{\text{time travelled}}$ = _____ $\dfrac{\text{km}}{\text{hours}}$ = _____ km/h

   e) Is the mean speed for the whole trip closer to 110 km/h or 60 km/h? _____

   Why does this make sense? _____

PDM8-18 Theoretical Probability — Review

This spinner has 4 regions, so there are 4 **outcomes**.

The spinner will land in

 , , , or

All 4 outcomes are **equally likely** to happen.

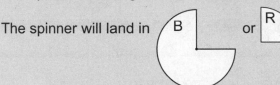

This spinner has 2 regions, so there are 2 **outcomes**.

The spinner will land in or

The 2 outcomes are **not** equally likely to happen.

1. How many different outcomes are there when you...

   a) roll a die? _____   b) flip a coin? _____   c) play hockey? _____

2. What are the possible outcomes for the spinner?

   a)

   The spinner lands in

   regions _1_, ___ ___ or ___

   There are ____ outcomes.

   b)
   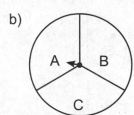

   The spinner lands in

   region _____

   There are ____ outcomes.

3. You draw a coloured marble from the box. How many different outcomes are there?
   Are the outcomes equally likely to happen?

   a)
   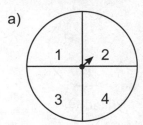

   _____ outcomes

   Equally likely? _yes_

   b)
   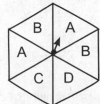

   _____ outcomes

   Equally likely? _____

4. You spin the spinner. How many different outcomes are there? Are the outcomes
   equally likely to happen?

   a)

   _____ outcomes

   Equally likely? _____

   b)
   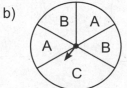

   _____ outcomes

   Equally likely? _____

   c)
   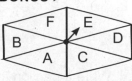

   _____ outcomes

   Equally likely? _____

   BONUS ▶

   _____ outcomes

   Equally likely? _____

There are 4 **equal** regions on the spinner, so there are 4 **equally likely** outcomes.

 You can spin red in 3 ways:

The probability of spinning red is P(Red) = $\dfrac{\text{\# of ways of spinning red}}{\text{\# of ways of spinning any colour}} = \dfrac{3}{4} = 3:4$

When outcomes are equally likely: P(Event A) = $\dfrac{\text{\# of outcomes that suit A}}{\text{\# of all outcomes}}$

5. How many ways are there to…

a)   draw a green marble? _____

_____

draw a marble of any colour? _____

_____

b) 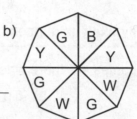   spin green? _____

_____

spin any colour? _____

_____

6. For each spinner, what is the probability (P) of spinning red?

a) 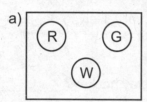   P(Red) = _____

b)   P(Red) = _____

c)   P(Red) = _____

d)   P(Red) = _____

7. If a dart always lands on the board with each region equally likely, what is the probability of hitting blue? Reduce your answer if possible.

a)

B	R
G	B

P(Blue) = _____

b)

B	R	G

P(Blue) = _____

c)

B	R	R
G	B	Y

P(Blue) = _____

d)

R	B	R	G
Y	Y	B	B

P(Blue) = _____

8. Add lines to divide the spinner to make all outcomes equally likely. Find the probability.

a)   P(Blue) = _____

b)   P(Red) = _____

c) 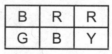   P(Yellow) = _____

d)   P(Green) = _____

9. Write a fraction that gives the probability of spinning…

a) the number 1   b) the number 3   c) an even number

d) an odd number   e) a number less than 5   f) a number greater than 5

Remember: A regular die is a cube with the numbers from 1 to 6 on its faces.

Dice can also come in different shapes and have different numbers on their faces.

10. a) List the numbers on a regular die. _____

   b) How many outcomes are there when you roll a regular die? _____

11. a) List the numbers on a regular die that are even. _____

   b) How many ways can you roll an even number? _____

   c) What is the probability of rolling an even number? _____

12. a) List the numbers on a regular die that are greater than 4. _____

   b) How many ways can you roll a number greater than 4? _____

   c) What is the probability of rolling a number greater than 4? _____

13. Match each net for a die to the correct statement.

A.

	4		
4	5	5	2
	3		

B.

	4		
1	6	4	5
	2		

C.

	3		
2	1	3	6
	3		

D.

	5		
3	2	5	1
	4		

_____ The probability of rolling a 4 is $\frac{1}{6}$.   _____ The probability of rolling an even number is $\frac{1}{2}$.

_____ The probability of rolling a 3 is $\frac{1}{2}$.   _____ The probability of rolling a 1 is the same as the probability of rolling a 5.

14. Write a fraction that gives the probability of spinning…

   a) the letter T   b) the letter N

   c) the letter E   d) a vowel

   e) a consonant   f) a letter that appears in the word "Canada"

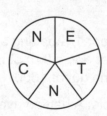

15. Cathie says the probability of rolling a 1 on a regular die is $\frac{1}{6}$, so the probability of rolling a 5 is $\frac{5}{6}$. Ella says the probability is $\frac{1}{6}$ for both numbers. Who is right? Explain.

16. Complete the net for a 12-faced die on which the probability of rolling an odd number is $\frac{1}{3}$ and the probability of rolling a 3 is $\frac{1}{4}$.

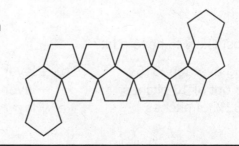

PDM8-19 Theoretical Probability

1. Circle the numbers that mean $\frac{3}{5}$.

   35% $\frac{5}{3}$ 0.3 $\frac{30}{50}$ 60% $\frac{3+4}{5+4}$ 3 out of 5 $\frac{3\times2}{5\times2}$ 9 out of 15 $\frac{60}{100}$ 9 out of 10

2. Express each probability as a fraction, a decimal, and a percentage.

   a) P(R) = $\frac{1}{2}$ = 0.5 = 50%

      P(W) = _____

      P(any colour) = _____

   b) P(R) = _____

      P(W) = _____

      P(G) = _____

3. Circle the numbers that can express probability.

   40% $\frac{1}{3}$ $\frac{3}{1}$ 0.58 $\frac{4}{7}$ $\frac{7}{4}$ 2.64

   $2\frac{1}{2}$ 1 : 5   2   −0.2   1   57.3% $\frac{31}{1000}$

   0.35   −2   0   +0.25   +1.37   2 : 7   325%

4. Describe an event that has a probability of…

   a) 100%   b) 50%   c) 0%

5. The probability of rain is often given as a percent. For each prediction below, write a fraction giving the probability that it will rain. Reduce your answer to lowest terms.

   a) 60% chance of rain   b) 35% chance of rain   c) 75% chance of rain

6. In baseball, a batting average is the ratio of the number of hits to the number of times a player has a turn at bat. Batting averages are decimals that can be changed to fractions out of 1000.

   Example: A batting average of .427 ($= \frac{427}{1000}$) means a player had 427 hits in 1000 times at bat.

   Find the probability of a hit given a player's batting average. Reduce your answers to lowest terms.

   a) .125   b) .300   c) .425   d) .256   e) .324

7. Which player is most likely to have a hit?

   a) Player A: batting average .315
      Player B: hits 3 out of 10 pitches
      Player C: hits 32% of pitches

   b) Player A: hits one quarter of pitches
      Player B: batting average .240
      Player C: hits 24% of pitches

DM8-20 Tree Diagrams

At sports camp, Erin has these choices: **Morning** – gymnastics or rowing
Afternoon – volleyball, soccer, or rugby

Erin draws a **tree diagram** so that she can see all the combinations of choices.

Step 1: She writes the name of her two morning choices at the ends of two branches.

Step 2: Under each of her morning choices, she adds three branches — one for each of her afternoon choices.

Step 3: Follow any path along the branches (from the top of the tree to the bottom) to find one of Erin's choices.

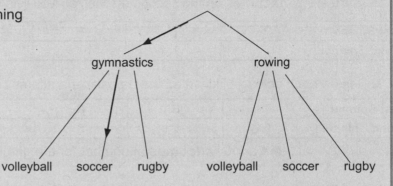

Example: The path highlighted by arrows shows gymnastics in the morning and soccer in the afternoon.

a) Complete the tree diagram to show all of the possible outcomes of flipping a coin (H = heads, T = tails) and then drawing a marble from a box that holds three marbles of different colours: R = red, G = green, Y = yellow.

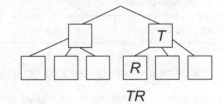

b) How many different combinations of outcomes are there? _____

Matthew's camp offers the following activities: **Morning** – drama or visual arts
Afternoon – dance or creative writing

Draw a tree diagram (like the one in Question 1) to show all the combinations of choices.

Draw a tree diagram to show all the combinations of numbers you could spin on the two spinners.

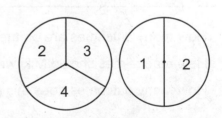

a) How many pairs of numbers add to four?
b) How many pairs of numbers have a product of four?

a) Look at the tree diagrams you drew above and fill in the table.

b) How can you calculate the total number of paths using the number of branches at each level? Explain.

c) Dean rolls two dice: a die with 20 faces and a die with 12 faces. He draws a tree diagram to see all the possible outcomes. How many paths will his tree diagram have?

Question	# of branches at the 1st level	# of branches at the 2nd level	Total # of paths
1	2	3	6
2			
3			

PDM8-21 Counting Combinations

Miki wants to know how many outcomes there are for a game with two spinners.

First spinnner 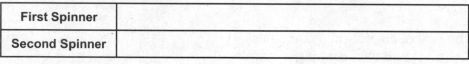 Second spinnner

Step 1: There are **3 outcomes** on the second spinner, so Miki lists each colour on the first spinner **3 times.**

First Spinner	R	R	R	Y	Y	Y
Second Spinner						

Step 2: Beside each colour, Miki writes the 3 possible outcomes on the second spinner.

First Spinner	R	R	R	Y	Y	Y
Second Spinner	1	2	3	1	2	3

The list shows that there are **6 outcomes** altogether for the game.

For each question below, answer parts a) and b), then list all of the possible combinations
Miki can spin to find the total number of outcomes for each game.

1.

First Spinner	
Second Spinner	

a) How many outcomes are on the second spinner? _____

b) How many times should Miki write W (for white) and R (for red) on his list? _____

c) How many outcomes does this game have altogether? _____

2.

First Spinner	
Second Spinner	

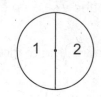

a) How many outcomes are on the second spinner? _____

b) How many times should Miki write R (for red), B (for blue) and W (for white) on his list? _____

c) How many outcomes does this game have altogether? _____

3.

First Spinner	
Second Spinner	

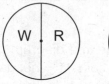

a) How many outcomes are on the second spinner? _____

b) How many times should Miki write 6, 7, and 8 on his list? _____

c) How many outcomes does this game have altogether? _____

4. These are the choices at art camp:

Morning – painting or music
Afternoon – drama, creative writing, or dance

Clare makes a chart so she can see all of her choices.
She starts by writing each of her morning choices
3 times.

a) Complete the chart to show all of Clare's choices.

b) Why did Clare write each of her morning choices
3 times?

Morning	Afternoon
painting	
painting	
painting	
music	
music	
music	

5. If you flip a coin, there are two outcomes: heads (H) and tails (T).
List all the outcomes for flipping a coin and spinning this spinner.

Coin						
Spinner						

6. Peter has a quarter (Q) and a dime (D) in his left pocket, and a dime (D) and a
nickel (N) in his right pocket. He pulls **one coin from each pocket**.

Make a T-table to show all the combinations of coins that Peter could pull out of
his pockets and the value of those combinations.

7. Make a T-table to show all the combinations of activities at a camp that offers the
following choices:

Morning – badminton, squash, or tennis   **Afternoon** – canoeing, swimming, or diving

8. a) Record all the scores you could get by throwing two darts at the dart board.
(If a dart lands outside the board, the score is 0.)

b) Find as many combinations as you can that give the same score.

c) How many combinations give a total of 4? Can you determine the probability of
scoring 4? Explain why or why not. (Hint: Are all outcomes equally likely?)

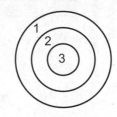

9. A tetrahedral die has 4 vertices numbered from 1 to 4. When you
roll this die, there is always a vertex on top. Make a chart to show
all the combinations for rolling this pair of tetrahedral dice.

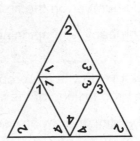

10. Without making a T-table, say how many combinations
there will be if you…

a) roll a pair of regular dice. _____

b) roll a regular die and draw a marble from a box with 35 marbles. _____

PDM8-22 Compound Events

Jade and Lara have a box of marbles.

1. Lara draws a marble from the box. She leaves the marble outside the box and draws a second marble. There are four marbles in the box for the second draw.

   a) List all the outcomes of Lara's second draw if on the first draw she draws…

   i) a green marble: _____G, B, B, B_____   ii) a blue marble: _____

   b) Does the list of possible outcomes of the second draw depend on the first draw? _____

2. Jade draws a marble from the box. She places the marble back in the box and draws a marble again.

   a) List all the outcomes of Jade's second draw, if on the first draw she draws…

   i) a green marble: _____   ii) a blue marble: _____

   b) Does the list of possible outcomes of the second draw depend on the first? _____

> Two events are **independent** if the outcomes of one event do not depend on the results of the other event.

3. Whose pair of draws is independent, Jade's or Lara's? _____

4. Are these pairs of events independent? Explain.

   a) Draw a marble from a box and spin a spinner.
   b) Pull two coins, one after the other (without replacing), from a bag of coins.
   c) Pick captains for two teams from a group of students.

> A combination of two or more events is called a **compound event**.

5. a) Write a set of ordered pairs to show all the combinations you could spin on the two spinners.

   b) How many outcomes are there? _____

   c) How many ways can you spin…

   i) a 1 on the first spinner and an R on the second? _____

   ii) an odd number on the first and a B on the second? _____

   d) Find the probability of spinning each situation in part c).   i) _____   ii) _____

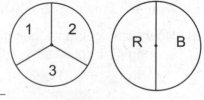

INVESTIGATION 1 ▶ How is the probability of a compound event connected to the probabilities of the individual events?

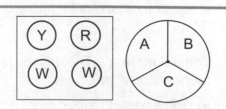

A. Find the probability of drawing each colour of marble from the box.

   P(R) = _____   P(W) = _____   P(Y) = _____

B. Find the probability of landing in each region on the spinner.

   P(A) = _____   P(B) = _____   P(C) = _____

Probability and Data Management 8-22

C. Use a tree diagram or a T-table to list all possible outcomes of spinning the spinner together with drawing a marble from the box.

How many possible combinations are there? _____

D. Find the probabilities.

P(A and R) = _____   P(A and W) = _____   P(B and Y) = _____   P(C and W) = _____

E. Compare the probabilities of the individual events with the probability of the compound event.

P(A) = _____, P(R) = _____,   P(A) = _____, P(W) = _____,

P(A and R) = _____   P(A and W) = _____

How can you get the probability of a compound event from the probabilities of the individual events? Check your conjecture with these probabilities:

P(B) = _____, P(Y) = _____,   P(C) = _____, P(W) = _____,

P(B and Y) = _____   P(C and W) = _____

The probability of a **compound event** consisting of two **independent events** is a product of the individual probabilities of the independent events: **P(A and B) = P(A) × P(B)**

---

6. Find the probability of each possible outcome for each spinner in Question 5. Use the formula above to check your answers in 5 d).

INVESTIGATION 2 ▶ Does the formula P(A and B) = P(A) × P(B) apply to non-independent events?

Bob and Nick each have a box like this: (R) (R) (G)

Bob draws two marbles from his box. Nick draws one marble, puts it back in his box, then draws a marble again.

A. Draw a tree diagram to show the possible outcomes of each person's draws.

B. Who has more possible outcomes, Bob or Nick? _____

C. Whose way of drawing two marbles is independent, Bob's or Nick's? _____

D. Use your tree diagrams to fill in the table.

	Total # of outcomes	# of ways to draw two green marbles	Probability of drawing two green marbles	# of ways to draw two red marbles	Probability of drawing two red marbles
Bob					
Nick					

E. What is the probability of drawing a single red marble from the box? P (Red) = _____

What does the formula for compound events give for P(Red and Red)? _____

Does the formula P(Red and Red) = P(Red) × P(Red) produce the correct answer for Bob's way of drawing marbles? For Nick's way of drawing marbles? Explain.

PDM8-23 Concepts in Probability

1. Linda has two dice: one with four vertices, marked 1 to 4, and the other with eight sides, marked 1 to 8.

   a) Make a T-table and list all the outcomes for rolling the two dice.

   b) Circle all the outcomes that add to 5.

   c) What is the probability of rolling a pair of numbers that add to 5?

   d) What is the probability of rolling 8 on one die and an even number on the other?

   e) Which of the probabilities in parts c) and d) could you find using the formula for the probability of compound events? Explain.

2. Joe and Ida each have three bills in their pockets: two $5 bills and a $10 bill. They each pull out one bill.

   a) What are all the possible combinations of two bills they could pull out?

   b) They need to pay $15 together. Which combinations of bills will be enough? What is the probability of Joe and Ida pulling out enough money if they each pull out one bill? Show your work.

   c) Joe and Ida need to pay $10 each. Are the events "Joe pulls out a $10 bill" and "Ida pulls out a $10 bill" independent? Find the probability of the compound event "Joe and Ida each pull out a $10 bill" using the formula and using a table.

First Die	Second Die
1	1
1	2
1	3
1	4
1	5
1	6
2	1
2	2
2	3
2	4
2	5
2	6

3. Simone made an organized list to find all possible outcomes for rolling two regular dice. This is **part** of the table she made.

   Why did Simone write the number 1 six times in her table? Complete Simone's table.

4. You roll 2 regular dice.

   a) What is the probability of rolling a total of…

      i) 4?   ii) 6?   iii) 7?   iv) 11?   v) 12?

   b) What is the probability of rolling…

      i) an even number total?   ii) two even numbers?   iii) two consecutive numbers?

   c) What two totals are you **least likely** to roll?

   d) What total are you **most likely** to roll?

5. Which outcome is more likely: A or B?

   a) **A** Roll 2 dice and get a total of 12.
      B Toss a coin 4 times and get 4 heads.

   b) **A** Roll 2 dice and get a total of 11.
      B Toss a coin 4 times and get 3 heads and 1 tail.

   c) Explain how you solved each problem in parts a) and b). How are the problems the same and how are they different?

PDM8-24 Experimental Probability

Theoretical probability is what should happen in any experiment. This is what you have been calculating so far. **Experimental probability** is what actually happens when you perform the experiment.

Experimental probability: $\text{Exp P(Event A)} = \dfrac{\text{\# of times A happened}}{\text{\# of experiments performed}}$

1. a) Write a set of ordered pairs to show all the combinations you could spin on these two spinners.

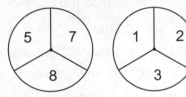

  b) Calculate the theoretical probability of spinning…

   i)   a 5 on the first spinner and a 3 on the second.   ii)   a sum of 10.

  c) Spin the spinners 30 times. How many times did you get each of the results in part b)? What is your experimental probability for each event?

  d) Is your experimental probability the same as the theoretical probability? Explain.

INVESTIGATION ▶ How does experimental probability change with the number of trials?

A. What is the theoretical probability of tossing two coins and getting two heads? How do you know?

B. Perform the experiment 5 times in a row. Then do it 5 more times and combine the results. Continue repeating the experiment and combining the results to fill in the table.

# of tosses of two coins	5	10	15	20	25
# of times 2 heads were tossed					
Exp P(2 heads)					

C. Make a line graph to show your results.

D. Draw a horizontal line on the graph at the height of the theoretical probability of tossing 2 heads. What can you say about the horizontal line and the line graph?

E. Do you expect to get the same result as everybody else? Explain.

F. Compare your results with a partner's.

  In 25 tosses, I tossed 2 heads _____ times.

  In 25 tosses, _____ tossed 2 heads _____ times.

  Did you get the same experimental probability? Explain.

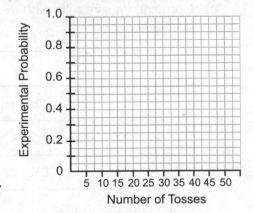

G. Combine your results of 25 tosses with the results of your partner. Add the data to your graphs.

  In 50 tosses, we tossed 2 heads _____ times.

  Calculate the experimental probability based on 50 tosses: Exp P(2 heads) = _____

  Which experimental probability of getting 2 heads is closer to the theoretical probability: the one using 25 tosses or the one using 50 tosses? _____

2. Karin plans to spin the spinner to see how many times it will land on yellow. Since $\frac{1}{3}$ of the spinner is yellow, Karin expects to spin yellow $\frac{1}{3}$ of the time, or 1 in each 3 spins.

a) What is the ratio of yellow spins to total spins that Karin expects to see?

_____ : _____

b) Use equivalent ratios to find how many times she should expect to spin yellow if she spins the spinner…

   i) 15 times   ii) 33 times   iii) 60 times   iv) 555 times

c) Karin spins the spinner 15 times and the spinner lands on yellow 8 times. Explain why this result does not contradict your answer in part b).

d) What was Karin's experimental probability of spinning yellow? _____

e) Karin thinks that if she spins the spinner 1500 times, she will get yellow about 800 times, because 8 : 15 = 800 : 1500. Is she correct? Explain Karin's mistake. What should she expect?

3. Take a box with 5 blue marbles, 3 red marbles, and 2 white marbles.

Experiment 1: Draw two marbles from the box.

Experiment 2: Draw one marble from the box, note the colour, and put the marble back. Draw a second marble.

a) How are the experiments the same and how are they different? Do you expect the theoretical probabilities to be the same?

b) Perform each experiment 10 times and find the experimental probability that both marbles are blue. Are the answers for the experiments the same or different?

c) Combine your results with the results of several classmates, and complete the table.

	Experiment 1	Experiment 2
Total number of trials		
Total number of times two blue marbles were drawn		
Exp P(2 blue marbles)		

Predict the theoretical probability of drawing two blue marbles in each experiment.

d) Find the theoretical probability of drawing two blue marbles in each experiment to check your prediction. Are the theoretical probabilities the same or different? How do the actual theoretical probabilities compare to your predictions? Did you expect this?

PDM8-25 Complementary Events

Two events that have no outcomes in common but account for all possible outcomes are called **complementary.** If Event A does **not** happen, then the event complementary to A happens.

Example: Event A: Rolling 5 or 3 on a regular die   Event B: Rolling 1, 2, 4, or 6 in a regular die
Events A and B are complementary.

1. Describe the event complementary to the given event.

a) rolling an odd number on a regular die

b) flipping heads on a coin

c) drawing a red marble from a bag with 3 red, 3 blue, and 1 white marbles

d) spinning red on this spinner

e) rolling a 1 on a regular die

f) drawing a red card from a deck of 52 cards

INVESTIGATION ▶ How are probabilities of complementary events related?

A. Find the probability of the events and complementary events in Question 1.
Write your answer in the table.

	a)	b)	c)	d)	e)	f)
Probability of the event						
Probability of the complementary event						

B. Look at the probabilities in each column. Make a conjecture about the probabilities of

complementary events. _____

C. What is the probability of a certain event (an event that always happens)? _____

Give an example of a certain event when you roll a die. Event A: _____

What is the complementary event to Event A? _____

What is the probability of the event complementary to A? _____

Does your answer fit with your conjecture in part B? _____

D. Explain why your conjecture in part B is true.

---

2. Find the probability that the event will not happen. It may be easier first to find the probability that the event will happen.

a) You will roll a sum more than 4 on a pair of regular dice.
b) You will spin an even number on the spinner shown.
c) A family with 2 children will have 2 girls.
d) You will roll a sum of 12 on a pair of regular dice.

3. The probability of rain is often given as a percent. For each prediction below, write a fraction giving the probability that it will not rain.

a) 60% chance of rain

b) 70% chance of rain

c) 20% chance of rain

PDM8-26 Samples and Sample Sizes

> If you collect information by surveying an entire population, you are using a **census**.
>
> If you survey only a part of the population, you are using a **sample**.

1. Would you use a sample or a census to find out…

   a) which movie 5 friends want to watch?
   b) who your school thinks should be school president?
   c) how smoking affects people's lungs?
   d) whether people in your home city would support an NHL hockey team?

   Explain your answers.

2. Dimitra wants to know whether the students in her grade want a pop machine at school. She asks everyone to drop a red marble in her jar for "yes" and a blue marble for "no."

   She counts the marbles and finds 18 blue marbles and 24 red marbles.

   a) How many people answered the survey? _____

      Did more people answer "yes" or "no"? _____

   b) Find 18 black playing cards and 24 red playing cards and shuffle them well.

      What colour of cards represents the blue marbles? _____

   c) Pick the top card. What colour do you expect it to be? _____

      What colour is it? _____ Did you pick the colour you expected to? _____

   d) What is the ratio of red cards to all cards in the whole set? _____

   e) Put the card back and shuffle again. This time, pick the top 5 cards.

      How many are black and how many are red? _____ black, _____ red

      What is the ratio of red cards to all cards in your sample? _____

   f) Put the cards back and shuffle again. This time, pick the top 10 cards.

      What is the ratio of red cards to all cards in your sample now? _____

   g) Put the cards back and shuffle again. This time, pick the top 20 cards.

      What is the ratio of red cards to all cards in your sample now? _____

   h) As you used larger sample sizes, did you get closer to the real ratio of red cards

      to black cards? _____

   i) Dimitra does not have time to survey all the students in her grade and only wants

      to survey a sample. How many people should be in her sample: 5, 10, or 20? _____

   j) How is shuffling the cards similar to picking people at random to survey?

INVESTIGATION ▶ You are conducting a survey. You ask a question that has 2 answers: "yes" and "no." How many people should you survey so that the fraction of people in your sample who answer yes is close to the fraction in the whole population who would answer yes?

A. A city has 10 000 people. Suppose that 2000 people in the whole city would answer yes.

What fraction of people in the whole city would answer yes? _____

B. We can label the people in the city with the numbers 1, 2, 3, 4, … , 10 000.

Use an online random number generator to randomly choose 5 numbers between 1 and 10 000.

_____ _____ _____ _____ _____

How is this like randomly choosing 5 people to survey? _____

_____

C. Sometimes a random number generator will provide the same number more than once. The generator allows you to choose whether you will keep repeated numbers.

How is choosing a repeated number like surveying the same person twice? Would you ever do that in a survey? Should you allow repeated numbers or not?

D. Which fraction below is the same as the fraction of "yes" answers in part A? _____

i)   The fraction of odd numbers in the set 1, 2, 3, 4, … , 10 000

ii) The fraction of multiples of 5 in the set 1, 2, 3, 4, … , 10 000

iii) The fraction of perfect squares in the set 1, 2, 3, 4, … , 10 000

E. In the chart below, the samples were generated using a random number generator.

Circle the multiples of 5 and complete the chart. Remember: A number is divisible by 5 if its ones digit is 0 or 5.

Sample Size	Sample	Number of multiples of 5 in the random sample	Fraction of multiples of 5 in the random sample
2	6347, 3071	0	0
3	4157, (355,) 6191	1	$\frac{1}{3}$
5	386, 2704, 9605, 1552, 4097		
5	7455, 6420, 1742, 1174, 1176		
10	1996, 3356, 7804, 924, 1237, 4206, 9031, 7483, 9444, 6906		
10	4086, 9086, 2394, 7978, 4313, 7094, 8527, 4375, 3893, 3732		

F. Create a random sample of 20 numbers from 1 to 10 000 using a random number generator.

_____	_____	_____	_____
_____	_____	_____	_____
_____	_____	_____	_____
_____	_____	_____	_____
_____	_____	_____	_____

G. How many numbers from your random sample are multiples of 5? _____

What fraction of numbers from your random sample are multiples of 5? _____

H. Combine your results with the results of other students in your class, as indicated in the chart.

Sample size	Number of multiples of 5	Fraction of multiples of 5 in sample
20 (my results)		
40 (with 1 partner)		
80 (group of 4)		
160 (group of 8)		
320 (group of 16)		

I. Look at your chart. As the sample size gets larger, does the fraction of multiples of 5 get closer to the actual fraction of multiples of 5 in the whole population? _____

J. Do you think the fraction of "yes" answers in a large enough random sample would be close to the actual fraction of "yes" answers in the whole population? _____

K. How large is large enough? Is a sample size of 40 large enough? 80? 160?

_____

_____

L. How would you change the investigation if $\frac{4}{5}$ of people in the city answered "yes"? Would it change your answer in part K? Explain.

_____

_____

_____

M. How would you change the investigation if the city had 100 000 people? Do you think it would change your answer in part K? Explain.

_____

_____

_____

PDM8-27 Bias in a Survey

1. A school principal wants to find out if students think that school should start and finish half an hour earlier, but she does not have time to ask everyone. She surveys two groups:

   A: The first 50 students who arrive in the morning.　　　YES　40　　　NO　10

   B: Five students from each of the ten classrooms.　　　YES　20　　　NO　30

   a) Why did the two surveys not get the same results?

   b) Which group's opinion will be more similar to the whole school's opinion?

   c) If there are 500 people in the school, how many do you think will want school to start and finish half an hour earlier?

   > A **representative sample** is similar to the whole population. A **biased sample** is not similar to the whole population because some parts are not represented.

2. Which sample in Question 1 is biased: A or B? How do you know?

3. Decide whether the samples are biased or representative. Explain the cause of any bias.

   a) A school (grades 1–8) is planning a party and wants to play music at the party. To find the most popular songs in the school, the school council surveys...

      • 40 grade 7 and 8 students
      • 5 students from each grade

   b) Scientists are comparing the heart rate of 15-year-olds before and after half an hour of exercise. They test the heart rate of...

      • 25 members of a school track and field team
      • 25 students from one class

   c) The government of Canada wants to know what percentage of Canadians shop regularly in the United States. They survey...

      • 1000 people living in Cornwall, Ontario, which is very close to the US border
      • 1000 people chosen randomly from the list of voters
      • 1000 people living in Iqaluit, Nunavut, which is very far from the US border

4. A city wants to build a new baseball stadium, a new swimming pool, or a new concert hall. Which of the following places is the best site for a survey? Why? What is wrong with the other three?

   • a beach
   • a music and video store
   • a professional soccer game
   • a shopping mall

5. Two students, Mickey and Helen, are running in student elections. They want to know how many of the school's 250 students will vote for them.

   • Mickey asks the 25 students in his class and finds that 15 will vote for him and 10 will not.

   • Helen gets a student list from the principal and asks every tenth student on the list. She finds that 15 will vote for her and 10 will not.

   a) Whose sample is more biased? Why?
   b) Who do you think will win the election? Why?

6. Daniel wants to know how many hours per day his classmates play video games. This is the question he asked the students in his class:

   | How many hours per day do you play video games? |
   | ☐ 0–8 hours per day   ☐ 8–16 hours per day   ☐ 16–24 hours per day |

   Explain why Daniel's survey results will be biased.

   Rewrite the survey so that the results will be less biased.

7. A town council is thinking of selling a city park and allowing a department store to build in its place. Two groups ask different questions:

   A: Are you in favour of having a new store in our town that will provide jobs for 50 people?

   B: Are you in favour of keeping our town quiet and peaceful by maintaining all of our parks?

   a) Which question was proposed by someone in favour of selling the park? Which question was proposed by someone against selling the park?

   b) Write a new survey question that does not already suggest an answer.

8. Student council is responsible for choosing music and ordering food for events. Most people enjoy the music, but not the food. Look at the two surveys:

Survey A	**Survey B**
1. Do you enjoy the music at the events?	1. Do you enjoy the food at events?
2. Is student council doing a good job?	2. Is student council doing a good job?
3. Do you enjoy the food at events?	3. Do you enjoy the music at events?

   a) What is the same about the two surveys?

   b) What is different about the two surveys?

   c) Which survey is more likely to suggest that student council is doing a good job? Why?

   d) How can the order of the questions on a survey affect the results?

PDM8-28 Surveys and Experiments

1. You want to find out what time people in your neighbourhood get up on weekday mornings.

   a) Write a question you would ask. What responses do you expect? Do you need an "other" category?

   b) Who would you survey? How would you choose your sample? What different types of people should you be sure to include? (e.g., males and females, people of different ages)

   c) What type of graph would you use to display your results? Explain.

2. You want to find out if people who take the bus to school take more or less time to get to school than people who walk to school.

   a) Write two unbiased questions you would ask people in your survey.
   b) Who would you survey? How would you choose your sample?
   c) What type of graph would you use to display your results? Explain.

3. You want to find out if taller people tend to get higher grades, lower grades, or the same grades as shorter people.

   a) How many questions would you put on your survey?
   b) What question(s) would you ask?
   c) Who would you survey? How would you choose your sample?
   d) What type of graph would you use to display your results? Explain.

4. You want to find out whether maple leaves grow proportionally, so you collect various maple leaves of different sizes and record their lengths and widths.

   a) What type of graph will you use to display your results?

   b) What would you expect the graph to look like if maple leaves do, in fact, grow proportionally?

5. You want to find out if people get better at throwing darts (in other words, they can throw darts closer to the target) with practice.

   a) What do you need to measure?

   b) How will you measure your results? What materials and equipment do you need?

   c) Will you need people to help you? What will they need to do?

   d) Should the distance between the thrower and the dart board be the same for all throws? How would it affect the results if the person throwing darts stands very close to the board at first and moves farther from the board after practising?

   e) What type of graph will you use to display your results? Explain your choice.

6. Design your own survey.

    a) Decide on your question. Predict the answer. Examples:

        • How much time do grade 8 students spend on homework?

        • Is there a relationship between the amount of time grade 8 students spend on homework and their final grade?

        • Is there a relationship between the amount of time a student spends on homework and the grade (K–12) they are in?

    b) Design an unbiased survey question with appropriate responses that will help you answer your main question.

    c) Draw the table you will use to record your results.

    d) Perform your survey.

    e) Choose and draw an appropriate type of graph to display your data.

    f) Summarize your conclusions. Did your results correspond with your predictions?

7. Design your own experiment.

    a) Decide on your question. Predict the answer. Examples:

        • Is the average of a school's performance on a math contest related to the percentage of students at the school who participate?

        • Does the height a ball bounces depend on the material the ball is made of?

        • Does the distance a block slides depend on the slope of the ramp?

    b) What do you need to measure? What materials and equipment will you need?

    c) How will you make sure your experiment gives reliable results? You will need to keep everything other than what you want to measure constant.

    d) Draw the table you will use to record your results.

Item #	Length	Width
1.		
2.		

    e) Perform your experiment.

    f) Choose and draw an appropriate type of graph to display your data.

    g) Summarize your conclusions. Did your results correspond with your predictions?